D1649080

Formal Development

of

Programs and Proofs

EDITED BY

EDSGER W. DIJKSTRA
The University of Texas at Austin

Addison-Wesley Publishing Company

Reading, Massachusetts • Menlo Park, California • New York
Don Mills, Ontario • Wokingham, England • Amsterdam • Bonn
Sydney • Singapore • Tokyo • Madrid • San Juan

This book is in the University of Texas at Austin Year of Programming Series.

005.1
F 723

Library of Congress Cataloging-in-Publication Data

Formal development of programs and proofs

(The UT year of programming series)
Bibliography: p.
Includes index.
1. Electronic Digital Computers—Programming—
Congresses. I. Dijkstra, Edsger Wybe. II. Series.
QA76.6.F657   1990   005.1   89-102
ISBN 0-201-17237-2

ABCDEFGHIJ—MA—89

The UT Year of Programming Series

Series editor: HAMILTON RICHARDS JR. The University of Texas at Austin

Concurrent Programming
   Editor: C. A. R. HOARE Oxford University

Logical Foundations of Functional Programming
   Editor: GERARD HUET INRIA Rocquencourt

Research Topics in Functional Programming
   Editor: DAVID TURNER University of Kent

Formal Development of Programs and Proofs
   Editor: EDSGER W. DIJKSTRA The University of Texas at Austin

The UT Year of Programming Series

The design for the books was commissioned by the publisher, Addison-Wesley. The designer was Jean Hammond, and the design was transformed into LaTeX style files by William H. Miner Jr. of TeX*niques* in Austin, Texas. The book was composed in LaTeX, primarily by the UT Year of Programming staff using Macintosh[1] SE personal computers, but also by several authors who supplied their manuscripts as TeX[2] or LaTeX source files. The Macintosh implementation of TeX —TeXTURES— is a product of Blue Sky Research of Portland, Oregon. Draft versions of the manuscript were printed on an Apple[3] LaserWriter II NTX printer, and the final copy was produced on a Linotronic 100[4] by Publishing Experts of Austin.

The typeface in which the book is set is Lucida[5], a product of Adobe Systems Incorporated, whose permission to use a beta version of the Lucida Math fonts is gratefully acknowledged; a few additional POSTSCRIPT characters were created using Fontographer.[6] Lucida was installed in LaTeX and TeXTURES by Buff Miner and by David Mallis of Publishing Experts; the value of their dedication and expertise is beyond calculation.

The publisher's vital assistance and patient encouragement were personified by Peter S. Gordon (Publishing Partner for Computer Science), Helen M. Goldstein (Assistant Editor), Helen M. Wythe (Production Administrator) and Mona Zeftel (Electronic Production Consultant).

1. Macintosh is a trademark of Apple Computer, Inc.
2. TeX is a trademark of the American Mathematical Society.
3. Apple and LaserWriter are registered trademarks of Apple Computer, Inc.
4. Linotronic 100 is a trademark of Allied Corporation.
5. Lucida is a registered trademark of Bigelow & Holmes.
6. Fontographer is a registered trademark of Altsys Corporation.

Contents

       Theorem   A. J. M. van Gasteren 49

7   A Problem on Bichrome 6-Graphs
       A. J. M. van Gasteren 55

8   Formal Program Transformations for VLSI Circuit
       Synthesis   A. J. Martin 59

9   Programs from Specifications   Joseph M. Morris 81

10 Piecewise Data Refinement   Joseph M. Morris 117

11 Exercises in Formula Manipulation   W. H. J. Feijen 139

12 Multiplication and Division of Polynomials
       Martin Rem 159

13 A Parallel Program that Generates the Möbius Sequence
       Martin Rem and Tom Verhoeff 171

14 Distribution and Inversion of Warshall's Algorithm
       Jan L. A. van de Snepscheut 183

15 A Distributed Algorithm for Mutual Exclusion:
       An Experiment in Presentation   Jan L. A. van de Snepscheut 195

16 The Derivation of a Proof by J. C. S. P. van der Woude
       Edsger W. Dijkstra 201

17 Fillers at the YoP Institute   Edsger W. Dijkstra 209

18 Influences (or Lack Thereof) of Formalism in Teaching
       Programming and Software Engineering   David Gries 229

       The Authors 237

       The Year of Programming on Videotape 242

Foreword

*T*his volume is a product of the 1987 University of Texas Year of Programming ("YoP"), an initiative of UT-Austin's Department of Computer Sciences underwritten by generous grants from Lockheed/Austin, an anonymous donor, and —principally— the U.S. Office of Naval Research.[7]

The Year of Programming's general objectives were

> to advance the art and science of programming by bringing together leading computing scientists for discussions and collaboration, and

> to disseminate among leading practitioners the best of what is known — and being discovered— about the theory and practice of programming.

These objectives grew out of the original proposal's statement of purpose:

> Programming includes all aspects of creating an executable representation of a problem [solution] ... from mathematical formulation to representation of an algorithm [for a] specific architecture.... The Year of Programming will ...address ...the conversion of programming into a mathematical ... discipline.

---

7. under Contract N00014-86-K-0763.

Almost from the outset, it was agreed that the Year of Programming would make its greatest contribution by steering away from topics and formats already well addressed by industrial concerns, government agencies, and the technical societies. Hence it was decided to leave such topics as programming psychology, sociology, and management to entities better qualified to deal with them, and to concentrate on those aspects of programming most amenable to scientific treatment.

As planning progressed, the YoP developed mainly into a series of Programming Institutes. Although each institute focused on a different sector of computing's scientific frontier, all proceeded from a conviction that good programming is the art and science of keeping things simple, and that the conversion of programming from a craft into a mathematical discipline requires an unorthodox type of mathematics in which the traditional distinction between "pure" and "applied" need not appear.

Each institute was organized by a scientific director recruited for his contributions to the art and science of programming or to the mathematics that it requires. Each director in turn enlisted a few colleagues—between four and a dozen or so—to assist him in discussing, refining, and presenting their school of thought. Over a period of one or two weeks, each institute team presented tutorials, research papers, and public lectures, and engaged in panel discussions and workshops. The institutes' audiences numbered from 30 to over 100, and converged on Austin from many parts of North America and Europe.

The selection criterion was wide enough to admit a broad variety of approaches, and many institute topics were considered. From a welter of conflicting schedules and commitments finally emerged six Programming Institutes, whose scientific directors and topics were as follows:

1. C. A. R. Hoare, Oxford University (visiting UT Austin for the academic year 1986–87). *Concurrent Programming*, 23 February–6 March.

2. David Gries, Cornell University. *Encapsulation, Modularization, and Reusability*, 1–10 April.

3. Gérard Huet, INRIA Rocquencourt. *Logical Foundations of Functional Programming*, 8–12 June.

4. Michael J. C. Gordon, Cambridge University, and Warren A. Hunt, Jr., University of Texas, Austin (co-directors). *Formal Specification and Verification of Hardware*, 8–17 July.

5. David A. Turner, University of Kent, Canterbury, U.K. *Declarative Programming*, 24–29 August.

6. Edsger W. Dijkstra, University of Texas, Austin. *Formal Development of Programs and Proofs*, 26–30 October.

The volume you hold in your hands is a product of the sixth Programming Institute. It is not a proceedings in the usual sense, for it is not a mere collection of materials brought to the Institute by its participants. Instead, it attempts to capture the essence of the institute as seen after the fact —and after some reflection— by its principal participants. Some of the articles do indeed closely resemble their authors' presentations in Austin; others were not presented at all, but are included here as indispensable background material. Still others represent work that was carried out either at the institute or as a result of it.

Whatever success YoP has achieved reflects primarily the caliber and dedication to excellence of the many computing scientists who contributed as scientific directors, lecturers, workshop participants, and authors. Enlisting such dedicated colleagues to serve as scientific directors was mainly the achievement of the YoP executive subcommittee's three leaders— James C. Browne, Edsger W. Dijkstra, and C. A. R. Hoare. Their task was greatly eased by the resources put at YoP's disposal by its sponsors, which made it possible for YoP to attract the very best scientific talent in the field; personifying the sponsors' support and encouragement were Charles Holland and Andre van Tilborg at the Office of Naval Research and Stephen Sherman at Lockheed. Finally the YoP Management Committee deserves great credit for its guidance, and for much sage advice and wise counsel, from YoP's earliest days.

Hamilton Richards Jr.

Preface

---

*Y*ou have in your hands the Proceedings of
the last YoP Institute, held in 1987 under the auspices of the department of
Computer Sciences of The University of Texas at Austin, which named 1987
"The Year of Programming". That is what the initials "YoP" officially stand
for, but they stand for much more: With the stream of visitors coming to
the successive Institutes, we in Austin quickly learned that they also stood
for the "The Year of Parties", and as soon as each Institute was over, each
contributor learned that they also stood for the "The Year of Proceedings".
During the preparation we realized that they would also denote "The Year of
Proofs", as is duly reflected in this Institute's title: "Formal Development of
Programs and Proofs".

The combination of the ingredients of this title is unavoidable. The only
thing a digital machine can do for us is to manipulate symbols; the program-
mable computer can do so only after it has been programmed; the only re-
liable way we know of designing such programs is by deriving them in a
process of symbol manipulation. Hence computing science is intrinsically
concerned with the boundary between human and mechanical symbol manipulation. In the human symbol manipulation, the program is derived by
choosing the structure of the formal proof that is going to demonstrate that

the functional specification will be met, and the program is then derived so as to fit the chosen correctness proof.

The unavoidability of the combination of said ingredients is obvious; it is less obvious, however, how to combine those ingredients into a workable methodology. Early efforts at formal program derivation quickly revealed that these efforts were much more promising than those of an a posteriori verification of existing programs (written in one way or another, but without formal verification in mind). They were encouraging to the extent that they justified the characterization of verification a posteriori as putting the cart before the horse; they were discouraging to the extent that they revealed that our manipulative abilities were hardly up to the task. Consequently, computing science found itself vividly interested in formal techniques.

That interest took many different forms, many of which are reflected in the various contributions to these proceedings. They range from theoretical underpinnings, via more general methodological and notational concerns, to the formal derivations of actual algorithms of all sorts.

The contribution of R. C. Backhouse reflects the renewed interest in the foundation of formal mathematics and in constructive type theory in particular, because, in that theory, proofs and programs are essentially treated on the same footing.

The contributions of A. J. M. van Gasteren and of E. W. Dijkstra hardly touch programming at all. They are concerned with the streamlining of the mathematical argument in general and reflect, for instance, how the experience gained in programming methodology can be transferred to doing mathematics in general. Here we see how, thanks to formalization, the shape of the formulae concerned almost dictates how to proceed with the calculational argument.

This heuristic aspect is further exemplified in the contributions of Wim H. J. Feijen, whose purpose is to show how to let the symbols do the work. His examples strikingly illustrate the economy of reasoning that can be obtained by never taking more into account than what is strictly needed for a next step; his derivations range from proofs of theorems to programs, sequential or not.

The remaining contributors focus their attention more specifically on (formal) aspects of the programming task.

Joseph M. Morris gives a mathematical theory that justifies the main patterns of stepwise refinement. He obtains a considerable simplification by treating functional specification and program logically on the same footing, the only difference being that the program is potentially more specific than the original specification and is so expressed as to make it interpretable as executable code.

Martin Rem (also reporting work of Tom Verhoeff) presents the derivation of a number of systolic algorithms; it is interesting to note that many fewer subscripts are used than a more naive approach would require.

Alain J. Martin's contribution presents the formal derivation of VLSI designs —down to the gate level!— for delay-insensitive circuitry, and, as such, reflects a major breakthrough in hardware design. Since his design methodolgy has led to actual designs of chips that immediately worked beautifully when they returned from the foundry, his contribution should dispel the myth that formal techniques work only for "toy problems".

David Gries and Jan L. A. van de Snepscheut derived algorithms, sequential and otherwise. They distinguished themselves from the other speakers in two ways. First, they both tackled the problem of presentation of sophisticated algorithms explicitly; they both took the (successful) experiment of explaining "with their hands in their pockets". (The experiment was fully in order. Abstaining from all visual aids might seem a handicap but it is not: It reduces the bandwidth of communication, and what is calculational reasoning, compared with verbal reasoning, other than a bandwidth reduction?) Second, they showed during the Institute formal techniques in action by deriving the inorder traversal of a binary tree and inverting that algorithm.

With a few minor exceptions, the contributions to these proceedings appear in the order of performance of the speakers. (For instance, David Gries's banquet speech, delivered on the last day but one, appears at the end of the proceedings.) The Institute extended over four and a half days, and each speaker had either a full morning or a full afternoon at his disposal and was, for instance, thus totally free in the timing of the refreshment breaks. Also, it was understood that each speaker was free to stop when, before his time was over, he felt that enough was enough. To this end I had prepared a number of "fillers", mostly in the expected presentation range of ten to twenty minutes. These fillers have been included at the end of these proceedings. (I mention this way of scheduling the Institute because it is somewhat unusual and was greatly appreciated by both speakers and audience. We can recommend it.) There is no specific significance in the order in which the half-day slots were allocated; the main principle was that speakers that could be expected to suffer from jet lag were given morning sessions and that I, as the Institute's Scientific Director, would get the last morning in which I could accommodate a discussion. The way in which the audience had seen programs being derived had differed so drastically from what the audience was used to and familiar with that the discussion predictably focused on the educational challenge implied, and this was as it should be. Too often, we see a failure to distinguish sufficiently clearly between the intrinsic problems of computing science and the difficulties resulting from the shortcomings of our various educational systems. In this respect, the Institute had been an exception, for —though all speakers were from academia— all through the week, these two different concerns had been rigorously separated.

The Institute closed with warm applause for Dr. Hamilton Richards Jr. and his staff, whose unwavering attention to all details of the organization of the Institutes had been a major factor in the success of the "The Year of Programming". Here, I add an equally warm appreciation for the painstaking care with which that same crew has provided the publisher with the camera-ready manuscript for this book.

Edsger W. Dijkstra

Constructive Type Theory

A Perspective from Computing Science

1

Roland C. Backhouse
Groningen University

1 Introduction

Renewed interest in the formal connection between programs and proofs has recently been stimulated by Per Martin-Löf's formalization of constructive mathematics. Although Martin-Löf is himself a philosopher rather than a computing scientist, his theory has attracted considerable attention among theoretical computing scientists (at least in Europe!). My own contribution to this institute is to try to explain his theory from my own perspective as a computing scientist. I have two specific objectives. The first is to demonstrate how the theory increases our understanding of constructive mathematics and the relation between programs and proofs. The second is to convey to you some of my enthusiasm for his system as a formal system for performing program construction.

In order to put his work into perspective I shall begin with a very brief review of some of the more important advances that have been made in the "mathematics of programming" since 1968. I have taken 1968 as the starting point since that was the year of a now-famous NATO conference on Software Engineering in Garmisch, West Germany. It was at that conference, I believe, that the term "software crisis" was coined. More importantly, it was at that conference that the computing community became publicly aware of the vital need for a theory of programming.

The four developments that I discuss are these:

data structuring,

functional programming,

logic programming, and

program verification.

The first of these, the introduction of type declarations (enumerated types, record structures, etc.) into programming languages is also, historically, the first to have had a significant impact on the way we program. C. A. R. Hoare's suggestions on data structuring [20], which were subsequently realized in the programming language Pascal, were made with the expressed aim of *"extend(ing) the range of programming errors which logically cannot be made".*

That this objective was achieved is undoubtedly true, but the notion of *strong typing* —the requirement that the left and right sides of all assignments (implicit or explicit) have identical type— introduced in Pascal to achieve that objective involved a severe penalty of inflexibility. For example, it is impossible to define in Pascal an identity function— a function that takes an arbitrary value as argument and returns the same value as result. It is, however, possible to write *separate* identity functions for integers, for Booleans, etc. This may not seem to be a very significant example; its significance becomes more apparent when one realizes that separate, but essentially identical, procedures are needed to search a list of widgets for a widget and to search a list of thingummyjigs for a thingummyjig.

One of the benefits of some functional programming languages was to liberate us from the straitjacket of strong typing without compromising Hoare's stricture on extending the range of errors which logically cannot be made. Thus in the language ML, developed by Robin Milner and his colleagues as part of the Edinburgh LCF system [18] one *can* define the identity function— it takes the form $id = \lambda x.x$ and has the *polymorphic* type $* \rightarrow *$, meaning that it maps an element of arbitrary type $*$ into an element of the same type $*$. Nevertheless, there is a strict regime governing type correctness of programs that prevents many involuntary errors. ("Polymorphic" means "having many forms," and indeed polymorphic functions appear in many languages but in the role of second-class citizens. For instance, the function **new** in Pascal is polymorphic since it returns a pointer of arbitrary type. The term was apparently invented by Christopher Strachey and is distinct from "overloading" such as occurs in the use of "+" to denote both integer and real addition [27]).

In spite of its undoubted advances there are still shortcomings in the type-definition mechanism in ML (and in Standard ML [28]). One such is that, for example, the addition and multiplication functions on integers both have the *same* type $int \times int \rightarrow int$ as does the integer division function, **div**. There is, thus, no mechanism in the language to record the different algebraic properties of addition and multiplication (the fact that 0 is the identity of the former and 1 the identity of the latter, etc.); nor is there any mechanism (in the type structure) to indicate that addition and multiplication are everywhere-defined functions whereas integer division is undefined when its second argument is zero.

Another shortcoming of the type mechanism in ML is that there is no notion of a *dependent* type, in which components of a type may depend on the values held by previously defined types. An example of a dependent type is the type semigroup. An element of the type semigroup is a set S, say, together with an associative binary operator +, say, defined on the elements of S. The point to note about this definition is that a semigroup has two components, the second of which has type $S \times S \rightarrow S$ which *depends* on the set, S, defined in the first component.

The third topic on my list, logic programming, is often identified with programming in Prolog. Prolog allows statements to be made in a limited form of the predicate calculus called Horn-clause form. Horn clauses are interpreted procedurally so that a set of one or more clauses describes a set of one or more recursive procedures. There is no doubt that Prolog has achieved a great deal in highlighting the value of formal logic to programming; my reference to logic programming is, however, to a rather broader understanding of the nature of programming as a mathematical activity requiring an unusual degree of formality and rigor.

The final topic on my list, program verification, is for me the most fundamental. But, although its development began about the same time as the development of data-structuring techniques, it is probably the topic that has had the least effect on the way that practicing programmers develop software. Its effects have been emasculated because the techniques of program verification have never been properly integrated into a programming language. It is still possible to write programs without having the slightest clue about program proofs, invariant properties, etc., and those few programmers who do have such knowledge often regard program proofs as a gross encumbrance and impossible to use except for "toy" problems.

I am impressed by Martin-Löf's theory because it seems to combine within the same framework many of the advances I have been discussing. It is a logical system, developed from Gentzen's system of natural deduction [16], that formalizes constructive mathematics in the style of Bishop [5]. It incorporates very powerful type-definition facilities, including the notion of dependent types mentioned earlier, and it embodies an extremely important principle, the so-called principle of "propositions as types". In the space that I have available I shall try to provide an account of the contribution that the theory might make to the very practical task of program construction.

1.1 *Propositions as Types*

In outline, Martin-Löf's theory is a formal system for making judgments about certain well-formed formulae. Such judgments take one of four possible forms. For the moment, however, I shall consider only one of these, the form

$p \in P$.

A judgment of the form $p \in P$ can be read in several different ways. In the sense of conventional computing science, it is read as "p has type P" or "p is a member of the set P". Examples of such judgments (introduced now so that I can use them very shortly) are

$0 \in \mathbb{N}$,

meaning "0 has the type natural number";

$red \in \{red, white, blue\}$,

meaning "red is an element of the enumerated type $\{red, white, blue\}$";

$\mathbb{N} \in U_1$,

and

$\emptyset \in U_1$.

Here U_1 stands for a universe of types, the first in a hierarchy of universes. Thus the judgment $\mathbb{N} \in U_1$ reads that the set of natural numbers is an element of the first universe, and the judgment $\emptyset \in U_1$ reads that the empty type is also such an element.

In "intuitionistic" or "constructive" logic the judgment form $p \in P$ admits a different reading. If P is a proposition (i.e., a well-formed formula constructed from the propositional connectives $\wedge$, $\vee$, etc.), then the judgment form $p \in P$ means that p is a summary of a (constructive) proof of P. In other words, proposition P is identified with the set (or "type") of its proofs. This is the idea generally attributed to Curry and Howard and called the principle of propositions-as-types. Table 1 illustrates the principle.[1]

---

1. The notation we are using for λ-expressions and function application is the conventional one [9, 34]. That is, function application is denoted by juxtaposition and associates to the left, and we assume that when a λ-term such as $\lambda x.q$ occurs in a larger expression q is taken as extending as far to the right as possible— to the first unmatched closing bracket or the end of the expression, whichever is first. Corresponding to the convention that function application associates to the left we have the convention that implication associates to the right. Thus $P \Rightarrow Q \Rightarrow R$ is read as $P \Rightarrow (Q \Rightarrow R)$.

Table 1. Propositions as types.

Proposition	Type	Type Name	Example
$P \Rightarrow Q$	$P \longrightarrow Q$	function space	$\lambda x.x \in A \Rightarrow A$ $\lambda x.\lambda y.x \in A \Rightarrow (B \Rightarrow A)$
$P \wedge Q$	$P \times Q$	Cartesian product	$\lambda x.\langle x, x\rangle \in A \Rightarrow (A \wedge A)$ $\lambda y.\mathbf{fst}\ y \in (A \wedge B) \Rightarrow A$
$P \vee Q$	$P + Q$	disjoint sum	$\lambda x.\mathbf{inl}\ x \in A \Rightarrow (A \vee B)$
$\exists(P, x.Q(x))$	$\sum(P, x.Q(x))$	dependent product	$\langle \mathbb{N}, 0\rangle \in \exists(U1, A.A)$ $\langle \mathbb{N}, \lambda x.x\rangle \in \exists(U1, A.A \Rightarrow A)$
$\forall(P, x.Q(x))$	$\prod(P, x.Q(x))$	dependent function space	$\lambda A.\lambda x.x \in \forall(U1, A.A \Rightarrow A)$
$\neg P$	$P \longrightarrow \emptyset$		$\lambda f.f\emptyset \in \neg\forall(U1, A.A)$

In constructive mathematics, a proof of $P \Rightarrow Q$ is a method of proving Q given a proof of P. Thus $P \Rightarrow Q$ is identified with the type $P \longrightarrow Q$ of (total) functions from the type P into the type Q. Assuming that A is a proposition, an elementary example would be the proposition $A \Rightarrow A$. A proof of $A \Rightarrow A$ is a method of constructing a proof of A given a proof A. Such a method would be the identity function of A, $\lambda x.x$, since this is a function that, given an object of A, returns the same object of A. The proposition $A \Rightarrow (B \Rightarrow A)$ provides a second, slightly more complicated, example of the constructive interpretation of implication. Assuming that A and B are propositions, a proof of $A \Rightarrow (B \Rightarrow A)$ is a method that, given a proof of A, constructs a proof of $B \Rightarrow A$. Now, a proof of $B \Rightarrow A$ is a method that from a proof of B constructs a proof of A. Thus, given that x is a proof of A the constant function $\lambda y.x$ is a proof of $B \Rightarrow A$. Hence the function $\lambda x.\lambda y.x$ is a proof of $A \Rightarrow (B \Rightarrow A)$.

To prove $P \wedge Q$ constructively, it is necessary to exhibit a proof of P and to exhibit a proof of Q. Thus the proposition $P \wedge Q$ is identified with the Cartesian product, $P \times Q$, of the types P and Q. That is, $P \times Q$ is the type of all pairs $\langle x, y\rangle$ where x has type P and y has type Q. For example, assuming that A and B are propositions, the proposition $(A \wedge B) \Rightarrow A$ is proved constructively as follows. We have to exhibit a method that given a pair $\langle x, y\rangle$, where x is an object of A and y is an object of B, constructs an object of A. Such a method is clearly the projection function **fst** that projects an object of $A \wedge B$ onto its first component. (The function **fst** is not a primitive of type theory but is expressed as $\lambda p.\mathbf{split}(p, (x, y).x)$. In general $\mathbf{split}(p, (x, y).e)$ splits a pair p into its two components and evaluates the expression e with the variables x and y bound to the respective components. Thus $\mathbf{split}(p, (x, y).x)$ splits p into its two components and then evaluates the expression x with x bound to the first component; i.e., it evaluates the first component.)

A constructive proof of $P \vee Q$ consists of either a proof of P or a proof of Q together with information indicating which of the two has been proved. Thus $P \vee Q$ is identified with the disjoint sum of the types P and Q. That is, objects of $P \vee Q$ take one of the two forms **inl** x or **inr** y, where x is an object of P, y is an object of Q, and the reserved words **inl** (inject left) and **inr** (inject right) indicate which operand has been proved. As elementary examples of provable propositions involving disjunction we take $A \Rightarrow A \vee B$ and $A \vee B \Rightarrow B \vee A$. The proposition $A \Rightarrow A \vee B$ is proved by the function $\lambda x.\textbf{inl}\ x$ that injects an argument x of type A into the left operand of $A \vee B$. The proposition $A \vee B \Rightarrow B \vee A$ is proved by the function $\lambda x.\textbf{when}(x, y.\textbf{inr}\ y, z.\textbf{inl}\ z)$.[2] In general the construct **when**$(x, y.e, z.f)$ is evaluated as follows. The argument x is evaluated; if it takes the form **inl** a then the expression e is evaluated with the variable y bound to a; if x takes the form **inr** b then the expression f is evaluated with the variable z bound to b. Thus **when**$(x, y.\textbf{inr}\ y, z.\textbf{inl}\ z)$ has the effect of transforming a value of the form **inr** b into **inl** b and vice versa.

The notation $\forall(P, x.Q(x))$ denotes a universal quantification. We prefer this notation to the more conventional $(\forall x \in P)Q(x)$ because it makes clear the scope of the binding of the variable x. In order to prove constructively the proposition $\forall(P, x.Q(x))$ it is necessary to provide a method that, given an object p of type P constructs a proof of $Q(p)$. Thus proofs of $\forall(P, x.Q(x))$ are functions (as for implication), their domain being P and their range, $Q(p)$, being dependent on the argument p supplied to the function. As an example the polymorphic identity function $\lambda A.\lambda x.x$ is a proof of the proposition $\forall(U_1, A.A \Rightarrow A)$.

The notion of *dependent* function space is often severely restricted if not completely unknown in conventional programming languages, even though the idea is commonplace in the space of real world problems. Examples would include the type of functions that input a number n and then return a number that is at least n, the type of functions that input a number n and then return a function that inputs an array of size n and outputs its maximum element, or a function that inputs the details of a person and then, depending on whether the person is living or dead, outputs that person's employment status or details of the person's estate.

A constructive proof of $\exists(P, x.Q(x))$ consists of exhibiting an object p of P together with a proof of $Q(p)$. Thus proofs of $\exists(P, x.Q(x))$ are pairs $\langle p, q \rangle$ where p is a proof of P and q is a proof of $Q(p)$.

The type $\exists(P, x.Q(x))$ is called a *dependent* type because the type of the second component, q, in a pair $\langle p, q \rangle$ in the type depends on the first component, p. For example, there are many objects of the type $\exists(U_1, A.A)$. Each consists

---

2. Later the name "$\vee$-*elim*" is used instead of "**when**". The latter is used for the moment in order to suggest its operational meaning. Similarly, "$\wedge$-*elim*" should have been used instead of "**split**".

of a pair $\langle A, a \rangle$ where A is a type and a is an object of that type. (Thus the proposition is interpreted as the statement "there is a type that is provable", or "there is a type that is nonempty".) The pair $\langle \mathbb{N}, 0 \rangle$ is an object of $\exists(U_1, A.A)$ since $\mathbb{N}$ is an element of U_1 and 0 is an element of $\mathbb{N}$. Two further examples are $\langle \{red, white, blue\}, red \rangle$ and $\langle \mathbb{N} \Rightarrow \mathbb{N}, \lambda x.x \rangle$.

Objects of the type $\exists(U_1, A.A)$ are the simplest possible examples of *algebras* (one or more sets together with a number of operations defined on the sets) since they each consist of a set A together with a single constant of A. Indeed algebras are good examples of the need for dependent types. A semigroup, for example, is a set S together with an associative binary operation on S. Thus a semigroup is a pair in which the type of the second component depends on the value of the first component.

Negation is not a primitive concept of type theory. It is defined via the *empty type*. The empty type, denoted $\varnothing$, is the type containing no elements. The negation $\neg P$ is defined to be $P \Rightarrow \varnothing$:

$$\neg P \equiv P \Rightarrow \varnothing$$

($\equiv$ stands for *definitionally equal to*). This means that a proof of $\neg P$ is a method for constructing an object of the empty type from an object of P. Since it would be absurd to construct an object of the empty type, this is equivalent to saying that it is absurd to construct a proof of P.

As an example of a provable negation, consider the proposition $\neg\forall(U_1, A.A)$. The proposition states that not every proposition (in U_1) is provable, or not every type is nonempty. The basis for its proof is very ordinary— we exhibit a counter-example, namely, the empty type $\varnothing$. Formally, we have to construct a function that maps an argument f, say, of type $\forall(U_1, A.A)$ into $\varnothing$. Now f is itself a function mapping objects, A, of U_1 into objects of A. So, for any type A, the application of f to A, denoted $f A$, has type A. In particular, $f \varnothing$ has type $\varnothing$. Thus the proof object we require is $\lambda f.f\varnothing$.

Some further examples of provable propositions may help to clarify the nature of constructive proof.

Functional composition proves the transitivity of implication:

$$\lambda f.\lambda g.\lambda x.g(f\, x) \in (A \Rightarrow B) \Rightarrow (B \Rightarrow C) \Rightarrow (A \Rightarrow C).$$

The propositional equivalent of currying:

$$\lambda f.\lambda x.\lambda y.f \langle x, y \rangle \in (A \wedge B \Rightarrow C) \Rightarrow (A \Rightarrow B \Rightarrow C)$$

and of uncurrying:

$$\lambda f.\lambda w.\mathbf{split}(w, (x, y).f\, x\, y) \in (A \Rightarrow B \Rightarrow C) \Rightarrow (A \wedge B \Rightarrow C).$$

Two more:

$$\lambda f.\lambda x.f(\textbf{inl } x) \in (A \vee B \Rightarrow C) \Rightarrow (A \Rightarrow C)$$

$$\lambda w.\textbf{when}(w, f.\lambda x.f(\textbf{fst } x), g.\lambda x.g(\textbf{snd } x))$$
$$\in [(A \Rightarrow C) \vee (B \Rightarrow C)] \Rightarrow [(A \wedge B) \Rightarrow C].$$

1.2 *An Example Derivation*

Martin-Löf's theory is defined by a number of natural deduction style [16] inference rules. For the purposes of illustration we consider just four rules for the moment. These are (simplified forms of) the rules for function introduction and elimination, and two rules for ∨-introduction.

$$\frac{\begin{array}{l} |[\ x \in A \\ \rhd\ f(x) \in B \\ ]| \end{array}}{\lambda x.f(x) \in A \Rightarrow B} \quad \Rightarrow\text{-introduction}$$

$$\frac{\begin{array}{l} a \in A \\ f \in A \Rightarrow B \end{array}}{f\,a \in B} \quad \Rightarrow\text{-elimination}$$

$$\frac{a \in A}{\textbf{inl } a \in A \vee B} \qquad \frac{b \in B}{\textbf{inr } b \in A \vee B} \quad \vee\text{-introduction}$$

The second of these rules (⇒-elimination) introduces the least amount of new notation and so is the easiest to begin with. It can be read in two senses—in a logical sense and in a computational sense. In a logical sense the rule states that if a is a proof of A and f is a proof of $A \Rightarrow B$, i.e., a method of going from a proof of A to a proof of B, then $f\,a$ —the result of applying the method f to the given proof a— is a proof of B. In a computational sense it states that if a has type A and f is a function from A to B then $f\,a$, the result of applying the function f to a, has type B.

The first rule (⇒-introduction) says how functions can be constructed. It has one premise— a so-called "hypothetical premise". Hypothetical judgments play an extremely important role in the theory and are indicated by the use of scope brackets ("|[" and "]|"). (This notation, borrowed from the book by Dijkstra and Feijen [13], is not used by Martin-Löf but is one that I have introduced in my own accounts of the theory. It is likely that a number of my colleagues in this institute will also use the same notation for their own purposes. Although there may be some differences in interpretation you will not go far wrong if you consider all uses as meaning the same.) A hypothetical judgment has two parts, first a number of assumptions and then a number of conclusions that can be made in the context of those assumptions. In the notation used here the assumptions are separated from the conclusions by the symbol '▷'. In a logical sense the rule may be read as "if assuming that x is a proof of A it is possible to construct a proof $f(x)$ of B then $\lambda x.f(x)$ is a proof of $A \Rightarrow B$." In a computational sense the rule is read differently: "If in a context in which x is an object of type A the object $f(x)$ has type B then the function $\lambda x.f(x)$ is an object of type $A \Rightarrow B$."

In general, $f(x)$ will be an expression containing zero or more free occurrences of x. Such occurrences of x become bound in the expression $\lambda x.f(x)$. Such binding of variables is always associated with the discharge of assumptions.

The last two rules say how to construct a proof of a disjunction or, equally, how to construct an element of a disjoint sum. To prove $A \vee B$ we exhibit a proof of A and tag it with the constant **inl**, or we exhibit a proof of B and tag it with the constant **inr**. Put another way, an element of the disjoint sum of types A and B is an element of A tagged by **inl** or an element of B tagged by **inr**. The constants **inl** and **inr** are called *injection functions* and stand for **in**ject **l**eft and **in**ject **r**ight, respectively.

We use these rules in the proof of the proposition

$$[(A \vee (A \Rightarrow B)) \Rightarrow B] \Rightarrow B.$$

Example 1.1

$$\lambda f.f(\mathbf{inr}(\lambda x.f(\mathbf{inl}\ x))) \in [(A \vee (A \Rightarrow B)) \Rightarrow B] \Rightarrow B$$

Derivation

0.0	‖[	$f \in [(A \vee (A \Rightarrow B)) \Rightarrow B]$
0.1.0	▷	‖[$x \in A$
	▷	% 0.1.0,**inl**-introduction %
0.1.1		$\mathbf{inl}\ x \in A \vee (A \Rightarrow B)$
		% 0.0,0.1.1, $\Rightarrow$-elimination %
0.1.2		$f(\mathbf{inl}\ x) \in B$
		]‖
		% 0.1.0, 0.1.2, $\Rightarrow$-introduction %
0.1		$\lambda x.f(\mathbf{inl}\ x) \in A \Rightarrow B$
		% 0.1, **inr**-introduction %
0.2		$\mathbf{inr}(\lambda x.f(\mathbf{inl}\ x)) \in A \vee (A \Rightarrow B)$
		% 0.0, 0.2, $\Rightarrow$-elimination %
0.3		$f(\mathbf{inr}(\lambda x.f(\mathbf{inl}\ x))) \in B$
	]‖	
		% 0.0, 0.3, $\Rightarrow$-introduction %
1		$\lambda f.f(\mathbf{inr}(\lambda x.f(\mathbf{inl}\ x))) \in [(A \vee (A \Rightarrow B)) \Rightarrow B] \Rightarrow B$

There is an ulterior motive for presenting the above as an example of proof derivation in constructive mathematics, namely, to explain the role of the law of the excluded middle. It is commonly —misleadingly— stated that this law is not valid in constructive mathematics. This is not so. What is valid is that there is no general method for establishing the law for an arbitrary proposition; a theory obtained by adding the law of the excluded middle to type theory would not be inconsistent. Indeed it is the case that the law of the excluded middle can never be refuted in constructive mathematics. Evidence for this is obtained from the above example. Specifically, by substituting ø for B and replacing $P \Rightarrow$ ø by $\neg P$ we obtain the tautology

$\neg\neg(A \lor \neg A).$

Quantifying over A we obtain

$\forall(U_1, A.\neg\neg(A \lor \neg A))$

and applying the result that "$\forall \neg \Rightarrow \neg \exists$" we obtain

$\neg\exists(U_1, A.\neg(A \lor \neg A)).$

We interpret the last proposition as the statement that it is impossible to exhibit a type, A, for which the law of the excluded middle does not hold.

The form $\neg\neg P$ is of interest because it asserts that P cannot be refuted. Other examples of propositions that are classically valid but cannot be generally established in constructive mathematics are the following:

$(A \Rightarrow B) \lor (B \Rightarrow A)$

$(A \Rightarrow B \lor C) \Rightarrow [(A \Rightarrow B) \lor (A \Rightarrow C)]$

$(\neg B \Rightarrow \neg A) \Rightarrow A \Rightarrow B$

For each such proposition P it is, however, the case that $\neg\neg P$ can be proven constructively. Indeed it is a theorem attributed by Kleene [22] to Glivenko [17] that if P is any tautology of the classical propositional calculus then the proposition $\neg\neg P$ is always constructively valid. For one method of modeling classical reasoning in a formal implementation of a constructive theory you are referred to [10].

2 *The Structure of the Rules*

The programmer is, in his everyday activities, a user of formal systems— operating systems, text-processing systems, and programming systems. The computing scientist is therefore, in his everyday activities, concerned with the construction and analysis of formal systems. What criteria should we use to assess a formal system? What is it that distinguishes an "elegant" formal system from an "inelegant" formal system? Certainly there have been many formalizations of constructive mathematics, but none has gained as much acclaim among the computing scientist community as that of Per Martin-Löf. I believe that it is because his system exhibits a certain elegance that others lack.

On first encounter, however, the universal reaction among computing scientists appears to be that the theory is formidable. Indeed, several have specifically referred to the overwhelming number of rules in the theory. On closer examination, however, the theory betrays a rich structure— a structure that is much deeper than the superficial observation that types are defined by introduction, elimination, and computation rules. Once recognized, this structure considerably reduces the burden of understanding. The aim of this section is, therefore, to convey that structure to you.

There is a very practical reason for wanting to recognize the inherent structure of the formal system. As programmers using a typed programming language we are strongly encouraged to introduce and exploit our own type structures. Such declared data types are intended to reflect the structure of the given data and are in turn reflected in the structure of the programs that we write (see for example [21]). Any formalization of constructive reasoning should also strongly encourage the introduction of new type structures, but of course in a disciplined way. That his theory is already open to extension is a fact that was clearly intended by Martin-Löf. Indeed, it is a fact that has been exploited by several individuals; Nordström, Petersson, and Smith [31] have extended the theory to include lists; they and Constable et al. [11] have added subset types, and Constable et al. have introduced quotient types; Nordström has introduced multi-level functions [29], Chisholm has introduced a very special-purpose type of tree structure [7], and Dyckhoff [15] has defined the type of categories.

(Objections to such extensions can be made on the grounds that they can always be encoded within the existing theory, in particular using the W-type [14], because they add to the complexity of the theory and because they might undermine the quality of the theory even to the extent of introducing inconsistencies. The experiences and arguments of others have convinced me that this view is wrong. In the context of this section, however, my main purpose is not to argue this view but to elucidate the structure of the rules as presented by Martin-Löf.)

The rules defining individual type constructors can be divided into five sets:

1. the formation rule,

2. the introduction rules,

3. an elimination rule,

4. computation rules, and

5. congruence rules.

The formation rule specifies how a type constructor may be parameterized by other types; the introduction rules say how to form elements of the type, and the elimination rule says how to reason about elements of the type (or equally, since reasoning is constructive, how to construct functions defined over the elements of the type). The elimination rule associates with the type constructor a so-called noncanonical object form; the computation rules then prescribe how to evaluate instances of this form. Finally, the congruence rules express substitutivity and extensionality properties. I shall not have time to discuss the congruence rules; in any case their formulation is relatively straightforward.

The main contribution that we make here is to describe a scheme for computing the elimination rule and computation rules for a newly introduced type constructor. In other words, we show that it suffices to provide the type formation rule and the introduction rules for a new type constructor; together these provide sufficient information from which the remaining details can be deduced. The significance of this result is that it has the twin benefits of reducing the burden of understanding and the burden of definition. It reduces the burden of understanding since we now need to understand only the formation and introduction rules and the general scheme for inferring the remaining rules. Conversely, the burden of definition is reduced since it suffices to state the formation and introduction rules, the others being inferred automatically.

The method of inferring the elimination rule from the introduction rules is described by way of examples rather than formally, although a formal method does indeed underlie our descriptions and should be evident.

2.1 *Lists*

The list type constructor should be familiar. The formation rule and two introduction rules are as follows:

$$\frac{A\ type}{List(A)\ type} \qquad \text{List formation}$$

$$\frac{A\ type}{[\,]\in List(A)} \qquad [\,]\text{-introduction}$$

$$A \ type$$
$$a \in A$$
$$l \in List(A)$$
_____   :-introduction
$$a : l \in List(A)$$

It is normal to omit the premises of the formation rule from the premises of the introduction rules. Thus the premise "*A type*" would normally be omitted from the [ ]- and :-introduction rules above. We shall follow the same practice in the remainder of this discussion.

The (single) elimination rule for a given type constructor performs two functions: It says how to reason about objects of the type, and it says how to define functions over objects of the type. (Because proofs are interpreted constructively these amount to the same thing.) The first premise (excluding the premises of the formation rule) of the elimination rule for type constructor Θ is therefore the statement that C, say, is a family of types indexed by objects of Θ. In other words C is postulated to be a property of objects of type Θ. The introduction rules represent the only way that canonical objects of the type may be constructed; so, in order to show that property C holds for an arbitrary object of type Θ, it suffices to show that it holds for each of the different sorts of canonical objects. There is thus one premise in the elimination rule for each of the introduction rules. Moreover the premises of an introduction rule become assumptions in the corresponding premise of the elimination rule.

In the case of lists there are just two sorts of canonical element, the empty list and composite lists consisting of a head element and a tail list. In order to prove that a property C is true of an arbitrary list, we thus have to show that it is true of the empty list and of composite lists. Equally, to define a function over lists, it suffices to define its value on the empty list and its value when applied to a composite list. The elimination rule is therefore as shown in Figure 1 (a).

In this rule the third premise is the one corresponding to [ ]-introduction; it is not hypothetical since, apart from the premises of list formation, there are no premises in the [ ]-introduction rule. The fourth premise corresponds to the :-introduction rule; it is hypothetical since the :-introduction rule has two premises in addition to the premises of list formation. To emphasize the way in which the premises of the introduction rule become assumptions of the corresponding premise in the elimination rule, we have used the same symbols, a and l, in the :-introduction rule and in the elimination rule.

Note that there is an additional assumption ("$h \in C(l)$") in the elimination rule arising from the fact that l is a recursive introduction variable.

The computation rules for a type introduce a third judgment form about which we need to make some preparatory remarks before going into the details of the computation rules for lists. The judgment form is

$$p = q \in P$$

and is read as "*p* and *q* are equal objects within the type *P*". Thus implicit in such a judgment are the judgments that *p* is an object of *P* and that *q* is an object of *P*.

Computation in the theory is lazy. That is, to evaluate an expression like *List-elim*(...), the first parameter is evaluated to its canonical form and then further evaluation involving the other parameters takes place. Since the introduction rules specify the only forms that the canonical objects of a type can take, it suffices to provide a computation rule corresponding to each of the introduction rules. For the *List* type constructor we must therefore explain how to evaluate expressions of the form *List-elim*([ ], ...) and of the form *List-elim*(*a* : *l*, ...). We do so by replacing the premise "*x* ∈ *List*(*A*)" in the List elimination rule by the premises of the introduction rule. Taking first the [ ]-introduction we obtain the computation rule shown in Figure 1 (b). Since there are no premises in the [ ]-introduction rule, the effect of the replacement is simply to reduce the number of premises by one. The conclusion of the rule is also straightforward to see. Note the parameter to the elimination hypothesis *C* in the conclusion.

The computation rule for composite lists is a little more difficult to understand. As before, the premise "*x* ∈ *List*(*A*)" in the elimination rule is replaced this time by the premises of the :-introduction rule. The construction of the conclusion of the rule is guided by its type part, viz., *C*(*a* : *l*). The right side of the equality must be an object of this type. But the last premise of the List

---

Figure 1.   (a) List-elimination; (b) [ ]-computation.

|[*w* ∈ *List*(*A*) ▷ *C*(*w*) *type*]| *x* ∈ *List*(*A*) *y* ∈ *C*([ ]) |[*a* ∈ *A*; *l* ∈ *List*(*A*); *h* ∈ *C*(*l*) ▷ *z*(*a*, *l*, *h*) ∈ *C*(*a* : *l*)]|	|[*w* ∈ *List*(*A*) ▷ *C*(*w*) *type*]| *y* ∈ *C*([ ]) |[*a* ∈ *A*; *l* ∈ *List*(*A*); *h* ∈ *C*(*l*) ▷ *z*(*a*, *l*, *h*) ∈ *C*(*a* : *l*)]|
List-elim(*x*, *y*, *z*) ∈ *C*(*x*)	*List-elim*([ ], *y*, *z*) = *y* ∈ *C*([ ])

elimination rule tells us how to construct such an object: We have to exhibit objects *a*, *l*, and *h* of appropriate type and, having done so, the expression $z(a, l, h)$ has type $C(a : l)$. The type of *h* is $C(l)$; to construct something of this type given that *l* has type *List(A)* we would use list elimination. Thus we obtain the rule shown in Figure 2.

One final comment should be made about the computation rules to avoid misunderstanding. The two rules above should be regarded as left-to-right rewrite rules for the purposes of evaluating an expression involving *List-elim*. As such the rules involve a recursive computation. The number of recursive evaluations of *List-elim* may, however, be smaller than the length of the given list— this occurs for example when the expression $z(a, l, h)$ contains no occurrences of the variable *h*. This is what is meant by saying that evaluation is "lazy". As a consequence, an expression may well contain occurrences of the constant *ø-elim* —discussed in Section 2.3 and for which no computation rules are given— without evaluation of the expression being in any way divergent.

2.2 *Disjoint sums*

We may now return to the disjoint sum type whose introduction rules were presented in Section 1.2. Since there are two introduction rules there are four premises in the elimination rule— the two standard premises, which postulate the existence of a family of types *C* and an object of the type, and one premise for each introduction rule (see Figure 3).

Figure 2.   :-computation.

$$
\begin{array}{l}
|[\quad w \in List(A) \\
\quad \triangleright\ C(w)\ type \\
]| \\
a \in A \\
l \in List(A) \\
y \in C([\ ]) \\
|[\quad a \in A;\, l \in List(A);\, h \in C(l) \\
\quad \triangleright\ z(a, l, h) \in C(a : l) \\
]| \\
\hline
List\text{-}elim(a : l, y, z) = z(a, l, List\text{-}elim(l, y, z)) \in C(a : l)
\end{array}
$$

Note how the premises of the introduction rules become assumptions in the corresponding premises of the elimination rule. Note also the parameterization of C in each of the premises.

There are two computation rules for $\vee$-*elim* objects, one for each sort of canonical object; they are given in Figures 4 and 5.

The operational understanding of $\vee$-*elim* is that $\vee$-*elim*$(t, a.e(a), b.f(b))$ picks out either $e(a)$ or $f(b)$ depending on the form taken by t. If it has the form **inl** p, then e is evaluated with the parameter a bound to p. On the other hand, if it has the form **inr** q, then f is evaluated with the parameter b bound to q.

2.3 *The empty set*

It is always instructive to consider extreme cases. Let us therefore consider the empty type. The formation rule is just the axiom:

$$\frac{\rule{2cm}{0.4pt}}{\emptyset \; type} \qquad\qquad \emptyset\text{-formation}$$

There are no introduction rules for the empty type (since it would be absurd to construct an element of the empty type). Thus there are no premises in the elimination rule other than the standard ones.

Figure 3. $\vee$-elimination.

$$
\begin{array}{l}
[\![\; w \in A \vee B \\
\;\rhd \; C(w) \; type \\
]\!] \\
d \in A \vee B \\
[\![\; a \in A \\
\;\rhd \; e(a) \in C(\textbf{inl} \; a) \\
]\!] \\
[\![\; b \in B \\
\;\rhd \; f(b) \in C(\textbf{inr} \; b) \\
]\!] \\
\hline
\vee\text{-}elim(d, a.e(a), b.f(b)) \in C(d)
\end{array}
$$

$$\frac{\begin{array}{l} [\![\ w \in \emptyset \\ \vartriangleright\ C(w)\ type \\ ]\!] \\ r \in \emptyset \end{array}}{\emptyset\text{-}elim(r) \in C(r)} \qquad \emptyset\text{-elimination}$$

This rule is easily recognized as the absurdity rule— if it is possible to establish an absurdity, then it is possible to establish any proposition whatever.

Since there are no introduction rules there are no computation rules. The object $\emptyset\text{-}elim(r)$ should thus be considered as a divergent computation.

2.4 *Finite Sets*

Suppose we wish to define a type constructor $\Im$ such that $\Im(A)$ is the type of finite subsets of A.[3] Any such subset can be constructed by listing its elements. Conversely, any list of elements of A may be regarded as a finite subset of A provided that we disregard the order of the elements and repeated occurrences of the same element. $\Im(A)$ is thus the quotient of *List(A)* with respect to the equivalence relation that defines two lists as equal if they have the same elements independent of order and number of repeated occurrences.

---

3. The material in this section is from [8], to which the reader is referred for further discussion.

Figure 4.   inl-computation.

$$\begin{array}{l} [\![\ w \in A \vee B \\ \vartriangleright\ C(w)\ type \\ ]\!] \\ a \in A \\ [\![\ a \in A \\ \vartriangleright\ e(a) \in C(\textbf{inl}\ a) \\ ]\!] \\ [\![\ b \in B \\ \vartriangleright\ f(b) \in C(\textbf{inr}\ b) \\ ]\!] \\ \hline \vee\text{-}elim(\textbf{inl}\ a, a.e(a), b.f(b)) = e(a) \in C(\textbf{inl}\ a) \end{array}$$

We define the type constructor ℑ by adding to the introduction rules for List two additional rules defining the above equivalence. In full the rules are as follows:

$$\frac{A \; type}{ℑ(A) \; type} \qquad ℑ\text{-formation}$$

$$\frac{}{\phi \in ℑ(A)} \qquad \phi\text{-introduction}$$

$$\frac{a \in A \quad s \in ℑ(A)}{a; s \in ℑ(A)} \qquad ;\text{-introduction}$$

$$\frac{a \in A \quad s \in ℑ(A)}{a; a; s = a; s \in ℑ(A)} \qquad \text{repetition}$$

Figure 5.   **inr**-computation.

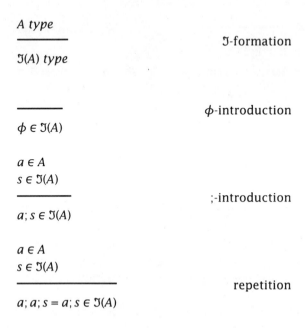

$$
\begin{array}{l}
|[\;\; w \in A \vee B \\
\;\; \triangleright \;\; C(w) \; type \\
]| \\
b \in B \\
|[\;\; a \in A \\
\;\; \triangleright \;\; e(a) \in C(\mathbf{inl}\; a) \\
]| \\
|[\;\; b \in B \\
\;\; \triangleright \;\; f(b) \in C(\mathbf{inr}\; b) \\
]| \\
\hline
\vee\text{-}elim(\mathbf{inr}\; b, a.e(a), b.f(b)) = f(b) \in C(\mathbf{inr}\; b)
\end{array}
$$

$$\frac{\begin{array}{l} a \in A \\ b \in A \\ s \in \mathfrak{J}(A) \end{array}}{a; b; s = b; a; s \in \mathfrak{J}(A)} \quad \text{order}$$

How should we construct the elimination rule for $\mathfrak{J}$? The best way to begin is to view the rule as a method of defining a function over objects of the type. If a function is to be truly a function then it must give equal values when applied to equal objects. Looking at it from the point of view of proofs, a proof that an object has some property must be independent of the way the object was constructed. Thus the $\mathfrak{J}$-elimination rule —shown in Figure 6— is constructed like the List-elimination rule but with two additional premises, one corresponding to the repetition rule and the other corresponding to the order rule.

The premise corresponding to the repetition rule,

Figure 6. $\mathfrak{J}$-elimination.

$$\frac{\begin{array}{l} |[\ w \in \mathfrak{J}(A) \\ \rhd\ C(w)\ type \\ ]| \\ x \in \mathfrak{J}(A) \\ y \in C(\phi) \\ |[\ a \in A; s \in \mathfrak{J}(A); h \in C(s) \\ \rhd\ z(a, s, h) \in C(a; s) \\ ]| \\ |[\ a \in A; s \in \mathfrak{J}(A); h \in C(s) \\ \rhd\ z(a,\ a; s,\ z(a, s, h)) = z(a, s, h) \in C(a; s) \\ ]| \\ |[\ a \in A; b \in A; s \in \mathfrak{J}(A); h \in C(s) \\ \rhd\ z(a,\ b; s,\ z(b, s, h)) = z(b,\ a; s,\ z(a, s, h)) \in C(a; b; s) \\ ]| \end{array}}{\mathfrak{J}\text{-}elim(x, y, z) \in C(x)}$$

$$\begin{aligned} &\mathbin{\|}[\ a \in \Lambda; s \in \mathfrak{I}(A); h \in C(s) \\ &\rhd\ z(a,\ a; s,\ z(a, s, h)) = z(a, s, h) \in C(a; s) \\ &]\mathbin{\|} \end{aligned}$$

is constructed as follows. The assumptions are derived from the premises of the repetition rule as in our discussion of lists. The judgment asserts that the proof object of $C(a; s)$ is the same whether we choose to evaluate it from $a; s$ or $a; a; s$. In the former case we evaluate $z(a, s, h)$, and in the latter case we evaluate $z(a,\ a; s,\ z(a, s, h))$.

The premise corresponding to the order rule,

$$\begin{aligned} &\mathbin{\|}[\ a, b \in A; s \in \mathfrak{I}(A); h \in C(s) \\ &\rhd\ z(a,\ b; s,\ z(b, s, h)) = z(b,\ a; s,\ z(a, s, h)) \in C(a; b; s) \\ &]\mathbin{\|} \end{aligned}$$

is constructed similarly.

2.5 *Polynomials over* $\{0, 1\}$

Consider now the representation of numbers in binary form. A binary numeral is a list of 1's and 0's in which leading 0's are insignificant. Thus $11 = 011 = 0011$ and so on. A binary numeral is, however, one particular interpretation of such a list. More generally we may regard such a list as denoting a polynomial; thus 11 denotes $1 \times x + 1$. Using Λ to denote the empty list, we can define a type, called P, say, of lists of 0's and 1's in which leading 0's are insignificant as follows:

$$\frac{}{\Lambda \in P} \qquad\qquad\qquad \Lambda\text{-introduction}$$

$$\frac{p \in P}{p0 \in P} \qquad\qquad\qquad 0\text{-introduction}$$

$$\frac{p \in P}{p1 \in P} \qquad\qquad\qquad 1\text{-introduction}$$

$$\frac{}{\Lambda 0 = \Lambda \in P} \qquad\qquad\qquad \text{leading zeroes}$$

Given these four introduction rules the elimination rule for P has four premises. The four premises state that to define a function over P it is necessary to consider three cases —the case where the argument is Λ, the case where it is of the form $p0$, and the case where it is of the form $p1$— and furthermore it is necessary to show that the insignificance of leading zeroes is respected. Specifically, we have the *P*-elimination rule shown in Figure 7.

3 *The Boyer-Moore Majority-Vote Algorithm*

3.1 *Preliminary Remarks*

This section is concerned with examining the relationship between the heuristics used in inductive proof and the heuristics used in the development of loop invariants [2, 13, 19] in algorithm design. Before we do so it is necessary to introduce two additional type structures, the natural numbers and the subset type [11, 30, 33]. Given the discussion in the previous section the type of natural numbers is easy to explain. There are just two introduction rules, the first asserting that 0 is a natural number, and the second asserting that the successor of m is a natural number whenever m is a natural number.

$$\frac{\rule{2cm}{0.4pt}}{0 \in \mathbb{N}} \qquad\qquad \text{0-introduction}$$

Figure 7. *P*-elimination.

$$\frac{\begin{array}{l} |[\;\; w \in P \\ \triangleright\;\; C(w)\ type \\ ]| \\ x \in P \\ y_1 \in C(\Lambda) \\ |[\;\; p \in P; h \in C(p) \\ \triangleright\;\; y_2(p, h) \in C(p0) \\ ]| \\ |[\;\; p \in P; h \in C(p) \\ \triangleright\;\; y_3(p, h) \in C(p1) \\ ]| \\ y_2(\Lambda, y_1) = y_1 \in C(\Lambda) \end{array}}{P\text{-}elim(x, y_1, y_2, y_3) \in C(x)}$$

$$\frac{m \in \mathbb{N}}{m+1 \in \mathbb{N}}$$ +1-introduction

The elimination rule for natural numbers is the familiar rule of simple mathematical induction. We leave as an exercise the reconstruction of the elimination and computation rules.

The subset type is less straightforward since it introduces a new concept, that of information loss. Quite early on in the application of the theory to computing science it was recognized that some proof objects have no computational content. Proof objects that witness equalities are the most obvious example, to which we can also add proof objects of negations and other propositions built with these two as basis. For this reason the subset type was introduced into the theory. The subset type is like the existential or $\sum$-type. To construct an object of the latter we have to construct a pair:

$$\frac{\begin{array}{l} a \in A \\ b \in B(a) \end{array}}{\langle a, b \rangle \in \exists(A, x.B(x))}$$ $\exists$-introduction

In the subset type the information contained in the proof of the second component is lost (the reason being that it very often carries no computational content):

$$\frac{\begin{array}{l} a \in A \\ B(a)\ \textbf{true} \end{array}}{a \in Set(A, x.B(x))}$$ Subset introduction

The judgment form P **true** means that P is a proposition that has been established to be true. This judgment form offers a possible mechanism for integrating other formal proof systems with that of type theory. One of the rules for establishing such a judgment should be, of course, that if P is constructively true then P is true:

$$\frac{p \in P}{P\ \textbf{true}}$$ Constructive truth

There is, however, no reason why one should not also allow instances of the law of the excluded middle to be **true** judgments:

$$\frac{}{P \vee \neg P\ \textbf{true}}$$ excluded middle

The elimination rule for subset types is, however, a little harder to use since the constructive evidence is unavailable (see Figure 8).

3.2 *Problem Statement*

The problem we use to illustrate algorithm development in Martin-Löf's theory of types is called the majority-vote problem. It may briefly be described as determining whether or not one of the candidates in a ballot has received a majority of the votes. The solution on which our development is based is described in [24] and is attributed therein to R. S. Boyer and J S. Moore.

Let us suppose that the number of votes cast in a ballot is n and that the votes are recorded in an array a of length n. To be completely formal, we further suppose that the candidates are drawn from the (nonempty) type A. Equality on A is necessarily decidable. Thus from now on we work within the following context:

$$
\begin{array}{ll}
|[& A \in U_1 \\
; & .eq. \in \forall(A, a.\forall(A, b.(a = b) \lor \neg(a = b)) \ \% \text{ We write } a.eq.b \\
; & n \in \mathbb{N} \\
; & a \in Set(\mathbb{N}, i.i < n) \longrightarrow A \\
; & x_0 \in A \\
\triangleright &
\end{array}
$$

In most ballots there are few candidates and many voters. Thus an obvious solution is to create a pigeonhole for each candidate and to put votes one by one into the pigeonholes. When all votes have been counted the number of votes of the candidate receiving most votes can be compared with n **div** 2. This means, however, that we must either assume known the number of candidates, allow for n candidates, or perform a preliminary analysis to determine the exact number of candidates. We obtain a much more elegant solution by doing none of these and abandoning the pigeonhole solution altogether.

Figure 8.   Subset elimination.

$$
\begin{array}{l}
|[\ w \in Set(A, x.B(x)) \\
\triangleright \ C(w) \ type \\
]| \\
x \in Set(A, x.B(x)) \\
|[\ a \in A; \ B(a) \ \textbf{true} \\
\triangleright \ c(a) \in C(a) \\
]| \\
\hline
c(x) \in C(x)
\end{array}
$$

The specification in type theory of the program we require is the following theorem:

$$Set(A, x.majority(x)) \vee \neg Set(A, x.majority(x)), \tag{0}$$

where

$$majority(x) \equiv \mathbf{N}(i : 0 \leq i < n : a\, i = x) > n \textbf{ div } 2.$$

Note that (0) is trivially true in classical mathematics; in constructive mathematics it is true only if one can provide a proof either of the proposition $Set(A, x.majority(x))$ —i.e., exhibit a candidate receiving a majority of votes— or of the proposition $\neg Set(A, x.majority(x))$. Note also that an object in the right summand of (0) carries no computational content. What is significant is that the specification is deterministic: Any two objects that achieve the specification must be equal.

3.3 *Solution Strategy*

In searching problems such as this a common strategy is to replace a proposition that may or may not be satisfiable by one that is always satisfiable but in such a way that a simple test on a satisfying instance determines whether the original proposition is satisfiable. This, for example, is the strategy adopted when a sentinel is added to the end of an array during a linear search for an element x. It is also the strategy used in specifying binary search, when we seek an index to a given array that separates all values of at most a given value x from those greater than x, rather than determining whether or not x occurs in the array [2]. And it is the strategy used in the Knuth-Morris-Pratt string-searching algorithm, where the search for a pattern in a string is replaced by the computation of a failure function [23]. In this case we recognize that an easily solved problem is that of determining whether or not a given candidate x occurs a majority of times in a. This problem has specification:

$$\forall(A, x.majority(x) \vee \neg majority(x)). \tag{1}$$

We leave it as an exercise for the reader to construct an object of (1).

Our solution to the majority-vote problem is based on combining a solution to (1) with a solution to the following:

$$Set(A, x.pm(n, x)), \tag{2}$$

where the predicate *pm* has yet to be defined. (The parameter n occurs in *pm* in anticipation of later developments.)

Comparing (2) with (0) immediately suggests a definition of *pm*:

$$pm(n, x) = majority(x) \vee \neg Set(A, x.majority(x)). \tag{3}$$

Of course a pair of objects of types (1) and (2) is not the same as an object of (0). However, such an object can be easily recovered. Specifically, the function

$$\lambda q.\textbf{split}(q, (f, p).\textbf{when}(f\, p, a.\textbf{inl}\, p, b.\textbf{inr}\, (\lambda x.x))$$

is of type (1) $\wedge$ (2) $\Rightarrow$ (0). This can be seen by the derivation shown in Figure 9 (which the reader may choose to skip).

The identifier "*pm*" is short for "possible-majority candidate." From (3) we observe that an object $x \in Set(A, x.pm(n, x))$ satisfies the property

$$\neg majority(x) \Rightarrow \neg Set(A, x.majority(x)) \tag{4}$$

Figure 9.   Derivation of majority-vote algorithm.

		% The abbreviation S is used throughout for %
		$Set(A, x.majority(x)) \vee \neg Set(A, x.majority(x))$
0.0	‖[	$f \in \forall(A, x.majority(x) \vee \neg majority(x))$
0.1	;	$p \in Set(A, x.pm(n, x))$
	▷	% $pm(n, x) \Rightarrow (\neg majority(x) \Rightarrow \neg Set(A, x.majority(x))$, %
		%exercise 1.13 (b)%
0.2		$p \in Set(A, x.\neg majority(x) \Rightarrow \neg Set(A, x.majority(x)))$
0.3.0	‖[	$x \in A$
0.3.1	;	$g \in \neg majority(x) \Rightarrow \neg Set(A, x.majority(x))$
	▷	% 0.0,0.3.0, $\forall$-elim %
0.3.2		$fx \in majority(x) \vee \neg majority(x)$
0.3.3.0	‖[	$a \in majority(x)$
	▷	% 0.3.0, 0.3.3.0, Subtype-intro, **inl**-intro %
0.3.3.1		**inl** $x \in S$
	]‖	
0.3.4.0	‖[	$b \in \neg majority(x)$
	▷	% 0.3.1,0.3.4.0, $\Rightarrow$-elim %
0.3.4.1		$gb \in \neg Set(A, x.majority(x))$
		% 0.3.4.1, example 2.1, **inr**-intro %
0.3.4.2		**inr**$(\lambda x.x) \in S$
	]‖	
		% 0.3.2,0.3.3,0.3.4, $\vee$-elim %
0.3.5		**when**$(fx, a.\textbf{inl}\, x, b.\textbf{inr}(\lambda x.x)) \in S$
	]‖	
		% 0.2,0.3, Subtype-elim %
0.4		**when**$(fp, a.\textbf{inl}\, p, b.\textbf{inr}(\lambda x.x)) \in S$
	]‖	

(since the right side of (3) formally implies (4)). Because a candidate obtaining a majority of votes is always unique, if one exists, (4) may be read as the statement that x excludes all other candidates from being in the majority.

3.4 *Invariants versus Inductive Hypotheses*

We choose to prove (2) by elimination on n (i.e., by induction over the natural numbers). The basis is trivial since no candidate can occur a majority of times among 0 votes: Thus we can straightforwardly exhibit an object of the right summand of (3) and any object will do as our possible-majority candidate. Problems occur when we try to perform the induction step. Suppose that $x \in Set(A, x.pm(k, x))$ for some $k \in \mathbb{N}$. How does one construct an object $y \in Set(A, x.pm(k + 1, x))$? It is clear that more information is needed about the object x— we must strengthen our induction hypothesis.

In programming terms our aim is simply to construct a loop of the form **for** $i := 1$ **to** n **do** that exhibits a possible-majority candidate at each iteration. The notion of inductive hypothesis corresponds directly to the notion of invariant property. Strengthening the inductive hypothesis corresponds to introducing additional auxiliary variables into the computation.

Too strong a hypothesis would be the conjunction of (0) and

$$\forall (A, x.majority(x) \vee \forall (x, \neg majority(x)) \Rightarrow pm(n, x))$$

since it defeats the purpose of introducing the predicate *pm*. (Such a hypothesis states that x is a possible-majority candidate if either it is a majority candidate or no value is a majority candidate. It is a hypothesis likely to be proposed by a mathematician with no regard for the computational efficiency of the proof.) Instead we wish to strengthen the induction hypothesis as little as possible.

Another hypothesis we might consider is that along with the possible majority candidate is known its number of occurrences in the array segment. This is both too strong and too weak. It is too weak to stand alone as an inductive hypothesis. It is too strong because if we do try to prove it inductively we are obliged to consider a hypothesis in which the number of occurrences of every candidate is known; i.e., we have to revert to the pigeonhole method.

The hypothesis we actually make is that not only is there a possible-majority candidate x but there is also an "estimate" of its number of occurrences in the array segment.

The information that the estimate must convey is when to discard one value and replace it by another. Suppose x is a possible-majority candidate for the first k votes. Then it is necessary to discard x as a possible-majority value for the first $(k + 1)$ votes if the number of occurrences of x among these votes does not guarantee that no other value is a possible-majority value. This will be so when the number of occurrences of x is at most $(k + 1)$ **div** 2.

This suggests that the estimate we maintain is an upper bound on the number of occurrences of x. Denoting the estimate by e we require:

$$no\text{-}of\text{-}occurrences(k, x) \leq e \qquad\qquad (5.1)$$

(where $no\text{-}of\text{-}occurrences(k, x) = \mathbf{N}(i: 0 \leq i < k: a\,i = x)$).

But this property alone is insufficient. We need to know that e is not a gross overestimate of the number of occurrences of x (the value $e = k$ satisfies (5.1)). The value e must also represent some limit on the number of occurrences of other candidates that precludes their being majority values. We propose therefore that e should also have the property:

$$\forall(A, y.(y = x) \lor no\text{-}of\text{-}occurrences(k, y) \leq k - e). \qquad\qquad (5.2)$$

The property (5.2) will imply the property $pm(k, x)$ if we also add the requirement:

$$k \leq 2 * e. \qquad\qquad (5.3)$$

In summary, the property we require to prove is

$$Set(A \times \mathbb{N}, (x, e).ind\text{-}hypo(n, x, e)) \qquad\qquad (6)$$

where $ind\text{-}hypo(k, x, e)$ is the conjunction of properties (5.1), (5.2), and (5.3).

We now have two tasks. The first is to prove (6) by induction. An object of (6) will therefore take the form $\mathbb{N}\text{-}elim(n, basis, (m, h)induction\text{-}step)$. The second task is to verify that the conjunction of properties (5) is indeed a stronger property than $pm(k, x)$. This is needed in order to show that the function **fst** maps an object of type (6) into the required object of type (2).

The second task is a problem of integer arithmetic and is one that we do not tackle here. We assume therefore that (the reader will verify)

fst $\in \forall((6), (x, e).pm(n, x))$.

Let us now turn to the inductive proof of (6). The basis is a trivial problem of integer arithmetic since we can exhibit an arbitrary candidate, x_0, say, as possible-majority candidate and 0 as the estimate of its number of occurrences.

For the induction step we assume that x and e satisfy properties (5) and show how to construct new values x' and e' satisfying (5)[$k := k + 1$]. (To be completely formal we should assume that z, say, is an object of (6) and then split z into its components x and e.) Consider now the effect of the inclusion of the kth vote, $a\,k$, in the votes cast.

If $a\,k = x$ the estimate e of its occurrences increases by one and x is retained as a possible-majority value. That is, $(x, e + 1) \in (6)[k := k + 1]$.

If, however, $a\,k \neq x$ the estimate e of x's occurrences remains constant and the situation is more complicated. One possibility is that $k = 2 * e$, and hence $k + 1 > 2 * e$. This clearly indicates that x is not a possible-majority value, and there is the possibility that some other value occurs a majority of times. The only value this could be is $a\,k$ since by the induction hypothesis no value y different from x is a majority value in the first k votes, and $a\,k$ is the only value whose number of occurrences has increased in the process of extending the array segment. An upper bound on the number of occurences of $a\,k$ is $k - e + 1$ since it occurs, by (5.2), at most $k - e$ times among the first k votes and, trivially, once more among the first $(k + 1)$ votes. Thus if $a\,k \neq x$ and $k = 2 * e$ the new possible majority value is $x' = a\,k$ and the new estimate is $e' = k - e + 1$ (which we observe equals $e + 1$).

The final possiblility is that although $a\,k \neq x$, the bound $k + 1 \leq 2 * e$ remains true. In this case $k + 1 - e$ is exactly one more than than $k - e$, and the number of occurrences of each element y in the first $(k + 1)$ votes is at most one more than its number of occurrences in the first k votes. Thus $(5)[k := k + 1]$ is true of $x' = x$ and $e' = e$.

Summarizing, the inductive step takes the form:

$$
\begin{aligned}
&\mathbf{if}\ \ a\,k = x \longrightarrow \langle x, e + 1 \rangle \\
&[\!]\ \ (a\,k \neq x) \wedge (2 * e = k) \longrightarrow \langle a\,k, e + 1 \rangle \\
&[\!]\ \ (a\,k \neq x) \wedge (2 * e > k) \longrightarrow \langle x, e \rangle \\
&\mathbf{fi}
\end{aligned}
$$

and the complete program (including a solution to (1)) takes the form shown in Figure 10.

4 *The Future of Type Structure*

The world of programming languages seems to be split into two quite distinct and antagonistic parts— the world of untyped languages and the world of typed languages. The best-known example of the former is probably Lisp, but it also includes Prolog, all command languages such as Cshell, and text-processing languages like TEX. The best-known example of the latter is probably Pascal, but it also includes modern functional languages like SML [28]. An illuminating account of the differences between Lisp and Pascal is afforded by the following quotation from the Foreword written by Alan J. Perlis to Abelson and Sussman's book, *Structure and Interpretation of Computer Programs* [1]:

> It would be difficult to find two languages that are the communicating coin of two more different cultures than those gathered around these two languages. Pascal is for building pyramids— imposing, breathtaking, static structures built by armies pushing heavy blocks into place. Lisp is for building organisms— imposing, breathtaking, dynamic structures built by squads fitting fluctuating myriads of simpler organisms into place.... In Pascal the plethora of declarable data structures induces a specialization within functions that inhibits and penalizes

casual cooperation. It is better to have 100 functions operate on one data structure than to have 10 functions operate on 10 data structures.

The tension that exists between the typed and type-free worlds will never,
in my view, be completely reconciled. Those of us who advocate typed languages are, in so doing, also advocating a discipline that ensures that the
structure of our "pyramids" is always evident. Discipline means constraint.
But there will always be a need for "throw-away" programs, "organisms" that
are used, perhaps quite intensively but for a short period of time and then
discarded.

Figure 10.   Majority-vote program.

```
split(
      ℕ-elim(n
             , < x₀, 0 >
             , (k, p).split(p
                           , (x, e).if  a k = x ⟶< x, e + 1 >
                                    ▯  (a k ≠ x) ∧ (2 * e = k) ⟶< a k, e + 1 >
                                    ▯  (a k ≠ x) ∧ (2 * e > k) ⟶< x, e >
                                    fi
                           )
             )
      , (x, e).
             (λx.when(
                      ℕ-elim(n, 0, (k, c)if a k = x ⟶ c + 1
                                       ▯ a k ≠ x ⟶ c
                                       fi
                      )
                      .gt.n div 2
                     , a.inl x
                     , b.inr b
                     )
             )x
      )
   ]|
```

Although the tensions will never be reconciled, the aim must surely be to bring the two sides closer and closer together. Such certainly is the aim of ML with its introduction of the notion of polymorphic type. Moreover, on the other side, no one would argue against the idea that a clearer structure would facilitate and not hinder the reuse of software.

Alongside the dichotomy between typed and type-free languages, most programmers would recognize a dichotomy between "static", or "compile-time", type checking and "dynamic", or "run-time", type checking. This view of type is, however, a severe impediment to future progress because there is indeed no such dichotomy; there is a trichotomy. There is a third time at which type checking can take place, and that is at development time.

There are many properties of a program that cannot be discovered either at run time or at compile time because of either theoretical or practical impossibility. I need mention only one— termination. Many would argue, however, that static type checking is an a priori requirement on any notion of type in programming languages, that such a machine check substantially increases the reliability of our programs. The truth is, though, that the most significant benefit of a well-defined type structure is the support it gives to organizing the development of programs, and that an experienced programmer will (or should?) never make major type errors in just the same way that he never makes major syntactic errors. The standards that we require of professional programmers should at least ensure that.

For there to be any progress in the exploitation of type structure in improving the quality of computer programs it is vital that it be linked to the development process rather than to issues of implementation. Martin-Löf's theory, with its concept of dependent types, has sufficiently enriched the language of types that they may be equated with specifications. There can be no going back to an impoverished, statically checkable language. The direction has been set for development-time type checking, and we must continue to pursue it.

References

[1] Abelson, H. and Sussman, G. J. with Sussman, J. *Structure and Interpretation of Computer Programs.* MIT Press, Cambridge, Mass., 1985.

[2] Backhouse, R. C. *Program Construction and Verification.* Prentice-Hall International, London, 1986.

[3] Backhouse, R. C. "Overcoming the mismatch between programs and proofs". Proceedings of Workshop on Programming Logic (Marstrand, 1–4 June), Dept. of Computer Sciences, Chalmers Univ. of Technology, Göteborg, Sweden, 1987.

[4] Beeson, M. J. *Foundations of Constructive Mathematics.* Springer-Verlag, Berlin, 1985.

[5] Bishop, E. *Foundations of Constructive Analysis.* McGraw-Hill, New York, 1967.

[6] Burstall, R. and Lampson, B. "A kernel language for abstract data types and modules". *Semantics of Data Types*, G. Kahn, D. B. MacQueen, and G. Plotkin, eds. Lecture Notes in Computer Science, vol. 173, pp. 1–50. Springer-Verlag, Berlin, 1984.

[7] Chisholm, P. "Derivation of a parsing algorithm in Martin-Löf's theory of types". *Science of Computer Programming 8* (1987), pp. 1–42 .

[8] Chisholm, P. "A theory of finite sets in constructive type theory". Dept. of Computer Science, Heriot-Watt Univ., Edinburgh, Scotland, 1987.

[9] Church, A. *The Calculi of Lambda-Conversion.* Annals of Mathematical Studies, vol. 6. Princeton Univ. Press, Princeton, 1951.

[10] Coquand, T. and Huet, G. "Constructions: A higher order proof system for mechanizing mathematics". EUROCAL 85 (April), Linz, Austria, 1985.

[11] Constable, R. L. et al. *Implementing Mathematics with the NuPRL Proof Development System.* Prentice-Hall, Englewood Cliffs, N. J., 1986.

[12] Courant, R. and Robbins, H. *What is Mathematics?* Oxford Univ. Press, London, 1941.

[13] Dijkstra, E. W. and Feijen, W. H. J. *Een Methode van Programmeren.* Academic Service, Den Haag, The Netherlands, 1984.

[14] Dybjer, P. "Inductively-defined sets in Martin-Löf's set theory". Programming Methodology Group, Dept. of Computer Sciences, Chalmers Univ. of Technology, Göteborg, Sweden, 1987.

[15] Dyckhoff, R. "Category theory as an extension of Martin-Löf's type theory". Dept. of Computational Science, Univ. of St. Andrews, Fife, Scotland, 1985.

[16] Gentzen, G. "Investigations into logical deduction". *The Collected Papers of Gerhard Gentzen*, M.E. Szabo, ed., pp. 68–213. North-Holland, Amsterdam, 1969.

[17] Glivenko, V. "Sur quelques points de la logique de M. Brouwer". *Bulletins de la classe des sciences 15*, 5, pp. 183–188. Academie Royale de Belgique, 1929.

[18] Gordon, M., Milner, R., and Wadsworth, C. *Edinburgh LCF.* Lecture Notes in Computer Science, vol. 78. Springer-Verlag, Berlin, 1979.

[19] Gries, D. *The Science of Programming.* Springer-Verlag, New York, 1981.

[20] Hoare, C. A. R. "Notes on data structuring". In *Structured Programming*, O.-J. Dahl, E. W. Dijkstra and C. A. R. Hoare, eds. Academic Press, New York, 1972.

[21] Jackson, M. A. *Principles of Program Design.* Academic Press, New York, 1975.

[22] Kleene, S. C. *Introduction to Metamathematics.* North-Holland, Amsterdam, 1952.

[23] Knuth, D. E., Morris, J. H., and Pratt, V. R. "Fast pattern matching in strings". *SIAM J. Computing 6* (1977), pp. 325–350.

[24] Misra, J. and Gries, D. "Finding repeated elements". *Science of Computer Programming 2* (1982), pp. 143–152.

[25] Martin-Löf, P. "Constructive mathematics and computer programming". *Proc. 6th Int. Congress for Logic, Methodology and Philosophy of Science*, L. J. Cohen et al., eds., pp. 153–175. North-Holland, Amsterdam, 1982.

[26] Martin-Löf, P. "Intuitionistic type theory". Notes by Giovanni Sambin of a series of lectures given in Padova, June 1980.

[27] Milner, R. "A theory of type polymorphism in programming". *J. Computer and System. Sciences 17* (1977), pp. 348–375.

[28] Milner, R. "The standard ML core language". *Polymorphism 2*, 2 (October 1985).

[29] Nordström, B. "Multilevel functions in type theory". Programming Methodology Group, Chalmers Univ. of Technology, Göteborg, Sweden (n.d.).

[30] Nordström, B. and Petersson, K. "Types and specifications". *Information Processing 83*, R. E. A. Mason, ed., pp. 915–920. Elsevier, North Holland, 1983.

[31] Nordström, B., Petersson, K., and Smith, J. "An introduction to Martin-Löf's type theory". Dept. of Computer Sciences, Chalmers Univ. of Technology, Göteborg, Sweden. Midsummer 1986.

[32] Petersson, K. "A programming system for type theory". Memo 21, Programming Methodology Group, Chalmers Univ. of Technology, Göteborg, Sweden, 1982.

[33] Petersson, K. "The subset type former and the type of small types in Martin-Löf's theory of types (Types and specifications part II)". Programming Methodology Group, Chalmers Univ. of Technology, Göteborg, Sweden, 1984.

[34] Stoy, J. *Denotational Semantics.* MIT Press, Cambridge, Mass., 1977.

[35] Turner, D. A. "A new implementation technique for applicative languages". *Software—Practice and Experience 9* (1979), pp. 31–49.

The Maximum-Segment-Sum Problem

2

David Gries
Cornell University

1 Introduction

All invention in the development of the algorithm presented here is the result of applying by-now-standard techniques in the formal development of algorithms. Required is only some skill with formal manipulation and with the standard techniques of developing program and proof hand in hand.

2 The Problem

Given is an array $b.(0..n-1)$ of integers, where $0 \le n$. We can compute the sum of the values of each segment $b.(i..j-1)$. Desired is the maximum such sum. The algorithm to be developed for this problem appeared in a paper by this writer [1].

Remark We use the period ' . ' for function application, and an array is viewed as a function. We also use currying: $S.i.j$ would traditionally be written $S(i,j)$.

We formalize the problem as follows. For i, j satisfying $0 \le i \le j \le n$, define

$$S.i.j = \sum(k: 0 \le i < j: b.k).$$

Then, execution of the program should store an integer in s to establish

$$R: \quad s = MAX(i, j: 0 \le i \le j \le n: S.i.j).$$

This formal definition makes clear that the empty segments $S.i.i$, for $0 \le i \le n$, are considered as segments of the array. The informal specification does not, and this is often a source of confusion and error.

3 *Development of a Simple Solution*

Each element of the array has to be referenced at least once in determining the maximum segment-sum. We decide to write an iterative algorithm. A loop invariant is developed by replacing constant n of R by a fresh variable h; it consists of two parts $P0$ and $P1$:

$P0$: $0 \le h \le n$,

$P1$: $s = MAX(i, j: 0 \le i \le j \le h: S.i.j)$.

And an algorithm is easily written using standard techniques:

```
s := 0;
var h := 0;
{invariant: P0 and P1}
{bound function: n − h}
do h ≠ n → s := MAX(i, j: 0 ≤ i ≤ j ≤ h + 1: S.i.j);
            h := h + 1
od .
```

4 *Transforming into a More Efficient Algorithm*

In the above algorithm, each iteration requires execution of an assignment to s, and a quick calculation reveals that the total time needed to execute all such assignments is proportional to n^2. We now eliminate the inefficiency.

First, rewrite the expression being assigned to s, taking advantage of $P1$:

$MAX(i, j: 0 \le i \le j \le h + 1: S.i.j)$

$=$ {split the range of the quantification}

$MAX(i, j: 0 \le i \le j \le h: S.i.j) \max MAX(i, j: 0 \le i \le j = h + 1: S.i.j)$

$=$ {replace the first term using invariant $P1$}

$s \max MAX(i, j: 0 \le i \le j = h + 1: S.i.j)$

$=$ {use the one-point rule to eliminate j}

s max MAX(i: $0 \le i \le h + 1$: $S.i.(h + 1)$)

At this point, we want to eliminate the expression

MAX(i: $0 \le i \le h + 1$: $S.i.(h + 1)$)

from the program. We would like to insert a fresh variable c defined by

$c = $ MAX(i: $0 \le i \le h + 1$: $S.i.(h + 1)$) .

However, variables s and c would then be defined on different initial segments of array b. To provide uniformity, we define c on the same initial segment as s, giving the additional loop invariant $P2$:

$P2$: $c = $ MAX(i: $0 \le i \le h$: $S.i.h$) .

$P2$ is established initially using $c := 0$. We replace the assignment to s by the assignment $s := s$ max c. However, before that assignment, the predicate

$c\ = $ MAX(i: $0 \le i \le h + 1$: $S.i.(h + 1)$)

has to be established. Hence, we rewrite the algorithm as

$s := 0$;
var $h, c := 0, 0$;
{invariant: $P0$ and $P1$ and $P2$}
{bound function: $n - h$}
do $h \ne n \rightarrow$ $c :=$ MAX(i: $0 \le i \le h + 1$: $S.i.(h + 1)$);
            $s := s$ max c;
            $h := h + 1$
od .

The next step is to simplify the expression being assigned to c. Using the fact that $P2$ holds at the place of the assignment, we rewrite this expression as follows:

MAX(i: $0 \le i \le h + 1$: $S.i.(h + 1)$)

$=$ {split the range of the quantification}

MAX(i: $0 \le i \le h$: $S.i.(h + 1)$) max MAX(i: $0 \le i = h + 1$: $S.i.(h + 1)$)

$=$ {in the first term, rewrite $S.i.(h + 1)$; in the second, use the one-point rule}

MAX(i: $0 \le i \le h$: $S.i.h + b.h$) max $S.(h + 1).(h + 1)$

$=$ {remove $b.h$ from the quantification}

MAX(i: $0 \le i \le h$: $S.i.h$) $+ b.h$ max $S.(h + 1).(h + 1)$

$=$ {in the first term, use $P2$; in the second, use def. of S}

$(c + b.h)$ max 0 .

The final algorithm, which is linear in n, is given below.

```
s := 0;
var h, c := 0, 0;
{invariant: P0 and P1 and P2}
{bound function: n − h}
do h ≠ n →   c := (c + b.h) max 0;
              s := s max c;
              h := h + 1
od .
```

Reference

[1] Gries, D. "A note on a standard strategy for developing loop invariants and loops".
     Science of Computer Programming 2 (1984), pp. 207–214.

Inorder Traversal of a Binary Tree and its Inversion

3

David Gries
Cornell University

Jan L. A. van de Snepscheut
Groningen University

This paper presents the derivation of an algorithm for producing the inorder traversal of a binary tree and then shows how to invert the algorithm. Given a sequence of values, the inversion produces, nondeterministically, any binary tree whose inorder traversal is that sequence.

The inorder traversal algorithm was presented by the first author at the Institute on Formal Development of Programs and Proofs in the 1987 UT Year of Programming. The second author derived the inversion with some help from the first author. The paper was written by the authors in alternating sentences.[1]

---

1. The original paper was handwritten during the Institute.

1 *The Inorder Traversal Algorithm*

Consider a finite binary tree t (say), which for our purposes is best defined recursively by

$$t \;=\; \varnothing \qquad\qquad \text{(i.e. } t \text{ is empty)} \quad \text{or}$$
$$t \;=\; (t.l,\ t.d,\ t.r)\,,$$

where $t.d$ is an integer and $t.l$ and $t.r$ are binary trees. By $\#t$ we denote the number of nodes in tree t.

We shall also be dealing with sequences of elements. The empty sequence is denoted by ϵ. Catenation of sequences and elements is denoted by juxtaposition. For S a sequence, $\#S$ denotes the number of elements in S.

The inorder traversal $in.t$ of t is a sequence of integers defined by

$$in.\varnothing \;=\; \epsilon$$
$$in.(t.l,\ t.d,\ t.r) \;=\; in.(t.l)\ t.d\ in.(t.r)\,.$$

We note that $\#t = \#(in.t)$.

We derive an iterative algorithm for storing the inorder traversal of a given finite binary tree t in a sequence variable Z, thus establishing

$$R : in.t = Z\,.$$

From the postcondition we obtain invariant P' by replacing Z with $Z\ in.t$ (so that Z can be initialized to the identity ϵ of catenation) and then replacing constant t with a fresh variable p :

$$P' : in.t = Z\ in.p\,.$$

The condition P' can be established using $Z, p := \epsilon, t$.

Determining the body of the loop requires investigation of the invariant. If $p \neq \varnothing$, using the definition of in, P' expands to

$$in.t = Z\ in.(p.l)\ p.d\ in.(p.r)\,,$$

and, if $p.l \neq \varnothing$, to

$$in.t \;=\; Z\ in.(p.l.l)\ p.l.d\ in.(p.l.r)\ p.d\ in.(p.r)\,.$$

Each replacement of the term $in.(\_)$ following Z by its definition introduces the expression $\_.d\ in.(\_.r)$ into the righthand side. We therefore introduce a fresh sequence variable S to contain the trees occurring in these pairs and generalize the loop invariant to

$$P : \;\; in.t = Z\ in.p\ x.S\,,$$

where x is defined by

$$x.\epsilon = \epsilon$$

$$x.(p\ S) = p.d\ in.(p.r)\ x.S\,.$$

The new invariant P is established by $Z, p, S := \epsilon, t, \epsilon$.

We now develop the loop. Under the condition $p \neq \varnothing$, P can be manipulated as follows:

$$
\begin{aligned}
in.t \ =\ & Z\ in.p\ x.S \\
=\ & \{\text{definition of } in\} \\
& Z\ in.(p.l)\ p.d\ in.(p.r)\ x.S \\
=\ & \{\text{definition of } x\} \\
& Z\ in.(p.l)\ x.(p\ S)\,.
\end{aligned}
$$

Hence P is maintained and $\#p$ (i.e. the number of nodes in tree p) is reduced by execution of

$$p, S := p.l,\ p\ S\,.$$

Under the condition $p = \varnothing \wedge S \neq \epsilon$, we introduce u and U that satisfy $S = u\ U$ and manipulate P:

$$
\begin{aligned}
in.t \ =\ & Z\ in.p\ x.(u\ U) \\
=\ & \{\text{definition of } in\} \\
& Z\ x.(u\ U) \\
=\ & \{\text{definition of } x\} \\
& Z\ u.d\ in.(u.r)\ x.U\,.
\end{aligned}
$$

Hence P is maintained and $\#t - \#Z$ is reduced by execution of

> **let** u, U **sat** $S = u\ U$;
> $Z, p, S := Z\ u.d,\ u.r,\ U\,.$

The algorithm is therefore

> $A:$ **var** $p: tree$;
> **var** $S: seq(tree)$;
> $Z, p, S := \epsilon, t, \epsilon$;
> **do** $p \neq \varnothing$ $\qquad \rightarrow p, S := p.l,\ p\ S$
> $[\!]$ $\ p = \varnothing \wedge S \neq \epsilon \rightarrow$ **let** u, U **sat** $S = u\ U$;
> $\qquad\qquad\qquad\qquad\qquad\qquad Z, p, S := Z\ u.d, u.r, U$
> **od**
> $\{P \wedge p = \varnothing \wedge S = \epsilon;\ \text{hence } R\}\,.$

From P it follows that $\#t \geq \#Z$, which implies that the set of pairs assumed by $(\#t - \#Z, \#p)$ is well founded under lexicographic ordering. Since both statements in the loop decrease $(\#t - \#Z, \#p)$, the algorithm terminates.

The simplicity of this algorithm and its description is a result of several design decisions: the use of a tree instead of its representation using pointers; the introduction of S as a sequence instead of a stack, with its operations *push* and *pop*; the decision to use the **let** statement, instead of referring to parts of Z and S using subscripting; and the recursive definition of x, which makes the derivations of the guarded commands and proofs of invariance of P almost trivial.

2 *Inversion of the Algorithm*

We now invert algorithm A, thus producing an algorithm V that, given a sequence Z, nondeterministically stores in p any tree satisfying $in.p = Z$. Algorithms A and V have the same invariant P. Constant t occurs in P and, in the case of V, we take t to be any tree whose inorder traversal is the given sequence Z.

Algorithm A terminates with $p = \emptyset$ and $S = \epsilon$. Hence, its inverse V begins by setting $p = \emptyset$ and $S = \epsilon$; note that this establishes invariant P. We invert the loop by inverting each of the guarded commands in isolation. In inverting a guarded command with its associated postcondition, the guard becomes the postcondition and vice versa. Consider the second guarded command:

$$\{p = \emptyset \wedge S = u\, U\}\ Z, p, S := Z\, u.d, u.r, U\ \{Z \neq \epsilon\}.$$

Denote the final value of Z by $Z = V\, v$. Inverting the command requires storing into Z, p, and S their initial values. For p this amounts to the assignment $p := \emptyset$, and for Z it is stripping off the last element v; i.e. $Z := V$. The inverse of $S := U$ is $S := u\, S$, provided we can construct tree u. We have $u.d = v$ and $u.r = p$, but we have no value available for $u.l$, so we leave it open. Thus the inverse command is

$$\{Z \neq \epsilon\}\ \textbf{let } V, v \textbf{ sat } Z = V\, v;$$
$$Z, p, S := V, \emptyset, (\_, v, p)\, S.$$

We verify that the command maintains P, no matter what tree is chosen for $\_$:

$$wp(\text{“}Z, p, S := V, \emptyset, (\_, v, p)\, S\text{”}, P)$$

=   {definition of P and wp}

$$in.t = V\ \ in.\emptyset\ \ x.((\_, v, p)\, S)$$

=   {definition of in}

$$in.t = V\ \ x.((\_, v, p)\, S)$$

=   {definition of x}

$$in.t = V \ \vee \ in.p \ x.S$$

$$= \quad \{Z = V \ \vee; \text{ definition of } P\}$$

$$P .$$

The precondition $Z \neq \epsilon$ ensures that the **let** statement is well defined.
  Consider the first guarded command in isolation:

$$\{p \neq \varnothing\} \ p, S := p.l, \ p \ S \ \{S \neq \epsilon\} .$$

Denote the final value of S by $S = u \ U$. Inverting the comand requires storing
into p and S their initial values. Inverting $S := p \ S$ requires simply deleting
the first element of S —using $S := U$. In terms of the values in p and S upon
termination of the above command, the tree

$$(p, u.d, u.r)$$

is to be stored into p. Thus the inversion of the command is

$$\{S \neq \epsilon\} \ \textbf{let} \ u, U \ \textbf{sat} \ S = u \ U ;$$

$$p, S := (p, u.d, u.r), U .$$

We verify that the command maintains invariant P:

$$wp(``p, S := (p, u.d, u.r), U", P)$$

$$= \qquad \{\text{definition of } P \text{ and } wp\}$$

$$in.t = Z \ in.(p, u.d, u.r) \ x.U$$

$$= \qquad \{\text{definition of } in\}$$

$$in.t = Z \ in.p \ u.d \ in.(u.r) \ x.U$$

$$= \qquad \{\text{definition of } x\}$$

$$in.t = Z \ in.p \ x.(u \ U)$$

$$= \qquad \{S = u \ U; \text{ definition of } P\}$$

$$P .$$

The precondition $S \neq \epsilon$ ensures that the **let** statement is well defined. Hence
the inverted program is

$$\forall : \textbf{var} \ p : tree;$$

$$\textbf{var} \ S : seq(tree);$$

$$p, S := \varnothing, \epsilon;$$

$$\textbf{do} \ Z \neq \epsilon \rightarrow \textbf{let} \ V, v \ \textbf{sat} \ Z = V \ v ;$$

$$Z, p, S := V, \varnothing, (\_, v, p) \ S$$

$$[] \quad S \neq \epsilon \rightarrow \textbf{let} \ u, U \ \textbf{sat} \ S = u \ U ;$$

$$p, S := (p, u.d, u.r), U$$

$$\textbf{od}$$

$$\{P \wedge Z = \epsilon \wedge S = \epsilon; \text{ hence } in.t = in.p\} .$$

Each guarded command reduces the pair $(\#Z, \#t - \#p)$, lexicographically speaking. Investigation of the invariant shows that the pair is bounded from below by $(0, 0)$. Hence the algorithm terminates.

Any tree whose inorder traversal equals the given sequence can be produced by an execution of algorithm V. The sole source of nondeterminism is in the selection of a guarded command if both guards are true.

Remark We neglected to state in invariant P that all elements of sequence S are nonempty trees. In both A and V this is required by the second guarded command; it is ensured by the initialization and both guarded commands.

A Hands-in-the-Pocket Presentation of a k-Majority Vote Algorithm

4

David Gries
Cornell University

This purely oral presentation of an algorithm, without the use of writing, is inspired by Jan L. A. van de Snepscheut's hands-in-the-pocket presentation a few hours ago of a mutual-exclusion algorithm [described elsewhere in this volume]. His algorithm was far more difficult to present than mine. His was a distributed algorithm; mine is sequential. It is a tribute to past advances that at least a few nontrivial algorithms can be presented in this fashion.

Remark This written version of the oral presentation will attempt to simulate the oral presentation by keeping the identifiers used to a minimum and by dealing only with extremely simple formulae. The reader can simulate the oral presentation by reading very slowly and never looking back, for the audience could not look back.

The algorithm was first described in a paper by D. Gries and J. Misra [1]. The presentation therein was due essentially to J. Misra.

Consider a bag of *n* values. We wish to find a candidate for the majority value —a value that occurs more than half the time in the bag, or more than $n \div 2$ times. Thus, if the bag has a majority value, then it is the candidate we have calculated.

Our algorithm doesn't tell us whether there *is* a majority value; it tells us only that *if* there is one, it is our calculated candidate. To tell whether there *is* a majority value, the number of occurrences of the candidate in the bag has to be counted.

Actually, it is just as easy to present an algorithm to calculate a set of *k*-majority candidates of a bag of size *n*. Suppose *k* is a positive integer. Then a value is a *k*-majority value if it occurs more than $n \div k$ times in the bag. Simple arithmetic indicates that there at most $k - 1$ *k*-majority values.

So, we describe an algorithm that constructs a bag with at most $k-1$ distinct values such that it is guaranteed to contain all *k*-majority values of the initial bag of size *n*.

Now, one algorithm would be to delete from the bag up to $n \div k$ occurrences of each distinct value in the bag. Since each distinct value is deleted as much as possible up to $n \div k$ times, only the *k*-majority values are left. However, that's a rather inefficient algorithm, so we'll do something different.

Let's define a *reduction* of a bag. Consider the operation of deleting *k* distinct values from the bag. Call a bag that results from performing this operation as much as possible, until the bag no longer contains *k* distinct values, a *reduction* of the bag. Note that a bag can have many different reductions, depending on which *k* distinct values are deleted at each step.

If the initial bag contains *n* occurrences of the same value, then the reduction is the initial bag. If the initial bag contains *n* distinct values, then any reduction contains *n* mod *k* of these values, and there are (*n* mod *k*)! different reductions.

We now prove a nice theorem. Any reduction of a bag contains all *k*-majority values of the bag. Why? In constructing a reduction for a bag, the operation of deleting *k* distinct values is performed as often as possible. It can be performed at most $n \div k$ times, because $n - k \times (n \div k)$ is less than *k* . Hence, in constructing a reduction, each value is deleted at most $n \div k$ times, so that any value that occurs more than $n \div k$ times in the initial bag is in the reduction.

So, our algorithm has only to construct a reduction for the initial bag.

Here's an important consideration. Suppose we have a bag *B* and a reduction for it. How do we construct a reduction for *B* unioned with one more value? Remember that the reduction for *B* contains at most $k - 1$ elements. Add the new value to the reduction, so it now contains at most *k* distinct elements. If the reduction does contain *k* distinct values, throw them out! The result is a reduction for *B* unioned with the new element.

The operation of constructing from a bag and its reduction a reduction for the bag unioned with a new element is a key step in our algorithm. The algorithm processes one element of the initial bag at a time, using a fresh bag-variable R. The algorithm maintains the invariant "variable R is a reduction of the elements processed thus far". Initially no elements have been processed, and since the only reduction of the empty bag is the empty bag, we initially set R to the empty bag. As each element is processed, the invariant is maintained by adding that element to R and then deleting k distinct elements from R, if possible. Upon termination, R contains a reduction for all processed elements, that is, for the initial bag, so by the theorem R contains all k-majority values.

Let's see how to represent R. For each distinct value in it, we need a pair consisting of that value and the number of times it occurs. These pairs —and there are at most $k - 1$ of them— can be kept in an AVL tree or 2–3 tree or something like that. Insertion of a value takes time order $\log k$, since R contains at most k distinct values. Testing whether R contains k distinct values can be done in constant time. Deleting k values takes time k, but the operation is done at most $n \div k$ times so that, in total, deletion contributes time order n. Hence, the algorithm takes time order $n \log k$.

Let's return to the case $k = 2$. Since $k = 2$, reduction R contains at most one distinct value. Represent R by a pair; the first component of the pair is the size of R and the second component of the pair is the value of all elements in R. Here's the algorithm for the case $k = 2$. Initially, set R to the pair $(0, any\ value)$. Process the elements of the initial bag one at a time, and with each perform the following operation to maintain the invariant that R contains a reduction for the processed elements. The operation has three disjoint cases:

> If the first component of the pair representing R is 0, then R is empty. Change the pair to $(1, the\ new\ value\ being\ processed)$.

> If the pair is (i, v), say, where $i > 0$ and v is the same as the value being processed, then add 1 to the first component of the pair.

> If the pair is (i, v) where $i > 0$ and v is different from the value being processed, then subtract 1 from the first component of the pair. This corresponds to inserting the value being processed into R and then deleting two distinct elements from R —the value being processed and one occurrence of the value that was in R.

The algorithm is obviously linear in the size of the initial bag.

Reference

[1] Gries, D. and Misra, J. "Finding repeated elements". *Science of Computer Programming 2* (November 1982), pp. 143–152.

A Small Problem on Rectangles

5

A. J. M. van Gasteren

A. J. M. van Gasteren
Waalre, The Netherlands

Through my fellow speakers at the Institute I learned about the following problem, communicated by one of the participants.

Consider a 3×6 rectangle: Both its perimeter and its area are 18. Similarly, a 4×4 rectangle has perimeter 16 and area 16. (It was said that the Sumerians considered 17 an evil number because it does not share this nice property with its neighbor integers.) The question now is whether there are any other integer-sided rectangles whose perimeter and area are the same; in other words: What are the integer solutions of equation

$$(x, y: x \cdot y = 2 \cdot (x+y) \ \wedge \ 0 \leq x \ \wedge \ 0 \leq y)?$$

The idea, of course, is to solve the problem in a nice way, which in this case means maintaining the symmetry between x and y. The simplest that comes to mind (at least to my mind) is to rewrite $x \cdot y = 2 \cdot (x+y)$ equivalently into something of the shape $(x-2) \cdot (y-2) = \ldots$, and that settles the matter: The equation becomes

$$(x, y: (x-2) \cdot (y-2) = 4 \ \wedge \ -2 \leq x-2 \ \wedge \ -2 \leq y-2).$$

Of the four integer factorizations of 4 into two factors, only $1 \cdot 4$, $2 \cdot 2$, and $(-2) \cdot (-2)$ have both their factors at least -2; hence the integer solutions for the unordered pair x, y are 3, 6 and 4, 4 and 0, 0.

The above argument has been recorded for its simplicity.

On the Formal Derivation of a Proof of the Invariance Theorem

6

A. J. M. van Gasteren
Waalre, The Netherlands

In this note we formally derive a proof for the invariance theorem. Our only concern here is the design of that proof from its specification: We wish to show to what extent the symbols can do the work. For the reader that has an interest in the theorem itself, we include a short appendix. (The contents of that appendix are, however, of no relevance to the argument below.)

Theorem

For

P and Q : predicates on some space;

t : a structure on that same space, t having its
             values in a partially ordered universe;

C : a subset of that partially ordered universe;

f : a predicate transformer;

we have that

$$[P \Rightarrow Q]$$

follows from the conjunction of

$(C, <)$ is well-founded (0)

$[P \wedge \neg(t \in C) \Rightarrow Q]$ (1)

$(\mathbf{A}x:: [P \wedge t = x \Rightarrow f.(P \wedge t < x)])$ (2)

$[f.Q \equiv Q]$ (3)

f is monotonic (4)

Square brackets denote universal quantification over the space; in (2), the outer quantification is over the anonymous partially ordered universe; structure t can be viewed as a function application in which both function and argument have been left implicit.

We shall prove the theorem by proving $[P \Rightarrow Q] \Leftarrow$ true, in a calculation starting at $[P \Rightarrow Q]$ and terminating at true, and using premises (0) through (4). We note that t, C, and f —unlike P and Q— occur only in the theorem's premises and not in consequent $[P \Rightarrow Q]$ or in true. This means that somehow they have to enter the calculation and disappear from it again. The same holds for universal quantifier $\mathbf{A}$ in (2).

We cannot say much about such introductions and removals until (0) and (4) are known in some more detail.

f is monotonic

$\equiv$ (4a)

for all Y and Z,

$[f.Y \Rightarrow f.Z] \Leftarrow [Y \Rightarrow Z]$.

By its shape, definition (4a) looks most suitable for removing fs from the calculation of $[P \Rightarrow Q] \Leftarrow$ true. Premise (3) —$[f.Q \equiv Q]$— seems suitable for both introduction and removal.

$(C, <)$ is well-founded

$\equiv$ (0a)

for each predicate S

$[(\mathbf{A}x: x \in C: S.x)$

$\equiv$

$(\mathbf{A}x: x \in C: S.x \Leftarrow (\mathbf{A}y: y \in C \wedge y < x: S.y))$

$]$.

The well-foundedness does not help us introduce or remove **A**s, but it allows us to rewrite one quantification equivalently into a formally weaker one (the lower quantification).

Since we do not have a rule for introducing **A** yet, it may be worthwhile to remember

$$[g.r \equiv (\textbf{A}x:\ x = r:\ g.x)] \text{ for any } r \text{ and function } g, \qquad (5)$$

the one-point rule.

We have one final remark before starting the calculation. In the derivation, there are only a few places where a design decision has to be taken. We give the derivation first and discuss the design decisions later. For the sake of easy reference, we label the steps that embody these decisions.

Proof   Instead of massaging $[P \Rightarrow Q]$, we massage the more general $[P \wedge Z \Rightarrow Q]$, for Z a predicate whose dependence on the given space is   (6) restricted to its dependence on t.

$\qquad [P \wedge Z \Rightarrow Q]$

$=\qquad \{(1), \text{ i.e., } [Q \equiv Q \vee (P \wedge \neg(t \in C))] \}$ (7)

$\qquad [P \wedge Z \Rightarrow Q \vee (P \wedge \neg(t \in C))]$

$=\qquad \{\text{reshuffling, aiming at the removal of one } P\}$

$\qquad [P \wedge Z \wedge \neg(P \wedge \neg(t \in C)) \Rightarrow Q]$

$=\qquad \{\text{De Morgan, negation}\}$

$\qquad [P \wedge Z \wedge (\neg P \vee t \in C) \Rightarrow Q]$

$=\qquad \{\text{complement rule}\}$

$\qquad [P \wedge Z \wedge t \in C \Rightarrow Q]$

$=\qquad \{(5) \text{ with } r := t,\ g.y := P \wedge Z_y^t \wedge y \in C \Rightarrow Q \text{ for any } y\}$ (8)

$\qquad [(\textbf{A}x:\ x = t:\ P \wedge Z_x^t \wedge x \in C \Rightarrow Q)]$

$=\qquad \{\text{trading, heading for (2)'s antecedent}\}$ (9)

$\qquad [(\textbf{A}x:\ Z_x^t \wedge x \in C:\ P \wedge x = t \Rightarrow Q)]$

$=\qquad \{\text{interchange of } \textbf{A} \text{ and } [\ ]\}$

$\qquad (\textbf{A}x:\ Z_x^t \wedge x \in C:\ [P \wedge x = t \Rightarrow Q])$

$\Leftarrow\qquad \{\text{see Intermezzo manipulating the term, monotonicity of } \textbf{A}\}$

$\qquad (\textbf{A}x:\ Z_x^t \wedge x \in C:\ [P \wedge t < x \Rightarrow Q])\ .$

Intermezzo

$\qquad [P \wedge x = t \Rightarrow Q]$

$\Leftarrow\qquad \{\text{heading for (2)'s consequent, transitivity of } \Rightarrow \}$

$$[P \wedge x = t \Rightarrow f.(P \wedge t < x)] \wedge [f.(P \wedge t < x) \Rightarrow Q]$$

=   {(2)}

$$[f.(P \wedge t < x) \Rightarrow Q]$$

=   {(3), preparing for removal of *f*s by (4)/(4a)}

$$[f.(P \wedge t < x) \Rightarrow f.Q]$$

⇐   {(4)/(4a)}

$$[P \wedge t < x \Rightarrow Q] .$$

Summarizing, we note that the only premise that has not been used yet is (0)/(0a), and that our calculation so far yields

$$[P \wedge Z \Rightarrow Q]$$

⇐   (10)

$$(\mathbf{A}x: Z_x^t \wedge x \in C: [P \wedge t < x \Rightarrow Q]) .$$

Now we can finish the calculation by

$$[P \Rightarrow Q]$$

⇐   {(10) with $Z := $ true}

$$(\mathbf{A}x: x \in C: [P \wedge t < x \Rightarrow Q])$$

=   {(0)/(0a) with $S.x := [P \wedge t < x \Rightarrow Q]$}

$$(\mathbf{A}x: x \in C: [P \wedge t < x \Rightarrow Q] \Leftarrow (\mathbf{A}y: y \in C \wedge y < x: [P \wedge t < y \Rightarrow Q]))$$

=   {(10) with $Z := t < x, x := y$}

$$(\mathbf{A}x: x \in C: \text{true})$$

=   {predicate calculus}

true.   □

On the design decisions

Our first design decision was to try to use each of the premises of the theorem only once, because in our experience duplicate usage can be a symptom of insufficient disentanglement of the argument. Here the decision led us to the isolation of lemma (10), i.e., to design decision (6): Before we had decided to massage the more general $[P \wedge Z \Rightarrow Q]$ instead of $[P \Rightarrow Q]$, our calculation contained a number of duplicate manipulations.

So design decision (6) helps avoid repetition and lengthiness, but the price we pay is that now the reader is confronted with this decision at a stage of the calculation at which he cannot yet see the need for it. In general we prefer to avoid such heuristic rabbits being pulled out of a hat as much as possible.

As for the design decision embodied in step (7): For this first step of the calculation at most two options look promising, viz., to introduce an **A** or to use (1); premises (0), (2), and (4) are not electable since there is no f or **A** in manipulandum $[P \wedge Z \Rightarrow Q]$, and introducing one f by (3) does not help much yet.

Of the two options, the introduction of **A** by (5) is, however, still a little premature because we do not know what to choose for r in (5). Hence we first exploit premise (4) in step (7), simplify, and then are ready in step (8) to introduce the universal quantifier.

Having introduced the **A**, we now have two options: using (0)/(0a) or first exploiting (2). The first choice would give us a long expression to which (2), (3), and (4) would still have to be applied, so for the sake of brevity we choose —in step (9)— to head for the exploitation of (2) first. After this decision, the rest of the calculation hardly leaves any more choice.

We note that the emergence of expression $[P \wedge t < x \Rightarrow Q]$ at the end of the intermezzo, where all premises except (0) have already been used, is a strong hint that $[P \wedge Z \Rightarrow Q]$ could be worth considering.

In summary, the design given above rests on three pillars: syntactic analysis of the formulae to be manipulated, familiarity with predicate calculus so as to be able to mold the formulae into a shape that is convenient for the manipulations to be performed, and the use of a few of our rules of thumb, such as trying to postpone usage until hardly anything else can be done.

Showing these three things at work was our main goal. We had proved our vehicle toward that goal —the invariance theorem— before, e.g., in [1]. It took us quite a few iterations to get the proof presented in that paper in a nice enough form; the design given here emerged with W. H. J. Feijen's cooperation, after he had suggested that in the mean time we should have learned to *construct* a proof inspired by the shape of the formulae.

Appendix

In the usual invariance theorem for the repetition, P is the invariant and t the variant function of repetition **DO** : **do** $B \rightarrow S$ **od**, whose semantics is considered equivalent to the semantics of **if** $B \rightarrow S$; **DO** [] $\neg B \rightarrow$ skip **fi**, viz., for all R

$$[wp.(\mathbf{DO}, R) \equiv (B \vee R) \wedge (\neg B \vee wp.(S, wp.(\mathbf{DO}, R)))].$$

For postcondition $R := P \wedge \neg B$ in particular, we have that $wp.(\mathbf{DO}, P \wedge \neg B)$ is a solution of $X : [X \equiv f.X]$, with

$$[f.X \equiv (B \vee P) \wedge (\neg B \vee wp.(S, X))].$$

(It is defined to be the strongest solution.)

That is what our premise (3) comes from. Premise (4), f's monotonicity, is usually formulated as

$wp.(S, ?)$ is monotonic.

Our premise (2) is the usual $(\mathbf{A}x:: [P \land B \land t=x \Rightarrow wp.(S, P \land t<x)])$, and our premise (1) is a (weakened) substitute for the traditional $[P \land B \Rightarrow t \in C]$. The latter two statements require a proof, which we leave to the reader. (Predicate calculus suffices.)

Reference

[1] Dijkstra, E. W. and van Gasteren, A. J. M. "A simple fixpoint argument without the restriction to continuity". *Acta Informatica 23* (1986), pp. 1–7.

A Problem

on

Bichrome 6-Graphs

7

A. J. M. van Gasteren
Waalre, The Netherlands

We present and discuss two expositions for the following problem. In a complete graph on six nodes each edge is either red or blue; demonstrate that such a colored graph contains at least two monochrome triangles. (Three nodes form a "monochrome triangle" if the three edges connecting them are of the same color.)

Exposition 0 This exposition first establishes the existence of one monochrome triangle as follows. Of the five edges meeting at some node X, at least three have the same color, say red. Calling their other endpoints P, Q, and R, respectively, we have that either triangle PQR is monochrome or it contains at least one red edge, PQ say. In the latter case triangle PQX is all red.

To establish the existence of a second monochrome triangle we assume that the existence of, say, an all-red triangle has been established. We mark each of its nodes A and each of the remaining nodes B.

Our first dichotomy is that triangle *BBB* is either monochrome or not. In the latter case *BBB* has at least one red edge and at least one blue edge; also, any second monochrome triangle is of the form *AAB* or *BBA*.

In this latter case the dichotomy is that either there is a monochrome triangle *AAB* —i.e., an all-red *AAB*, since *AAA* is all red— or there is not. In the latter case we hence have that at each *B* fewer than two red *BA*-edges meet; hence at each *B* at least two of the three *BA*-edges are blue. From these and a blue *BB*-edge, the existence of which we have not exploited yet, we find an all-blue *BBA*-triangle: Of the at least 2 + 2 blue *BA*-edges meeting at the endpoints of a blue *BB*-edge, two meet at the same *A* (on account of the pigeon-hole principle), thus yielding a blue *BBA*.

The above proof —though not long yet sufficiently detailed— is unattractive because of its case analysis and its destruction of all sorts of symmetry. The trouble already starts with "at some node *X*", which by naming one node destroys the symmetry among the nodes. The next harm is done by the introduction of the three distinct names *P*, *Q*, and *R*: The subsequent "*PQ* say" shows how the naming inappropriately breaks the symmetry. (The use of subscripted names would not have been any better.) Then the more symmetric nomenclature *AAA/BBB* is used, which somewhat smooths the presentation of the second part of the argument, but still we have the *A*'s versus the *B*'s. By distinguishing a first and a second monochrome triangle we had to distinguish three cases for the second, viz., whether it shares zero, one, or two nodes with the first triangle. The symmetry we lost almost from the start is the symmetry between the colors. All these distinctions render any generalization of the exposition to graphs with more nodes very unattractive if not impossible.

Exposition 1 is based on two decisions: to maintain the symmetry between the colors and among the nodes, even to the extent that we shall try to leave them anonymous.

Exposition 1   We head for a counting argument to establish a lower bound on the number of monochrome triangles, because such arguments are more likely to maintain symmetry. To that purpose we wish to characterize either monochrome triangles or bichrome ones, whichever is simpler. We have this choice because in the complete 6-graph the total number of triangles is fixed, viz., 20. Hence (20– an upper bound on the number of bichrome triangles) is a lower bound on the number of monochrome triangles.

To investigate which is easier to characterize, we note that for a monochrome triangle we need three edges of equal color; for a bichrome one, however, two differently colored edges meeting at a node suffice.

The latter being the simpler characterization, we give it a name —a *bichrome V* is a pair of differently colored edges meeting at a node— and investigate its properties. Bichrome V's and bichrome triangles satisfy

each bichrome triangle contains two bichrome V's;

different bichrome triangles contain different bichrome V's.

Consequently (an upper bound on) the number of bichrome triangles is at most half (an upper bound on) the number of bichrome V's.

Finally, in order to compute an upper bound for bichrome V's, we note that from the five edges meeting at a node at most 3×2 bichrome V's (meeting at that node) can be constructed. Hence the total number of bichrome V's is at most 6×6; the total number of bichrome triangles is at most $36/2$; and hence the number of monochrome triangles is at least $20 - 18$, i.e., at least two.

In the above argument, the "invention" enabling us to maintain the symmetries is, of course, the notion of a "bichrome V". It does, however, not come out of the blue: It is the result of our realizing the option to count bichrome triangles and the decision to keep things simple. Neither of the two circumstances should be surprising.

The bichrome V effectively hides the individual colors, and rightly so, because their only role is to express equality and difference of color. In this respect we note that two edges of different color form the simplest ensemble that is invariant under color inversion.

Formal Program Transformations for VLSI Circuit Synthesis

8

Alain J. Martin
California Institute of Technology

No more fiction to us: We calculate.
—Nietzsche

Introduction

We have developed a method for the synthesis of delay-insensitive VLSI circuits based on formal program transformations. The computation to be implemented is initially formulated as a concurrent program —a set of communicating processes— that has been proved to meet its specification. The program transformations replace the original description of the computation with a semantically equivalent one which can be directly implemented as a network of VLSI operators.

We shall not present the complete synthesis method, which has already been the subject of a series of lectures at the YoP Institute on Concurrent Programming; rather, we shall concentrate on those program transformations that are the most interesting from the point of view of formal derivations and that also turn out to be the crucial step of the method.

In particular, we want to illustrate how a small number of heuristics and a set of simple rules for the manipulation of uninterpreted formulae can be applied very effectively to this new area of programming. (As a justification of this claim, let us mention that the method has been applied to the design of a number of rather complicated chips. All the chips that have been fabricated have been fully functional at the first try. They have also been found to be efficient and robust.)

The step we shall describe takes as its "source code" a collection of straight-line programs, each implementing a total ordering of elementary actions. The "object code" to be produced is another implementation of the same ordering of actions from which all explicit sequencing has been removed.

Although we could describe this step in isolation, we have preferred to explain briefly how the source program is obtained. In particular, we want to justify, on the basis of previous transformations, the rules and properties that are used in the formal manipulations. The description of the previous steps will be both concise and incomplete; a more detailed presentation can be found in the proceedings of the YoP Institute on Concurrent Programming [1].

1 *The Program Notation*

Originally, the programs are expressed as a collection of concurrent processes communicating through channels. The following subset of the notation will be needed for the programs used as examples. (How algorithms are derived so as to meet their specification falls outside the scope of this presentation.)

1.1 *Communication*

Atomic actions are communication actions on channels. Channels have local names: For instance, a channel between two processes p and r will be called X in p and Y in r. A communication action on the channel is denoted by X in p and by Y in r. Communication actions on a channel are used as synchronization primitives. The pair (X, Y) of communication commands fulfills the axioms

$$cX = cY$$

$$\neg qX \lor \neg qY, \qquad\qquad (0)$$

where cA denotes the number of completed A-actions, and qA is the predicate "an A-action is suspended".

Our definitions of completion and suspension of a communication action are quite different from those in use: We have realized that we can use *any* definitions that satisfy all of the properties of these notions that are used in the correctness proofs. We consider a matching pair of communication actions to be *completed* when they are both initiated; and between initialization and completion, an action is *suspended*. Obviously those definitions fulfill the two axioms (0). Moreover, they allow us to talk about two actions being completed at the same time without having to appeal to those actions being coincident in time.

1.2 *Probe*

The probe is a Boolean primitive command on channels. Given a channel (X, Y), the *probe of* X, denoted by $\overline{X}$, is defined as follows:

$$\overline{X} \;\Rightarrow\; qY$$
$$qY \;\Rightarrow\; \diamond\overline{X},$$

where $\diamond P$ means *P holds eventually.*

1.3 *Control Structures*

We will use the following control structures.

> Sequencing, represented by the semicolon. (This notation will be slightly abused in the sequel, as the semicolon will be used to represent both the mechanism that enforces sequencing between two actions and the logical ordering relation.)

> Nonterminating repetition, for example,

> $$*[L; R].$$

> Selection mechanism on probes (guarded commands), for example,

> $$[\overline{L} \;\rightarrow\; S0$$
> $$\;[\!]\overline{R} \;\rightarrow\; S1$$
> $$\;].$$

A frequently used program structure is the nonterminating repetition, as in

$$*[[\overline{L} \;\rightarrow\; S0$$
$$\;[\!]\overline{R} \;\rightarrow\; S1$$
$$\;]].$$

2 *Handshaking Expansion*

Handshaking expansion is the transformation that replaces communication actions on a channel by their implementation in terms of a sequence of elementary actions. This sequence is called a handshaking protocol.

The elementary actions are of two types: simple assignments to a Boolean variable, and *waits*. The assignments $x := \textbf{true}$ and $x := \textbf{false}$ are denoted by $x\!\uparrow$

and $x\downarrow$, respectively. The *wait* command $[B]$, where B is a Boolean expression, stands for $[B \rightarrow skip]$.

Channel (X, Y) is implemented by the two processes

$$*[[xo]; yi\uparrow; [\neg xo]; yi\downarrow]$$

and

$$*[[yo]; xi\uparrow; [\neg yo]; xi\downarrow] .$$

Initially, xo, xi, yo, yi are **false**. (In the sequel, we will assume that all variables are initialized to **false** unless specified otherwise.)

2.1 *Two-Phase Handshaking*

Consider the sequences:

$$Ux \equiv xo\uparrow; [xi]$$
$$Uy \equiv [yi]; yo\uparrow$$
$$Dx \equiv xo\downarrow; [\neg xi]$$
$$Dy \equiv [\neg yi]; yo\downarrow .$$

Given the initialization of all handshake variables to **false**, a matching pair (X, Y) of communication actions can be implemented by Ux for X and Uy for Y.

Once the communication implemented by Ux and Uy has been completed, all handshake variables are **true**; therefore, the next matching pair of communication actions has to be implemented by Dx and Dy. Because of the difficulty of detecting syntactically which X- or Y-actions follow each other in an execution, we prefer in general to use a simpler implementation known as "four-phase handshaking".

2.2 *Four-Phase Handshaking*

In a four-phase handshaking, all X-actions are implemented as $Ux; Dx$; all Y-actions are implemented as $Uy; Dy$.

Both the two-phase and four-phase protocols have the property that, for a matching pair (X, Y) of actions, the implementation is not symmetrical in X and Y. One implementation is called "active" and the other "passive". The four-phase implementation with X active and Y passive is

$$X \equiv xo\uparrow; [xi]; xo\downarrow; [\neg xi] \tag{1}$$
$$Y \equiv [yi]; yo\uparrow; [\neg yi]; yo\downarrow . \tag{2}$$

The implementation of the probe is

$$\overline{X} \equiv xi \qquad \overline{Y} \equiv yi. \tag{3}$$

Because of the implementation of the probe, the X-action matching the probe $\overline{Y}$ has to be implemented as active; thus, the Y-action matching this X (this Y-action is said to be "probed") has to be implemented as passive.

Apart from this restriction, the choice of whether an action should be implemented as active or passive is arbitrary, except that an active implementation should match a passive one.

The following properties of the handshaking protocol will be used in the formal program transformations.

Property 1

The semicolons following $xo\uparrow$ and $xo\downarrow$ in (1) and the semicolon following $yo\uparrow$ in (2) are not used to enforce sequencing between those assignments and the following wait-actions. In the sequel, we will refer to them as "superfluous semicolons".

Property 2

In (1) and (2), Dx and Dy are used only to reset all variables to **false**. Hence, provided that the cyclic order of the actions of (1) and (2) is maintained, the sequences Dx and Dy can be inserted at any place in the program of each of the processes without invalidating the semantics of the communication involved. However, modifying the order of these two actions relative to other actions may introduce a deadlock.

This manipulation of handshaking actions is called "reshuffling". For instance, a sequence $xo\uparrow$; $[xi]$; $xo\downarrow$; $[\neg xi]$; S can be reshuffled as

$$xo\uparrow;\ [xi];\ S;\ xo\downarrow;\ [\neg xi]$$

or

$$xo\uparrow;\ [xi];\ xo\downarrow;\ S;\ [\neg xi].$$

3 *Production Rules*

Since in VLSI concurrency is free and sequencing is costly, we shall implement sequencing as restricted concurrency. More precisely, we shall transform a program described in the "handshaking expansion" notation —a very sequential description!— into a semantically equivalent description in which explicit sequencing has disappeared. This description is called a *production-rule set*. Sets of production rules are readily implemented as networks of VLSI operators.

A "production rule" is a construct of the form

$$G \mapsto S,$$

where G is a Boolean expression and S is either an elementary assignment ($x\uparrow$ or $x\downarrow$) or an unordered set of elementary assignments.

The production rule must be *stable*; i.e., once G holds, it must remain invariantly **true** until completion of S. A program is described as a production-rule set, which is an unordered collection of production rules represented as

$$G0 \mapsto S0$$
$$G1 \mapsto S1$$
$$G2 \mapsto S2 \,.$$

A production-rule set is a nonterminating repetition, each step of which is the concurrent execution of any nonempty set of *fireable* production rules. A production rule is fireable (or *enabled*) when its guard is **true**. The selection of fireable production rules is weakly fair. Interfering production rules, i.e., production rules modifying the same variable, should be *mutually exclusive*.

Since we are using production-rule sets to implement sequential processes, the production-rule sets we construct are such that at most one production rule of a set is fireable at any time. This restriction facilitates the implementation of both stability of the guards and mutual exclusion among interfering production rules. For example, the two processes implementing channel (X, Y) in the previous section can be compiled into the four production rules

$$xo \mapsto yi\uparrow$$
$$\neg xo \mapsto yi\downarrow$$
$$yo \mapsto xi\uparrow$$
$$\neg yo \mapsto xi\downarrow \,.$$

The four rules are stable because of the way they are used in the handshaking protocol. The first two rules correspond to the *wire* operator $xo \underline{w} yi$. The last two rules correspond to the wire $yo \underline{w} xi$. Hence a channel is implemented by two wires.

4 *Production-Rule Expansion*

Production-rule expansion is the transformation from a handshaking expansion to a set of production rules. It is the most crucial and most difficult step of the compilation since it requires enforcing sequencing by semantic means. It consists of three steps:

state assignment,

guard strengthening, and

symmetrization.

4.1 *Example One:* Q-*Element*

Consider the simple process Q, which we call a "Q-element":

$$Q \equiv *[[\overline{L} \rightarrow R; L]],$$

where L and R are channels. Since L is probed, it must be passive. If we want to compose Q-processes together, R must be active since it will match a passive L. The handshaking expansion gives

$$* [[li]; \; ro\uparrow; \; [ri]; \; ro\downarrow; \; [\neg ri]; \; lo\uparrow; \; [\neg li]; \; lo\downarrow] . \tag{4}$$

We now consider the handshaking expansion as the specification of the implementation: Any implementation of the program has to satisfy the ordering defined by (4). The next step is to construct a production-rule set that satisfies the ordering of (4).

We start with the production-rule set that is syntactically derived from (4):

$$li \; \mapsto \; ro\uparrow$$
$$ri \; \mapsto \; ro\downarrow$$
$$\neg ri \; \mapsto \; lo\uparrow$$
$$\neg li \; \mapsto \; lo\downarrow .$$

The execution of a production rule is called *effective* if it changes the value of a variable; otherwise, it is called *vacuous*. Vacuous executions of production rules can be ignored.

The production-rule set satisfies the handshaking-expansion specification if, and only if, the order of execution of effective production rules matches the *program order*, i.e., the order of the corresponding transitions in the handshaking expansion. (As a clue to the reader, production rules of a set are listed in program order.)

If program-order execution is not guaranteed for the syntactic production-rule set, our technique strengthens some rules' guards to enforce program-order execution. In our example, program order is not guaranteed for the syntactic production-rule set: Since $\neg ri$ holds initially, the third production rule can be executed first. This is also true for the fourth production rule, but the execution of the fourth rule in the initial state is vacuous. Because all handshaking variables of R are back to **false** when R is completed, we cannot find a guard for the transition $lo\uparrow$. Hence, we cannot distinguish the state following R from the state preceding R.

This is a general problem, since it arises for each unshuffled communication action. The task of transforming the handshaking expansion so as to make each state unique —a state is unique when there exists a predicate in terms of variables of the program that holds only in this state— is called *state assignment*.

4.2 *State Assignment with State Variables*

Let us return to our example. To define uniquely the state in which the transition $lo\uparrow$ is to take place, the first technique consists in introducing a state variable, say x, initially **false**. Q becomes

$$* [[li]; \ ro\uparrow; \ [ri]; \ x\uparrow; \ [x]; \ ro\downarrow; \ [\neg ri]; \ lo\uparrow; \ [\neg li]; \ x\downarrow; \ [\neg x]; \ lo\downarrow] \ . \qquad (5)$$

Observe that (5) is semantically equivalent to (4), since the two sequences of actions that are added to (4) (namely, $x\uparrow; [x]$ and $x\downarrow; [\neg x]$) are equivalent to a **skip**.

There are several places where the two assignments to the state variable can be introduced. In general, a good heuristic is to introduce those assignments at such places that the alternation between waits and assignments is maintained.

4.3 *State Assignment with Reshuffling*

Another way to find a valid guard for $lo\uparrow$ is to use Property 2 of the handshaking expansions to reorder the actions of (5). For instance, we can postpone the second half of the handshaking expansion of Q —i.e., the sequence $ro\downarrow; [\neg ri]$— until after $[\neg li]$. We get

$$* [[li]; \ ro\uparrow; \ [ri]; \ lo\uparrow; \ [\neg li]; \ ro\downarrow; \ [\neg ri]; \ lo\downarrow] \ . \qquad (6)$$

Now the syntactic production rule expansion is already "program ordered":

$$li \mapsto ro\uparrow$$
$$ri \mapsto lo\uparrow$$
$$\neg li \mapsto ro\downarrow$$
$$\neg ri \mapsto lo\downarrow \ .$$

5 *The Basic Algorithm for Guard Strengthening*

We consider a straightline handshaking expansion and assume that state assignment has been performed. Hence, each state of the handshaking expansion is now unique.

We also assume that each assignment to a variable, such as $x\uparrow$ or $x\downarrow$, occurs at most once in the program. This restriction is easily enforced by renaming; in the case of a program

$$p \equiv \ldots x\uparrow; \ldots; \ x\downarrow; \ldots; \ x\uparrow; \ldots; \ x\downarrow; \ldots$$

we can rename the variable as

$$p' \equiv \ldots \ x1\uparrow; \ldots; \ x1\downarrow; \ldots; \ x2\uparrow; \ldots; \ x2\downarrow; \ldots \ .$$

We first perform the handshaking expansion of p'. We then observe that since $\neg x1 \lor \neg x2$ holds at any time, we can combine $x1$ and $x2$ by the two rules

$$x1 \lor x2 \;\longmapsto\; x\uparrow$$
$$\neg x1 \land \neg x2 \;\longmapsto\; x\downarrow \;.$$

If we treat the cases of selection and repetition separately, we do not have to consider disjunctions in wait-actions. Hence we can construct all production-rule guards as conjunctions; disjunction will be introduced next in the symmetrization step.

5.1 *First Method: Weakening Strong Guards*

Since each state of the handshaking expansion is uniquely defined, the set of production rules in which each guard is the strongest predicate in this state is ordered.

The set of strongest guards is constructed mechanically by determining in each state the value of all variables that are defined in that state: The strongest predicate in that state is the conjunction of all terms that are true in that state. We can then simplify the guards by using program invariants of the form $P \Rightarrow R$ to replace $P \land R$ by P. (This method has been proposed and used by Huub Schols.)

5.2 *Second Method: Strengthening Weak Guards*

The second method, which we have been using most of the time, starts with the weakest set of guards and strengthens them until the production rule set is ordered.

For each assignment, the initial guard of the production rule is the wait action that precedes it in the handshaking expansion. When the assignment —say, S— is preceded by another assignment, we introduce the net effect of the preceding assignment as wait action:

$x\uparrow; S$ is replaced by $x\uparrow; [x]; S$

$x\downarrow; S$ is replaced by $x\downarrow; [\neg x]; S$.

For each assignment, we define two sets of states:

1. the *firing set*, which is the set of all states in which the guard of the assignment holds; and

2. the *conflicting set*, which is the set of all states in which the firing of the assignment must be disallowed. For assignment S, let S' be the complementary assignment. The conflicting set is the set of contiguous states starting at the state preceding S' and ending at the state preceding the assignment that precedes S.

The "window of S" is the intersection of the firing set and the conflicting set of S. The window set must be empty ("the window is closed"). If it is not, we shrink the firing set of S (by strengthening the precondition) until the intersection is empty.

Because each state can be uniquely characterized in terms of the program variables, it is always possible to close the window of each assignment by strengthening the guards. There may be several possible ways to strengthen a guard. We choose the one that is the simplest (least number of variables) and that is best suited for symmetrization of the rules, which is explained later.

As an example of the use of the algorithm, we prove a theorem that identifies standard production rules that need not be strengthened. This result significantly reduces the number of cases to be considered.

Theorem 1

Production rule $xi \mapsto xo\downarrow$ of the active expansion of communication action X and production rule $\neg xi \mapsto xo\downarrow$ of the passive expansion of communication action X have empty window sets.

Proof   The active handshaking expansion of X is

$xo\uparrow;\ [xi];\ xo\downarrow;\ [\neg xi]$.

For $xi \mapsto xo\downarrow$, the firing set starts at the precondition of $xo\downarrow$ and ends at the postcondition of $xo\downarrow$. The conflicting set starts at the precondition of $xo\uparrow$ and ends at the postcondition of $xo\uparrow$. Observe that even with reshuffling these two sets are disjoint: The window is closed.

The passive handshaking expansion of X is

$[xi];\ xo\uparrow;\ [\neg xi];\ xo\downarrow$.

For $\neg xi \mapsto xo\downarrow$, the firing set starts at the precondition of $xo\downarrow$ and ends at any place before $[xi]$. The conflicting set starts at the precondition of $xo\uparrow$ and ends at the postcondition of $xo\uparrow$. Again, even with reshuffling, the window is always closed.   □

A similar theorem holds for standard production rules involving state variables.

Theorem 2

For state variable u, introduced as follows in the active handshaking expansion of X:

$$xo\uparrow;\ [xi];\ u\uparrow;\ [u];\ xo\downarrow;\ [\neg xi],\qquad\qquad(7)$$

the production rules $xi \mapsto u\uparrow$ and $u \mapsto xo\downarrow$ have empty window sets. For state variable u introduced as follows in the passive handshaking expansion of X:

$$[xi]; \ xo\uparrow; \ [xo]; \ u\uparrow; \ [u]; \ [\neg xi]; \ xo\downarrow, \tag{8}$$

the production rule $xo \mapsto u\uparrow$ has an empty window set. The same results hold if any of the variables involved is replaced by its complement.

The proof, which is similar to that of Theorem 1, is omitted. The results of Theorem 2 indicate that passive handshaking is more difficult to deal with than active handshaking.

Let us now complete the production-rule expansion of the Q-element. Since x has been introduced to distinguish the preceding state $ro\uparrow$ from the preceding state $lo\uparrow$, we can immediately strengthen the guard of $ro\uparrow$ with $\neg x$ and the guard of $lo\uparrow$ with x. We get

$$\neg x \wedge li \mapsto ro\uparrow \tag{9}$$

$$ri \mapsto x\uparrow \tag{10}$$

$$x \mapsto ro\downarrow \tag{11}$$

$$x \wedge \neg ri \mapsto lo\uparrow \tag{12}$$

$$\neg li \mapsto x\downarrow \tag{13}$$

$$\neg x \mapsto lo\downarrow \ . \tag{14}$$

It is easy to check in (5) that the strengthenings of the guards of (9) and (12) close the two windows. We further observe in (5) that the introduction of $x\uparrow$ in the handshaking expansion of R, and the introduction of $x\downarrow$ in the handshaking expansion of L both fulfill property (7) of Theorem 2. Hence, according to Theorem 2, (10), (11), (13), and (14) are ordered, and the above handshaking expansion is program ordered.

6 *Operator Reduction*

The last step of the transformation implements sets of production rules that modify the same variable (or a common set of variables) with a VLSI operator. Any pair of rules

$$b1 \mapsto z\uparrow$$
$$b2 \mapsto z\downarrow$$

that are stable and mutually exclusive can be implemented by —or is the specification of— a simple VLSI operator. (In practice, there is a limit to the number of input variables that can appear in $b1$ and $b2$, but we need not be concerned with this limit here.)

Since we have enforced mutual exclusion between any two interfering rules, and stability of each rule, we can implement any set of production rules directly. (We shall later extend the repertoire of operators to include one special operator taking care of production rules that are not mutually exclusive, and another for cases where a production rule is not stable.) The simple operators (both mutually exclusive and stable) can be partitioned into two classes:

1. the *combinational* operators for which $b1 \lor b2$ holds at any time, and

2. the *state-holding* operators for which $\neg b1 \land \neg b2$ may hold at some time.

State-holding operators are slightly more difficult to realize than combinational operators because the current value of the output variable z has to be maintained when $\neg b1 \land \neg b2$ holds; in most cases, this requires extra circuitry.

For this reason, a last transformation, called "symmetrization", will be performed on the production rule set to minimize the number of state-holding operators.

7 Symmetrization

Symmetrization is performed on two guards $b1$ and $b2$ when one of the two guards, say, $b1$, is already in the form $x \land \neg b2$. If x holds as a precondition of the rule $b2 \mapsto z\downarrow$, the guard $b2$ is equivalent to $\neg x \lor b2$.

Now the two guards are complements of each other; i.e., the operator is combinational. Of course, weakening guard $b2$ is a dangerous transformation since we may introduce a new state where the guard holds. We have to check that this does not occur by checking the following invariant.

Given the new rule $\neg x \lor b2 \mapsto z\downarrow$, $\neg z$ must hold in any state where $\neg x \land \neg b2$ holds; i.e., we have to check the invariant truth of

$$x \lor b2 \lor \neg z .$$

7.1 Operator Reduction of the Q-element

For the direct implementation of Q, the symmetrization of (9) and (11), and (12) and (14) gives

$$\neg x \land li \mapsto ro\uparrow \tag{9}$$

$$ri \mapsto x\uparrow \tag{10}$$

$$\neg li \lor x \mapsto ro\downarrow \tag{11}$$

$$x \land \neg ri \mapsto lo\uparrow \tag{12}$$

$$\neg li \mapsto x\downarrow \tag{13}$$

$$ri \lor \neg x \mapsto lo\downarrow . \tag{14}$$

Rules (9) and (11) correspond to the *and*-operator $(\neg x, li) \triangle ro$, rules (10) and (13) correspond to the flip-flop $(ri; li)$ **ff** x, and rules (12) and (14) correspond to the *and*-operator $(x, \neg ri) \triangle lo$. The resulting circuit is shown in Fig. 1.

For the second implementation of Q, with reshuffling of actions (see (6)), the production-rule set can be reduced directly: The first and third rules specify wire *li w ro*; the second and fourth rules specify wire *ri w lo*.

Comparing the two circuits, we observe that the reordering of handshaking actions leads to a simpler implementation. This observation is true in general, although the gain is not always as drastic as in this case. We also observe that reordering handshaking actions modifies the behavior of the circuit concerning its synchronization with its environment. Hence, the choice to reorder actions is a choice in favor of a simpler circuit at the cost of modifying the original synchronization behavior of the circuit, in general, for the worse.

8 *Process Factorization*

The second example is used to introduce the technique of process factorization. The idea is to decompose a process, say, p, described as a handshaking expansion into a number of processes $p0, p1, \ldots, pn$ such that the parallel composition $(p0\|p1\| \ldots \|pn)$ is equivalent to p, i.e., implements the same handshaking sequence as p.

Factorization obeys two rules:

Rule 1

Each output variable belongs to exactly one factor process. (Hence factorization reduces the number of output variables per process.) Input variables may be shared by several factor processes.

Rule 2

Two adjacent actions $\alpha; \beta$ of the original process are put into two different processes during factorization if, and only if, the semicolon between α and

---

Figure 1. Direct implementation of the Q-element.

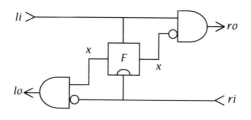

β is superfluous. Two cases fulfill this condition:

1. the two adjacent actions $\{\neg x\}\, x\uparrow;\ [x]$ and the two adjacent actions $\{x\}\, x\downarrow;\ [\neg x]$ for internal variable x, and

2. the pairs of handshaking actions $xo\uparrow;\ [xi]$ and $xo\downarrow;\ [\neg xi]$ for an active implementation, and the pair of handshaking actions $yo\uparrow;\ [\neg yi]$ for a passive implementation. (This is a direct consequence of Property 1.)

8.1 *Example Two: Two-to-Four Phase Converter*

The following process converts a passive two-phase handshaking on channel L into an active four-phase handshaking on channel R. First observe that the converter cannot be specified as a buffer $*[L;R]$. Indeed, let (L',R') be the channel on which the converter is to be inserted. This channel maintains the relation $\underline{c}L' = \underline{c}R'$. The converter should leave it unchanged. But if $0 \le \underline{c}L - \underline{c}R \le 1$, then $0 \le \underline{c}L' - \underline{c}R' \le 1$ holds after insertion of the converter. Hence, we have to implement the converter such that $\underline{c}L = \underline{c}R$; i.e., we have to interleave the handshaking of L and R in such a way that L and R are completed at the same time. We get

$$conv \equiv *[[li];\ ro\uparrow;\ [ri];\ ro\downarrow;\ [\neg ri];\ lo\uparrow;\ [\neg li];\ ro\uparrow;\ [ri];\ ro\downarrow;\ [\neg ri];\ lo\downarrow]\,.$$

(There are several ways to interleave the handshake sequences of two actions so as to make their completions coincide. Again, we have chosen the one in which the waits and the assignments alternate.) We first try to factorize *conv* into two processes, $p1$ and $p2$. We get

$$p1 \equiv *[[li];\ ro\uparrow;\ldots$$
$$p2 \equiv *[[ri];\ ro\downarrow;\ldots\,.$$

Here the factorization fails since it violates Rule 1. Rule 1 is violated because actions $ro\uparrow$ and $ro\downarrow$ follow each other as output actions in *conv*. We can separate the two output actions $ro\uparrow$ and $ro\downarrow$ by inserting a vacuous sequence $u\uparrow;\ [u]$ on a newly introduced internal variable u. (Initially, $u =$ **false**.) We introduce this sequence after the first $[ri]$; for reasons of symmetry, we introduce the sequence $u\downarrow;\ [\neg u]$ after the second $[ri]$. The transformed program is

$$conv' \equiv *[\,[li];\ ro\uparrow;\ [ri];\ u\uparrow;\ [u];\ ro\uparrow;\ [\neg ri];\ lo\uparrow;$$
$$[\neg li];\ ro\uparrow;\ [ri];\ u\downarrow;\ [\neg u];\ ro\uparrow;\ [\neg ri];\ lo\downarrow$$
$$]\,.$$

Now, we can apply factorization Rule 2 without violating Rule 1. We get

$$p1 \equiv *[[li];\ ro\uparrow;\ [u];\ ro\downarrow;\ [\neg li];\ ro\uparrow;\ [\neg u];\ ro\downarrow]$$
$$p2 \equiv *[[ri];\ u\uparrow;\ [\neg ri];\ lo\uparrow;\ [ri];\ u\downarrow;\ [\neg ri];\ lo\downarrow]\,.$$

It is easy to verify that $(p1\|p2)$ = *conv'*. Since the sequences $u{\uparrow}$; [*u*] and $u{\downarrow}$; [¬*u*] are both equivalent to a *skip* in *conv'*, $(p1\|p2)$ = *conv*.

Process $p2$ can immediately be identified as a standard process called a toggle, represented by the infix operator *ri* **tog** $(u; lo)$. For $p1$, we first strengthen the guards as follows:

$$p1 \equiv *[[¬u \wedge li]; ro{\uparrow}; [li \wedge u]; ro{\downarrow}; [¬li \wedge u]; ro{\uparrow}; [¬li \wedge ¬u]; ro{\downarrow}].$$

The validity of this transformation relies on invariants from *conv'*; it cannot be justified by properties of $p1$ only.

Now $p1$ can be identified with a difference operator, (u, li) **dif** *ro*, also called an *exclusive-or*. The corresponding circuit is shown in Fig. 2.

The kind of process factorization we have described in the previous section is very helpful but can, in principle, be avoided by applying the standard technique for production-rule expansion. One case of process factorization that cannot be avoided is when a process has to be decomposed into two or more processes, one of which is given. For reasons that will become clear in a moment, we call this transformation "process quotient".

9 *Production Rule Expansion of a Set of Guarded Commands*

Let us now address the problem of compiling a set of guarded commands. A canonical program for a process is:

Figure 2.   Two-to-four phase converter.

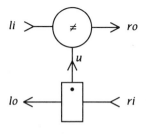

$$*[[\,B_0 \;\rightarrow\; S_0$$
$$[\![\,B_1 \;\rightarrow\; S_1$$
$$\cdots$$
$$[\![\,B_n \;\rightarrow\; S_n$$
$$]\!]\ .$$

First, each guarded command is compiled independently. Then the different guarded commands' production-rule sets are merged. The merging has to enforce mutual exclusion between the different sets: First, all guards B_0 through B_n have to be made mutually exclusive in the initial state. (When this is not possible, as in the next example, arbiters have to be introduced.) Second, execution of command S_i must leave all guards B_j, $j \neq i$, **false**. Third, interference between the production rules of the selected command and the production rules of the "dormant" commands must be excluded. Let us again use an example to illustrate the method.

10 *Example Three: Resource Arbitration*

Two independent processes compete for mutually exclusive access to a shared resource, e.g., a store. The "resource arbiter", *res,* selects a request from one of the two processes A and B. Before granting the resource S to the selected process, *res* activates a so-called "transfer module" associated with the process. The transfer module (T for A and R for B) prepares parameters for the shared resource that is activated after the transfer module activity has terminated. The resource arbiter process can be described as

$$res \;\equiv\; *[[\,\overline{A} \;\rightarrow\; T;S;A$$
$$[\![\,\overline{B} \;\rightarrow\; R;S;B$$
$$]\!]\ .$$

(We have used the same name for a process communicating with *res* and for the channel through which *res* communicates with the process.)

10.1 *Handshaking Expansion*

As usual, the handshaking expansion is straightforward: A and B are passive; T, R, and S are active. The specification of the problem allows T, R, and S to be reshuffled as follows:

$$res \;\equiv\; *[[\,ai \rightarrow to{\uparrow}; [ti]; so{\uparrow}; [si]; ao{\uparrow}; [\neg ai]; to{\downarrow}; [\neg ti]; so{\downarrow}; [\neg si]; ao{\downarrow}$$
$$[\![\,bi \rightarrow ro{\uparrow}; [ri]; so{\uparrow}; [si]; bo{\uparrow}; [\neg bi]; ro{\downarrow}; [\neg ri]; so{\downarrow}; [\neg si]; bo{\downarrow}$$
$$]\!]\ .$$

Since the requests for the resource on the two channels A and B are independent of each other, ai and bi can both be **true** at the same time. Since the problem is symmetrical in A and B, there is no symmetrical way to strengthen the two guards so as to make them mutually exclusive. An asymmetrical solution would replace ai by $ai \land \neg bi$, but it introduces unstable guards. Hence, we will have to implement production rules that are either not mutually exclusive or unstable.

For the symmetrical solution, we have just one operator that implements two guards that are not mutually exclusive: the basic "arbiter". It is described by the handshaking expansion

$$(x, y)\ \textbf{arb}\ (u, v) \equiv *[[x \rightarrow u\uparrow; [\neg x]; u\downarrow$$
$$[]y \rightarrow v\uparrow; [\neg y]; v\downarrow$$
$$]]\ .$$

It is easy to verify that if $\neg u \land \neg v$ holds initially, then $\neg u \lor \neg v$ is invariantly **true**.

Since the two guards ai and bi are not mutually exclusive, it seems reasonable to introduce the arbiter $(ai, bi)\textbf{arb}(u, v)$, where u and v are "new" internal variables introduced just for defining the arbiter. (What else could we do? It seems very difficult to use other variables of res as output variables of the arbiter.) Let arb be this arbiter. We now have to find a process X, such that

$$(X \| arb) = res\ .$$

Since arb is entirely defined, we would like to be able to perform the inverse operation of $\|$, or "process quotient", so as to compute X as

$$X = (res \div arb)\ .$$

A way to perform this division is to remove all actions of arb from res and then check to see whether the result fulfills $(X \| arb) \equiv res$. (We will omit the discussion about when such a quotient is possible.)

To perform the division as suggested, res should be extended to contain all actions of arb, so that the orders of actions are compatible in arb and in res', which is the extended version of res.

Given the ordering of actions in arb, the only way to extend res is as

$$res' \equiv *[[ai \rightarrow u\uparrow; [u]; to\uparrow; \dots [\neg ai]; u\downarrow; [\neg u]; to\downarrow; \dots ao\downarrow$$
$$[]bi \rightarrow v\uparrow; [v]; ro\uparrow; \dots [\neg bi]; v\downarrow; [\neg v]; ro\downarrow; \dots bo\downarrow$$
$$]]\ .$$

Now, by deleting the actions of arb from res', we get

$$X \equiv [res]_{u,v}^{ai,bi}\ .$$

It is easy to verify that $(X \| arb)$ is a valid implementation of res.

10.2 *Implementation of* X

Next, we shall implement each guarded command independently —thanks to the symmetry of the problem, we only have to do the job once!— and then we shall enforce the mutual exclusion between the two production rule sets, if necessary. The handshaking expansion of X is

$$*[[u \rightarrow to\uparrow; [ti]; so\uparrow; [si]; ao\uparrow; [\neg u]; to\downarrow; [\neg ti]; so\downarrow; [\neg si]; ao\downarrow$$

$$[]v \rightarrow ro\uparrow; [ri]; so\uparrow; [si]; bo\uparrow; [\neg v]; ro\downarrow; [\neg ri]; so\downarrow; [\neg si]; bo\downarrow$$

$$]] .$$

The two guards are mutually exclusive, but v may become true as soon as $[\neg u]$ has been completed in the first guarded command. Hence, there is a window in the first guarded command where the second guard may be true. The window starts after $[\neg u]$ and ends after $ao\downarrow$.

Since ao holds all through the window and $\neg ao$ holds in the initial state, we strengthen the second guard as $\neg ao \wedge v$; and symmetrically, we strengthen the first guard as $\neg bo \wedge u$.

Thanks to the reshuffling, the production rule expansion is straightforward:

$$\neg bo \wedge u \mapsto to\uparrow$$
$$ti \mapsto so\uparrow$$
$$si \mapsto ao\uparrow$$
$$\neg u \mapsto to\downarrow$$
$$\neg ti \mapsto so\downarrow$$
$$\neg s \mapsto ao\downarrow .$$

And similarly for the second guarded command:

$$\neg ao \wedge v \mapsto ro\uparrow$$
$$ri \mapsto so\uparrow$$
$$si \mapsto bo\uparrow$$
$$\neg v \mapsto ro\downarrow$$
$$\neg ri \mapsto so\downarrow$$
$$\neg si \mapsto bo\downarrow .$$

10.3 *Interference between Guarded Commands*

Interference can occur only among guarded commands that share variables or communication actions. Since the two guarded commands share communication action S, we must eliminate interferences between production rules of the two commands that use the variables so and si.

First, we observe that production rule $\neg ri \mapsto so\downarrow$ can fire at any point of the handshaking expansion of the first command since it fires vacuously in the initial state of the second guarded command. Its window is exactly the conflicting set of $so\uparrow$, which we close by strengthening the guard with $\neg ti$; and similarly for production rule $\neg ti \mapsto so\downarrow$ of the first guarded command. We strengthen both rules as

$$\neg ti \wedge \neg ri \mapsto so\downarrow \ .$$

Next, we observe that production rule $si \mapsto bo\uparrow$ of the second guarded command can be enabled during execution of the first guarded command, and production rule $si \mapsto ao\uparrow$ of the first guarded command can be enabled during execution of the second guarded command. The strengthening of those two rules gives

$$ri \wedge si \mapsto bo\uparrow$$
$$ti \wedge si \mapsto ao\uparrow \ .$$

After further symmetrization, the two production-rule sets become

$$u \wedge \neg bo \mapsto to\uparrow$$
$$ri \vee ti \mapsto so\uparrow$$
$$ti \wedge si \mapsto ao\uparrow$$
$$bo \vee \neg u \mapsto to\downarrow$$
$$\neg ri \wedge \neg ti \mapsto so\downarrow$$
$$\neg si \mapsto ao\downarrow$$

and

$$v \wedge \neg ao \mapsto ro\uparrow$$
$$ti \vee ri \mapsto so\uparrow$$
$$ri \wedge si \mapsto bo\uparrow$$
$$ao \vee \neg v \mapsto ro\downarrow$$
$$\neg ti \wedge \neg ri \mapsto so\downarrow$$
$$\neg si \mapsto bo\downarrow \ .$$

The operator reduction gives the set of operators

$$(ai', \neg bo) \triangle to$$
$$(ri, ti) \veebar so$$
$$(si; ti) \ \mathbf{aC} \ ao$$
$$(bi', \neg ao) \triangle ro$$
$$(si; ri) \ \mathbf{aC} \ bo \ .$$

The final circuit for *res* is shown in Fig. 3.

11 *Conclusion*

We have described a set of program transformations used in the synthesis of self-timed VLSI circuits from program specification. In particular, we have shown how a set of simple rules for manipulating uninterpreted formulae can be applied very effectively to this new area of program development.

The simplicity and generality of the two program notations we have introduced (production-rule expansion and handshaking expansion) make them amenable to algebraic manipulation. However, we have tried to avoid falling into the pitfall of oversimplification: For instance, unlike notations based on trace theory, the handshaking expansion maintains the difference between wait-actions and assignments. This difference turns out to be crucial in the program transformations performed.

These program transformation techniques make it possible for the designer to modify and refine a design while maintaining its correctness. Each "legal" transformation guarantees that the resulting program is semantically equivalent to the source program, providing the designer with a "safety net" that enables him to explore a much larger solution space than more traditional design techniques do.

12 *Postscriptum (April 1989)*

Formal methods are regularly disparaged on the ground that they have been demonstrated only on "toy examples", and are "obviously inapplicable

Figure 3. The final circuit for *res*.

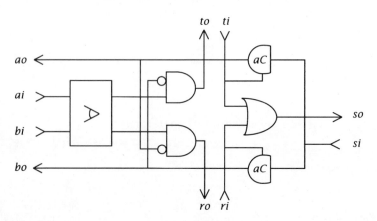

to real-world problems". This fallacious argument is difficult to refute when applied to programming because of the obfuscating effect of adjusting a new design to the idiosyncrases of an existing software and hardware system.

Fortunately, the VLSI medium offers the designer a "clean slate" to work with: Given a specification and a piece of silicon wafer —and the excellent services of the MOSIS silicon foundry— one can demonstrate the advantages claimed for a new design method practically in isolation, which makes it worthwhile to invest some time in sizable examples.

Hence every significant example that we have used in our research — distributed mutual exclusion, queues, stack, routing automata for communication network, $3X+1$ engine— has been fabricated in CMOS technology. They have all been found to be correct on "first silicon". They are also very robust, and surprisingly fast, given the low level of circuit optimization applied. For instance, the $3X+1$ engine, constructed by Tony Lee, is a special-purpose processor consisting of a state-machine and an 80-bit-wide datapath. It contains approximately 40,000 transistors and operates at over 8 MIPS (millions of instructions per second) in 2μm CMOS technology.

At the moment of writing this postscriptum, we have just completed the design and fabrication of the first asynchronous general-purpose microprocessor (see [2]). It is a 16-bit RISC-like architecture with independent instruction and data memories. It has 16 registers, 4 buses, an ALU, and two adders. The size is about 20,000 transistors. Two versions have been fabricated: one in 2μm CMOS, and one in 1.6μm CMOS. (On the 2μm version, only 12 registers were implemented in order to fit the chip on an 84-pin 6600μm$\times 4600\mu$m pad frame.)

The chips are entirely delay-insensitive, with the sole exception of the interface with the memories. In the absence of available memories with asynchronous interfaces, we have simulated the completion signal from the memories with an external —off-chip— delay.

In spite of some missing connections in the layout (floating n-wells), the 2μm version runs at 12 MIPS. The 1.6μm version runs at 18 MIPS. (These figures are based on measurements from sequences of ALU instructions without carry. They take no advantage of the overlap between ALU and memory instructions.) Those performances are quite encouraging given that the design is very conservative: no pass-transistors, static gates, dual-rail encoding of data, completion trees, etc.

Only 2 of the 12 2μm chips passed all tests, but 34 out of the 50 1.6μm chips were found entirely functional.

We have tested the chips under a wide range of values for the voltage level encoding the high boolean value (*VDD*). At room temperature, the 2μm version is functional in a voltage range from 7V down to 0.35V! It reaches 15 MIPS at 7V. We have also tested the chips cooled in liquid nitrogen. The 2μm version reaches 20 MIPS at 5V and 30 MIPS at 12V. The 1.6μm version reaches

30 MIPS at 5V. Of course, these measurements are made without adjusting any clocks (there are none), but simply by connecting the processor to a memory containing a test program and observing the rate of instruction execution.

The low power consumption —145mW at 5V and 6.7mW at 2V— compared to traditional designs, is due to the fact that our synthesis method produces the minimal set of transitions (production rules) necessary to implement a given computation.

Acknowledgments

Acknowledgments are due to my students Steve Burns and Pieter Hazewindus for their comments on the manuscript and to David Long for his implementation of the algorithm for production-rule expansion.

The research described in this paper was sponsored by the Defense Advanced Research Projects Agency, DARPA order number 6202, and monitored by the Office of Naval Research under contract number N00014-87-K-0745.

References

[1] Martin, A. J. "Programming in VLSI: From communicating processes to self-timed VLSI circuits". *Concurrent Programming* (Proceedings of the 1987 UT Year of Programming Institute on Concurrent Programming), C. A. R. Hoare, ed. Addison-Wesley, Reading, Mass., 1989 (to appear).

[2] Martin, A. J., Burns, S. M., Lee, T. K., Borkovic, D., and Hazewindus, P. J. "The design of an asynchronous microprocessor". In *Decennial Caltech Conference on VLSI*, C. L. Seitz, ed. MIT Press, Cambridge, Mass., 1989.

Programs
from
Specifications

9

Joseph M. Morris
University of Glasgow

---

0 Introduction

The making of a program begins with a specification, which in the first instance is a precise, and typically formal, statement of what is required of the program. But if we take the view that the programmer is obliged to make evident that his program realizes the specification —and we do— then the relationship between specifications and programs becomes more intimate. At the very least the specification is the standard against which the programmer verifies that his program is correct. But experience has taught us that it is difficult to verify an arbitrary program after the fact, and that it is better to employ a methodology that makes the correctness argument a natural accompaniment of programming, the program and the proof developing together. Rather than being an extra burden on the programmer, the correctness argument turns out to be of great heuristic value: Not only is the program correct, but it is made more quickly, and as often as not it is more efficient than a solution constructed less methodically [3, 4, 8, 9]. Our purpose here is to expose the mathematical laws underlying this approach to programming in the belief that they will enable us to employ it more effectively.

The role of the specification in our approach is central, because it guides the development of the program at each stage. More precisely, we are taking the view that programming consists in transforming a specification into a program according to mathematical laws that ensure that correctness is preserved. Of course, because we do not make a program in one giant leap but in a succession of small steps, in practice the transformation is a composition of many small transformations. The first transformation is applied to the given specification, the outcome of the final transformation is a program, and in between, each transformation is applied to a hybrid specification/program. But that is a complicated view of things, which we simplify by choosing to regard everything from specification to program as a specification. Programs are a subset of specifications. Of course we will choose the specification language and its program subset so that the former has power of expression and the latter has ease of implementation, but the choice doesn't matter much as far as the theory is concerned. Typically, certain constructs of the specification language are designated as "nonalgorithmic", and a program is defined as a specification employing no nonalgorithmic components.

We shall attach a formal semantics to specifications with the result that programs and specifications now inhabit the one semantic framework. We then define a relation $\sqsubseteq$ on specifications such that $s \sqsubseteq t$ is a formalization of "specification t preserves the intention behind specification s"—in other words, a customer asking for s would be willing to accept t. The programming task is: Given a specification s, find a program p satisfying $s \sqsubseteq p$. We do so via a sequence of specifications $s_0, s_1, \ldots, s_n$ satisfying $s = s_0 \sqsubseteq s_1 \sqsubseteq \cdots \sqsubseteq s_n = p$. Clearly relation $\sqsubseteq$ must be transitive. Furthermore, we would dearly like each s_{i+1} to be derived from s_i by application of one of a fairly small bag of mathematical laws. Finally, we would like the laws to be useful in practice— for example, they should have simple formulations and should not require inordinate amounts of writing in their application. An important attribute of the laws in this regard is that of "componentwise applicability"— the property that allows us to transform a specification by successively transforming small pieces of it in turn. We will develop a collection of transformations in which each transformation consists in replacing some construct in the current specification with a component that is "more algorithmic".

Our aims are modest: We want to make a point —that a formal calculus of programming is a useful thing— rather than construct an "industrial strength" calculus. Consequently the specification language will be fairly simple. It will be an extension of the programming notation of "guarded commands" [4], which we enrich to the extent that we can specify small programs such as those in [3, 4, 8, 9] in a couple of lines, and we will develop the formal calculus to the extent that we can profitably use it to develop such programs.

1 *Specifications and Programs*

We will describe a simple specification language, a subset of which we will identify as a programming language. The language is based on the notation of guarded commands, and its semantics are given by predicate transformers. It is best if the reader has some familiarity with these issues; they are well described in [3, 4, 8, 9].

The syntax and semantics of the language will make much use of "assertions", i.e., predicates in which the program variables may occur free (in the present context it is more proper to speak of "specification variables", but we will stick with the existing terminology). We will let $x, y, x_0, x0, \ldots$ stand for program variables. The set of possible values that the variables of a specification may collectively assume is called the "state space" of the specification; assertions may be interpreted as boolean-valued functions on the state space. Capital letters, possibly subscripted, will stand for assertions; T and F denote the assertions satisfied by all states and by no state, respectively. The notation [X] stands for X universally quantified over its free program variables (bear in mind that in manipulations of [X] we may be employing the properties of universal quantifiers). For variables x_i and expressions e_i, $0 \leq i < n$, $X(x_0, \ldots, x_{n-1}/e_0, \ldots, e_{n-1})$ denotes X in which all free occurrences of the x_i's are replaced by the corresponding e_i's; for e an expression $e(x_0, \ldots, x_{n-1}/e_0, \ldots, e_{n-1})$ is defined similarly. The symbols **A** and **E** are the universal and existential quantifiers, respectively. The small letters s, t, u, v, w —possibly subscripted— stand for statements of the specification language. $Tx, Ty, \ldots$ stand for types, and $e, e_0, e0, \ldots$ stand for expressions. Function application is denoted by an infix period, which has the highest operator precedence. The logical operators grouped in order of decreasing precedence are $\neg$; $\wedge$, $\vee$; $\Rightarrow$; and $\equiv$.

2 *Statements*

We describe the syntactic form of the statements of the specification language, together with some informal semantics; the semantics are described formally in the next section.

A "block" statement introduces variables and delimits their scope; for example,

$$[\![x: Tx; \; y: Ty; \; s]\!]$$

introduces variables x of type Tx and y of type Ty with scope delimited by the brackets; any positive number of variables may be introduced in a single block statement. We will assume —to avoid rather long-winded and mundane technical details— that the variables introduced in a block statement are given names that do not conflict with names in surrounding blocks. Common abbreviations —such as $x, y: Tx$ for $x: Tx; \; y: Tx$— are admitted. The allowable types of variables are not made explicit: Certainly the familiar primitive types such as **int**, **bool**, **char**, ... and structured types such as bounded sequences are admitted, but so also —because the language is a specification language— are such types as sets and unbounded sequences.

Simple assignment has the form $x := e$ and concurrent assignment the form $x_0, x_1, \ldots, x_{n-1} := e_0, e_1, \ldots, e_{n-1}$; these have the usual semantics.

The statement having no effect is **skip**. The statement **abort** is the maximally nondeterministic statement; i.e., its operational behavior is completely unpredictable, and it may even fail to terminate. The statement **miracle** is the magic statement that knows exactly what we want and does it.

Composition of statements s and t is denoted by $s; t$ as usual. The if- and do-statements have the respective forms

> **if** $P_0 \rightarrow s_0$ [] $P_1 \rightarrow s_1$ [] $\cdots$ [] $P_{n-1} \rightarrow s_{n-1}$ **fi**
>
> **do** $P \rightarrow s$ **od** ,

with n a positive integer. (The form $X \rightarrow s$ is called a "guarded command", X being the "guard".) Any assertion may be used as a guard. The if- and do-statements have the usual semantics.

The "assert" statement has the form $\{X\}$; it behaves like **skip** if X holds and otherwise like **abort**. It is customary to omit the semicolon when composing an assert statement with other statements.

The "nondeterministic assignment" statement has the form $x :- P$ and means "assign to x a value such that P holds after the assignment". For example $x :- x > 0$ asks for x to be assigned a positive value. We allow x' to occur in the P of $x :- P$ to denote the value of x before the assignment. For example $x :- x > x'$ asks for the value of x to be incremented. A variation of nondeterministic assignment has the form $x\langle e\rangle :- P$ and the meaning "assign to x a value such that P holds and the value of e is not changed by the assignment". For example $x\langle x \bmod 2\rangle :- x > 0$ asks for x to be assigned a positive value without changing its even/odd parity. For a more interesting example we make a brief incursion into "bag theory".

A "bag" b on type Tx is a function $b: Tx \rightarrow$ **nat**; the value of $b.x$ for x of type Tx is called the "number of occurrences of x in b". For bags b, c on Tx and x of type Tx we define $\in$, $\cup$, $\cap$, $-$, $+$, $\subseteq$, $\#$ thus:

$x \in b \equiv b.x > 0$

$(b \cup c).x \equiv b.x \textbf{ max } c.x$ $(b \cap c).x \equiv b.x \textbf{ min } c.x$

$(b - c).x \equiv (b.x - c.x) \textbf{ max } 0$ $(b + c).x \equiv b.x + c.x$

$b \subseteq c \equiv (\textbf{A}x: x \in Tx: b.x \leq c.x)$

$\#b \equiv \#\{\langle x, i\rangle: x \in Tx \land 0 \leq i < b.x\}$.

For any sequence d we let dom.d denote its domain. We associate with every sequence d a bag (on the same base type as d) denoted by bag.d and defined bag.$d.x \equiv \#\{i : i \in \text{dom}.d \land d.i = x\}$.

(Note that we write $d.i$ rather than $d[i]$ or d_i, and that function application associates to the left.) We allow sequences as arguments in place of bags in the above definitions of $\in$, $\cup$, etc., it being understood that the associated bag is intended. Bag theory supplies a useful notation for talking about sequences. For example, "x occurs in the sequence d" can be expressed as $x \in d$:

Lemma 2.0
For d a sequence and x a value in its base type

$$x \in d \equiv (\mathbf{E}\, i\colon i \in \text{dom}.d\colon d.i = x).$$

Proof   (See the note on proofs that follows.)

$\qquad x \in d$

$=\qquad$ "definition of $\in$ on sequences"

$\qquad x \in \text{bag}.d$

$=\qquad$ "definition of $\in$ on bags"

$\qquad \text{bag}.d.x > 0$

$=\qquad$ "definition of bag.d"

$\qquad \#\{i\colon i \in \text{dom}.d \land d.i = x\} > 0$

$=\qquad$ "set theory"

$\qquad \neg(\{i\colon i \in \text{dom}.d \land d.i = x\} = \varnothing)$

$=\qquad$ "set equality"

$\qquad \neg(\mathbf{A}\, i\colon\colon i \in \text{dom}.d \land d.i = x \equiv i \in \varnothing)$

$=\qquad$ "$i \in \varnothing \equiv$ false"

$\qquad \neg(\mathbf{A}\, i\colon\colon i \in \text{dom}.d \land d.i = x \equiv \text{false})$

$=\qquad$ "calculus"

$\qquad \neg(\mathbf{A}\, i\colon\colon \neg(i \in \text{dom}.d \land d.i = x))$

$=\qquad$ "de Morgan"

$\qquad (\mathbf{E}\, i\colon\colon i \in \text{dom}.d \land d.i = x)$

$=\qquad$ "introduce range"

$\qquad (\mathbf{E}\, i\colon i \in \text{dom}.d\colon d.i = x)$. $\square$

Note on proofs   Hints for the justification of proof steps are written within double quotes. The hint "calculus" records an appeal to rules of predicate calculus that are presumed to be familiar; the rules are presented, for example, in [3, 6, 9]. The word "substitution" hints at the elementary laws of substitution of variables, and "semantics" hints at the predicate transformer semantics of specifications to be presented later. In reducing a demonstrandum to "true" we may use $\Leftarrow$; $A \Leftarrow B$ is the same as $B \Rightarrow A$.

For the promised example of nondeterministic assignment we offer, for d a sequence variable

$$d\langle\text{bag}.d\rangle :- (\mathbf{A}\,i,j: i \in \text{dom}.d \,\wedge\, j \in \text{dom}.d: i \le j \Rightarrow d.i \le d.j)\,.$$

This asks for the elements of d to be rearranged so that the sequence in d is sorted; the $\langle bag.d\rangle$ clause is necessary to ensure that the final sequence is a permutation of the original sequence.

Nondeterministic assignment applies to lists of variables as well as just single variables. For example $x, y :- x > y$ asks for assignments to x and y such that x exceeds y. Information that can be inferred from the types of variables will not usually be made explicit in assertions. For example, with x a variable of type **int** we may write $x :- \text{T}$ instead of $x :- x \in \textbf{int}$.

The "minor miracle" is a statement with form $(P \to s)$; when P holds it behaves like s, and otherwise it behaves like **miracle**. It will turn out to be quite useful in constructing if-statements.

The input statement has the form $x?P$. Semantically we regard $x?P$ as equivalent to $x :- P$, its special form being an informal request not to refine it (with an assignment statement, for example). It indicates that we are looking for a program that is good for all values of x that satisfy P. We may write read.x instead of $x?T$. The output statement has the form write.e. Semantically we regard write.e as an assignment of e to an implicit global variable. Our view of input/output is admittedly simple, the simplifications being made because the details, although of practical importance, are not essential for our purposes. Here is an example:

```
[  d: seq of int; x: int; i: int;
   read.d;  read.x;
   if  (E i: i ∈ dom.d: d.i = x) → i :- d.i = x
   [] ¬(E i: i ∈ dom.d: d.i = x) → i := −1
   fi;
   write.i
]
```

("**int**" denotes the type of integers, and "**seq** of Tx" denotes the type of sequences on Tx with domain an initial segment of the natural numbers).

The specification language has many important omissions —procedures, parameters, and modules for example— but it suffices for the purpose at hand, namely, to show how specifications can be transformed into programs with mathematical rigor. The programming language is a defined subset of the specification language. Just what the program subset is is not crucial, except that it should be a relatively small subset —for otherwise the programming task becomes trivial or even empty— and yet not too small— for then programming might be impossible. We adopt as our programming language a Pascal-like subset of the specification language: It employs only familiar programming types— + on integers and ∧ on booleans are admitted for example, but not ∑ and **A**, no nondeterministic assignment statements, and no **miracle** statements. This is essentially the programming language of "guarded commands" [4].

3 *Formal Semantics*

Intuitively, a specification characterizes a set of (deterministic) computations. The set may be empty, as with $x :- F$, for example; or it may contain just one computation, as with $x :- x = 0$; or it may contain a few, as with $x :- 0 \leq x < 10 \land x \in$ **int**; or it may be very large, as with **abort**, which describes the set of all computations. We take it that a customer who gives us specification s to implement is asking for a program whose possible computations are a subset of those described by s.

We make a specification s having in mind some final state or set of states that the computations described by s should establish; a predicate describing the desired final state(s) is called a "postcondition" of the specification. A "precondition" of a specification s with respect to a postcondition R is a predicate characterizing a set of initial states such that the computations described by s when started in any of these states will terminate in a state satisfying R. The "weakest precondition" of s with respect to R —denoted by $s.R$— is the maximal such precondition. Semantically, specifications are functions on assertions mapping postconditions to weakest preconditions. The predicate $[P \Rightarrow s.Q]$, therefore, says that if any computation described by s is executed in any initial state satisfying P, then the computation will terminate in a state satisfying Q. It is usual to write $wp(s, R)$ rather than $s.R$, but we prefer not to make explicit the distinction between specifications as syntactic and semantic objects for the sake of notational brevity. Except for loops, which will be considered later, Fig. 1 defines $s.X$ by structural induction on s. The reader who finds Fig. 1 difficult to understand should consult [3, 4, 8, 9] for example. The term $(\mathbf{E} i: : i = e)$ in the definition of $x := e$ is a requirement that e be well defined, and similarly for concurrent assignment. The definition of block statements implies that variables are initialized to some arbitrary value although this does not necessarily accord with practice.

Convention   It is to be assumed unless the contrary is explicitly indicated that the P in $x, y :- P$ and $x, y\langle e\rangle :- P$ contains no free occurrences of x', y'.

Figure 1.   Definition of *s.X.*

---

s.X ≡

- *s* is **skip**
  X

- *s* is **abort**
  F

- *s* is **miracle**
  T

- *s* is $x := e$
  $(\mathbf{E}\, i :: i = e) \wedge X(x/e)$

- *s* is $x_0, x_1, \ldots := e_0, e_1, \ldots$
  $(\mathbf{E}\, i_0, i_1, \ldots :: i_0 = e_0 \wedge i_1 = e_1 \wedge \ldots) \wedge X(x_0, x_1, \ldots / e_0, e_1, \ldots)$

- *s* is $x, y :- P$
  $(\mathbf{A}\, x, y :: P \Rightarrow X)(x', y'/x, y)$

- *s* is $x, y(e) :- P$
  $(\mathbf{A}\, x, y :: P \wedge e = e' \Rightarrow X)(x', y'/x, y)$ where e' denotes $e(x, y/x', y')$

- *s* is $[\![x\colon Tx;\ y\colon Ty;\ t]\!]$
  $(\mathbf{A}\, x, y\colon x \in Tx \wedge y \in Ty\colon t.X)$

- *s* is $\{P\}$
  $P \wedge X$

- *s* is $t; u$
  $t.(u.X)$

- *s* is **if** $P_0 \to s_0 \;[\!]\; P_1 \to s_1 \;[\!]\; \cdots \;[\!]\; P_{n-1} \to s_{n-1}$ **fi**
  $(\mathbf{E}\, i\colon 0 \le i < n\colon P_i) \wedge (\mathbf{A}\, i\colon 0 \le i < n\colon P_i \Rightarrow s_i.X)$

- *s* is $(P \to t)$
  $P \Rightarrow t.X$

Hence we will mostly take $(\mathbf{A}x, y :: P \Rightarrow X)$ for $x, y :- P.X$.

The semantic functions for specifications are called "predicate transform-ers"; among their important properties are "conjunctivity" and "monotonic-ity":

Theorem 3.0

Specifications are conjunctive, i.e. $[s.X \wedge s.Y \equiv s.(X \wedge Y)]$.

Proof   The proof —at this stage for specifications without loops— is by structural induction on s and is left to the reader. See [9] for examples of the style.   □

Theorem 3.1

Specifications are monotonic, i.e., $[X \Rightarrow Y] \Rightarrow [s.X \Rightarrow s.Y]$.

Proof   The proof follows easily from Theorem 3.0 and is done in [9].   □

Other useful properties that the reader may easily prove are that compo-sition is associative and has **skip** as left and right identity.

It is shown in [9] that every program p obeys the laws of "the excluded miracle", i.e.,

$$[p.F \equiv F]$$

and "continuity", i.e.,

$$[p.(\mathbf{E}\,i: i \in \mathbf{nat}: P_i) \equiv (\mathbf{E}\,i: i \in \mathbf{nat}: p.P_i)]$$

for all sequences $\langle P_0, P_1, \ldots \rangle$ such that $[P_i \Rightarrow P_{i+1}]$ for all $i \in \mathbf{nat}$. Specifications, however, do not obey these laws. The statement **miracle** clearly violates the law of the excluded miracle, while $x :- x \in \mathbf{nat}$ exhibits what is called "un-bounded nondeterminacy", which is known to exclude continuity [5].

The semantics of iteration require some further notions. Let the relation $\leq'$ on assertions be defined by

$$X \leq' Y \equiv [X \Rightarrow Y].$$

The reflexivity, antisymmetry, and transitivity of $\leq'$ follow immediately from elementary laws of predicate calculus, and so $\leq'$ is a partial ordering. Now given set C partially ordered by $\leq$ and any B, $B \subseteq C$, an element u of C is an "upper bound" of B if $(\mathbf{A}x: x \in B: x \leq u)$; u is a "least" upper bound if $u \leq v$ for every upper bound v of B. A "complete lattice" is a set partially ordered by $\leq$ such that all its subsets have least upper bounds with respect to $\leq$. Any set of assertions $\{B_j : j \in J\}$, J any index set, has least upper bound $(\mathbf{E}j: j \in J: B_j)$; the proof of this is an exercise in predicate calculus that we leave to the reader. In summary, assertions partially ordered by $\leq'$ constitute a complete lattice.

Let C be a set partially ordered by $\leq$, and let $f: C \to C$ be a function; then c, $c \in C$, is a "fixpoint" of f if $f.c = c$, and a "least" fixpoint if in addition $c \leq d$ for all fixpoints d of f. The least fixpoint of function f, when it exists, is denoted by $(\mu x: f.x)$. Function $f: C \to C$, where C has a partial ordering $\leq$, is "monotonic" if $x \leq y \Rightarrow f.x \leq f.y$ for all $x, y \in C$; cf. Theorem 3.1. We can now state the well-known "Knaster-Tarski" theorem:

Theorem 3.2

Let C partially ordered by $\leq$ be a complete lattice; then for any monotonic function $f: C \to C$

(*i*) f has a least fixed point

(*ii*) $f.c \leq c \Rightarrow (\mu x: f.x) \leq c$ for all $c \in C$.

Proof   See [12].   □

Now for the semantics of iteration:

do $Q \to s$ **od** . $X = (\mu Y: (Q \wedge s.Y) \vee (\neg Q \wedge X))$.

The reader may easily show, using Theorem 3.1, that $(Q \wedge s.Y) \vee (\neg Q \wedge X))$ is a monotonic function of Y on the lattice of assertions; hence by Knaster-Tarski the preceding definition is a good one.

Let Asn denote the set of assertions. We say function $g:$ Asn $\to$ (Asn $\to$ Asn) is "conjunctive" if

$$[g.W.X \wedge g.Y.Z \equiv g.(W \wedge Y).(X \wedge Z)]$$

for all W, X, Y, Z. It is clear that if $g.X.Y$ is conjunctive then it is conjunctive, and hence monotonic, in each argument separately (that conjunctivity implies monotonicity is proved in [9]).

Lemma 3.0

Let $g.X.Y$ be conjunctive and $h.X$ stand for $(\mu Y: g.X.Y)$; $h.X$ is conjunctive.

Proof   We show $[h.P \wedge h.Q \equiv h.(P \wedge Q)]$ for all P, Q.

(*i*) $[h.(P \wedge Q) \Rightarrow h.P \wedge h.Q]$

   $=$ "definition of $h.(P \wedge Q)$"

   $[(\mu Y: g.(P \wedge Q).Y) \Rightarrow h.P \wedge h.Q]$

   $\Leftarrow$ "Knaster-Tarski"

   $[g.(P \wedge Q).(h.P \wedge h.Q) \Rightarrow h.P \wedge h.Q]$

   $=$ "g conjunctive"

   $[g.P.(h.P) \wedge g.Q.(h.Q) \Rightarrow h.P \wedge h.Q]$

$=$ "*h.P* and *h.Q* are fixpoints"

$[h.P \wedge h.Q \Rightarrow h.P \wedge h.Q]$

$=$ "calculus"

true

(*ii*) $[h.P \wedge h.Q \Rightarrow h.P \wedge h.Q]$

$=$ "calculus"

$[h.P \Rightarrow \neg h.Q \vee h.(P \wedge Q)]$

$=$ "definition of *h.P*"

$[(\mu Y: g.P.Y) \Rightarrow \neg h.Q \vee h.(P \wedge Q)]$

$\Leftarrow$ "Knaster-Tarski"

$[g.P.(\neg h.Q \vee h.(P \wedge Q)) \Rightarrow \neg h.Q \vee h.(P \wedge Q)]$

$=$ "calculus"

$[g.P.(\neg h.Q \vee h.(P \wedge Q)) \wedge h.Q \Rightarrow h.(P \wedge Q)]$

$=$ "*h.Q* a fixpoint"

$[g.P.(\neg h.Q \vee h.(P \wedge Q)) \wedge g.Q.(h.Q) \Rightarrow h.(P \wedge Q)]$

$=$ "*g* conjunctive, calculus"

$[g.(P \wedge Q).(h.Q \wedge h.(P \wedge Q)) \Rightarrow h.(P \wedge Q)]$

$=$ "*h.(P $\wedge$ Q)* a fixpoint"

$[g.(P \wedge Q).(h.Q \wedge h.(P \wedge Q)) \Rightarrow g.(P \wedge Q).(h.(P \wedge Q))]$

$=$ "*g* monotonic in second argument"

true   □

Proof of Theorem 3.0 completed   Let **DO** stand for **do** $Q \rightarrow s$ **od**.
Then **DO**.X is $(\mu Y: g.X.Y)$ where $g.X.Y$ is $(Q \wedge s.Y) \vee (\neg Q \wedge X)$. Under the inductive
hypothesis that *s.Y* is conjunctive, it is easy to show that *g.X.Y* is conjunctive.
Hence by the preceding lemma **DO**.X is conjunctive.   □

4 *Refinement*

We have taken the view that no semantic distinction is to be made between specifications and programs. We view programming as constructing a
sequence of specifications, the first one being supplied by the customer and
each one thereafter being a "more algorithmic" derivative of its predecessor.
The final member of the sequence is a program. The business of passing from
a specification to its successor in the developmental chain is called "refinement", and we proceed to give a formal explication of this process.

The specification language is richer than the programming language in two regards: It has a richer set of statements and a richer set of data types. The activity of reducing exotic statements to executable form is called "procedural refinement", whereas "data refinement" is concerned with replacing fancy data types with data types of the programming language. Here we set down the laws of procedural refinement; data refinement is described elsewhere [11].

That specification t is an acceptable substitute for specification s is denoted by $s \sqsubseteq t$, defined

$$s \sqsubseteq t = (\mathbf{A}X:: [s.X \Rightarrow t.X]).$$

For the operational motivation behind this definition, fix on any state σ of the state-space (common to s and t) and any postcondition R. If all computations described by s establish R when started in state σ, then the same can be said of the computations described by t if $s \sqsubseteq t$. The programming task is viewed as constructing a sequence of specifications $s_0, s_1, s_2, \ldots$ (s_0 being given) such that

$$s_0 \sqsubseteq s_1 \sqsubseteq s_2 \sqsubseteq \cdots$$

It will become clear as we proceed that this is indeed a reasonable formulation of what we do intuitively when we make a program. It is desirable that refinement should proceed "stepwise", i.e., that deriving each s_{i+1} from s_i is just a small step. Stepwise refinement is possible because of two properties of $\sqsubseteq$. The first is that $\sqsubseteq$ is transitive, indeed:

Theorem 4.0
$\sqsubseteq$ is a partial ordering.

Proof   Routine.   □

The second property of interest is that of "monotonic replacement":

Theorem 4.1
Let $s(w/u)$ stand for the specification got by replacing statement w in s with u, and similarly for $s(w/v)$. Then

$$u \sqsubseteq v \Rightarrow s(w/u) \sqsubseteq s(w/v).$$

Proof   The proof proceeds by structural induction, and is carried out for programs in [9]; the extension of the proof to specifications is left to the reader.   □

The transitivity of $\sqsubseteq$ allows us to carry out each step from s_i to s_{i+1} in isolation and yet to be guaranteed that the final program is a refinement of the initially given s_0. Monotonic replacement allows us to refine a specification by refining its components in isolation; the refinements of the components can then be "slotted in" to the specification—without any additional work— and in this way we achieve a large refinement by a succession of smaller ones. For example, we can prove $x :- x > 0 \sqsubseteq x := 1$ and $y :- y > x \sqsubseteq y := x \div 1$; hence by monotonic replacement we may conclude

$$x :- x > 0; \; y :- y > x \;\sqsubseteq\; x := 1; y := x + 1 \, .$$

It may appear that the definition of $s \sqsubseteq t$ as a boolean rather than a predicate is too coarse, for although t may not be a universally acceptable substitute for s it may well be acceptable in a particular context. For example, it can be shown that it is not the case that $x :- x > 0 \sqsubseteq$ **skip** , yet we should expect that such a refinement is acceptable in **if** $x > 0 \rightarrow x :- x > 0 \;[\!]\; x \le 0 \rightarrow x := x + 1$ **fi** . Suppose that for specifications s, t we were to introduce predicate $s \Rightarrow t$ to denote the weakest precondition such that t may replace s, defined

$$s \Rightarrow t \;=\; (\mathbf{A}X :: s.X \Rightarrow t.X) \, .$$

If assertion P characterizes the state of the computation preceding s —call P the "context" of s— then t may be substituted for s if $[P \Rightarrow (s \Rightarrow t)]$. But this connection between context and replacement can be described using $\sqsubseteq$; in fact it is easy to show that

$$[P \Rightarrow (s \Rightarrow t)] \;=\; \{P\} s \;\sqsubseteq\; t \, .$$

If follows that the assert statement supplies the context in which replacement takes place. The refinement rules for each statement s will be presented below as refinement rules for $\{P\}s$ where P stands for an arbitrary assertion. Here are some elementary rules for introducing, manipulating, and removing assert statements:

Theorem 4.2 ("assertions theorem")

(*i*)	$s = \{T\} s$
(*ii*)	$\{P\} s = \{P\} s \{Q\}$ if $[P \Rightarrow s.Q]$
(*iii*)	$\{P\} \{Q\} = \{P \wedge Q\}$
(*iv*)	$\{P\} s \sqsubseteq t \equiv \{P\} s \sqsubseteq \{P\} t$
(*v*)	$\{P\} \sqsubseteq \{Q\}$ if $[P \Rightarrow Q]$
(*vi*)	$\{P\} \sqsubseteq$ **skip** .

Proof   The proofs are elementary; as an example we prove (*ii*). For arbitrary X,

$$\{P\} s \{Q\}.X$$

=   "semantics of assert statement, composition"

$\{P\}\, s.(Q \wedge X)$

=   "semantics of assert statement, composition"

$P \wedge s.(Q \wedge X)$

=   "s conjunctive"

$P \wedge s.Q \wedge s.X$

=   "$[P \Rightarrow s.Q]$"

$P \wedge s.X$

=   "semantics of assert statement, composition"

$\{P\}\, s.X$.   □

Part (*iv*) of the above theorem is used when we refine a component s in a succession of steps, each time appealing to the original context even though we do not explicitly carry it along. Part (*vi*) shows that correctness is not affected by removing assert statements. More particular rules for introducing assert statements are presented below, where we consider the refinement rules pertaining to each statement of the language.

5 *If-Statements*

For n a positive integer we let

   if ($[\!]$ i: $0 \le i < n$: $Q_i \to s_i$) **fi**

abbreviate

   if $Q_0 \to s_0$ $[\!]$ $Q_1 \to s_1$ $[\!]$ $\cdots$ $[\!]$ $Q_{n-1} \to s_{n-1}$ **fi** .

There are two ways to introduce an if-statement into a specification:

Theorem 5.0 ("choice theorem")

If $\{P\}\, s \sqsubseteq (Q_i \to t_i)$ for $0 \le i < n$ (0)

and $[P \Rightarrow (\mathbf{E}\, i:\ 0 \le i < n:\ Q_i)]$,   (1)

then $\{P\}\, s\ \sqsubseteq\ $ **if** ($[\!]$ i: $0 \le i < n$: $Q_i \to t_i$) **fi** .

Proof

   $\{P\}\, s \sqsubseteq$ **if** ($[\!]$ i: $0 \le i < n$: $Q_i \to t_i$)**fi**

=   "definition $\sqsubseteq$, X arbitrary, semantics"

   $[P \wedge s.X \Rightarrow (\mathbf{E}\, i:\ 0 \le i < n:\ Q_i) \wedge (\mathbf{A}\, i:\ 0 \le i < n:\ Q_i \Rightarrow t_i.X)]$

=   "(1)"

   $[P \wedge s.X \Rightarrow (\mathbf{A}\, i:\ 0 \le i < n:\ Q_i \Rightarrow t_i.X)]$

$=$ "calculus, antecedent does not contain *i* free"

$(\mathbf{A}\,i\colon\ 0 \le i < n\colon [P \wedge s.X \Rightarrow (Q_i \Rightarrow t_i.X)])$

$=$ "semantics, X arbitrary, definition $\sqsubseteq$"

$(\mathbf{A}\,i\colon\ 0 \le i < n\colon \{P\}\,s\ \sqsubseteq\ (Q_i \rightarrow t_i))$

$=$ "(0)"

true . $\square$

For example, suppose we are to refine $m \mathrel{:\!-} m = x\ \mathbf{min}\ y$ where the infix operator **min** yields the minimum of its integer arguments. We may show first that $m \mathrel{:\!-} m = x\ \mathbf{min}\ y\ \sqsubseteq\ (x.{\le}\,y \rightarrow m := x)$ and second that $m \mathrel{:\!-} m = x\ \mathbf{min}\ y \sqsubseteq$ $(y \le x \rightarrow m := y)$, and hence conclude from the choice theorem, because $[x \le y \vee y \le x]$, that $m \mathrel{:\!-} x\ \mathbf{min}\ y\ \sqsubseteq\ \mathbf{if}\ x \le y \rightarrow m := x\ [\!]\ y \le x \rightarrow m := y\ \mathbf{fi}$.

Theorem 5.1 ("if-theorem")

If $[P \Rightarrow (\mathbf{E}\,i\colon\ 0 \le i < n\colon Q_i)]$
then $\{P\}\,s\ \sqsubseteq\ \mathbf{if}\ (\ [\!]\ i\colon\ 0 \le i < n\colon Q_i \rightarrow \{P \wedge Q_i\}\,s)\ \mathbf{fi}$.

Proof   Exercise. $\square$

The if-theorem replaces the problem of implementing s with the problem of implementing it n times— but the new problems are (presumably) easier than the original one because the new contexts are stronger.

We may need to rewrite the guards of an if-statement, perhaps to remove quantifiers, or on efficiency grounds:

Theorem 5.2

If $(\mathbf{A}\,i\colon\ 0 \le i < n\colon [P \Rightarrow (Q_i \equiv R_i)])$
then $\{P\}\,\mathbf{if}\ (\ [\!]\ i\colon\ 0 \le i < n\colon Q_i \rightarrow s_i)\ \mathbf{fi}\ \sqsubseteq\ \mathbf{if}\ (\ [\!]\ i\colon\ 0 \le i < n\colon R_i \rightarrow s_i)\ \mathbf{fi}$.

Proof   Exercise. $\square$

Assert statements may be introduced into if-statements in the obvious way:

Theorem 5.3

$\{P\}\quad\mathbf{if}\ (\ [\!]\ i\colon\ 0 \le i < n\colon Q_i \rightarrow s_i)\ \mathbf{fi}\ \sqsubseteq$

$\mathbf{if}\ (\ [\!]\ i\colon\ 0 \le i < n\colon Q_i) \rightarrow \{P \wedge Q_i\}\,s_i)\ \mathbf{fi}$.

Proof   Routine. $\square$

Theorem 5.3, and similar theorems to be presented below, allow us to strengthen a context and so make subsequent refinements easier—but this does not mean that in developing a program we should rewrite the current text so that the assert statement is explicitly included. Rather, theorems like 5.3 are used in program development to appeal to some context even though that context is not written explicitly in an assert statement preceding the component being refined.

Theorem 5.4 ("if-distribution")

$$\textbf{if } (\, []\, i\colon\, 0 \le i < n\colon\, Q_i \to s_i)\, \textbf{fi};\ \ t$$

=

$$\textbf{if } (\, []\, i\colon\, 0 \le i < n\colon\, Q_i \to s_i;\ t)\, \textbf{fi}\,.$$

Proof   Routine.   ☐

6 *Prescriptions*

The construct $\{P\}\, x :\!- Q$ —called a "prescription"— is ubiquitous, being the mechanism by which many small programs are specified; it says in effect: Given that the initial state satisfies P, establish Q while changing the values of no variables other than x. Before introducing the main theorem concerned with refining prescriptions, we define:

$$s.\langle e \rangle = (\mathbf{A}\, k\colon\, k = e\colon\, s.\mathrm{T} \Rightarrow s.(e = k))\,.$$

Operationally, $s.\langle e \rangle$ is the weakest precondition such that when s terminates, the value of expression e is the same as its inital value. When we write a variable x as in $x :\!- Q$ we allow that x may stand for a list of variables; when it matters whether x stands for a single variable or a list of variables we will be explicit about it.

Theorem 6.0 ("prescription theorem")
Let y be a list of the program variables not occurring in x; then

$$\{P\}\, x :\!- Q \sqsubseteq s\ \ \equiv\ \ [P \Rightarrow s.Q \wedge s.\langle y \rangle]\,.$$

(If the list y is empty then $s.\langle y \rangle$ is taken to be T.)

Theorem 6.0 is important in several regards. The traditional way to specify a small program [3, 4, 8, 9] is to supply a precondition P and a postcondition R with the request to make a program s satisfying $[P \Rightarrow s.R]$, whereas we express the task as one of finding an s satisfying $\{P\}\textbf{all} :\!- R \sqsubseteq s$ where **all** stands for a list of all the program variables. The prescription theorem guarantees these requirements are one and the same. As a specification mechanism prescriptions have the advantage of making clear what freedom we have in assigning to variables. Indeed Theorem 6.0 assures us that we have formally captured constraints on assignments because it implies that our rules will never let us derive an implementation of $\{P\}\, x :- Q$ that leaves variable $y0$ with a value different from its original value if $y0$ does not occur in x. The practical use of Theorem 6.0 is in deriving useful rules for refining prescriptions. The proof of the prescription theorem will use the following lemmas.

Lemma 6.0

If s assigns to no variables occurring free in assertion P then $[P \wedge s.\mathrm{T} \Rightarrow s.P]$. (By "s assigns to x" is meant that x occurs on the left of an assignment or nondeterministic assignment in s, or it is the argument of a read statement in s.)

Proof   By a routine structural induction on s.   □

Lemma 6.1

Letting y stand for a list of the free program variables of assertion P,

$$[P \wedge s.\mathrm{T} \wedge s.\langle y \rangle \Rightarrow s.P]\,.$$

Proof

$\qquad [P \wedge s.\mathrm{T} \wedge s.\langle y \rangle \Rightarrow s.P]$

$= \qquad$ "$s.\langle y \rangle$"

$\qquad [P \wedge s.\mathrm{T} \wedge (\mathbf{A}i\colon\ i = y\colon s.\mathrm{T} \Rightarrow s.(i = y)) \Rightarrow s.P]$

$= \qquad$ "calculus"

$\qquad [(\mathbf{A}i\colon\ i = y\colon P \wedge s.\mathrm{T} \wedge s.(i = y)) \Rightarrow s.P]$

$= \qquad$ "1-point rule"

$\qquad [(\mathbf{A}i\colon\ i = y\colon P(y/i) \wedge s.\mathrm{T} \wedge s.(i = y)) \Rightarrow s.P]$

$\Leftarrow \qquad$ "Lemma 6.0"

$\qquad [(\mathbf{A}i\colon\ i = y\colon s.(P(y/i)) \wedge s.(i = y)) \Rightarrow s.P]$

$= \qquad$ "s conjunctive"

$\qquad [(\mathbf{A}i\colon\ i = y\colon s.(P(y/i) \wedge i = y)) \Rightarrow s.P]$

$= \qquad$ "calculus"

$\qquad [(\mathbf{A}i\colon\ i = y\colon s.(P \wedge i = y)) \Rightarrow s.P]$

$\Leftarrow \qquad$ "s monotonic"

$\qquad [(\mathbf{A}i\colon\ i = y\colon s.P \Rightarrow s.P)]$

$= \qquad$ "calculus"

$\qquad$ true .   □

Lemma 6.2

Letting y stand for a list of the free program variables of P,

$$[s.Q \wedge s.\langle y \rangle \wedge P \Rightarrow s.R] \Leftarrow [Q \wedge P \Rightarrow R].$$

Proof

$\qquad [s.Q \wedge s.\langle y \rangle \wedge P \Rightarrow s.R]$

$= \qquad$ "calculus, s conjunctive"

$\qquad [s.Q \wedge s.T \wedge s.\langle y \rangle \wedge P \Rightarrow s.R]$

$\Leftarrow \qquad$ "Lemma 6.1"

$\qquad [s.Q \wedge s.P \Rightarrow s.R]$

$= \qquad$ "s conjunctive"

$\qquad [s.(Q \wedge P) \Rightarrow s.R]$

$\Leftarrow \qquad$ "s monotonic"

$\qquad [Q \wedge P \Rightarrow R].$ $\quad \square$

Proof of Theorem 6.0   We prove $\{P\} x :\!- Q \sqsubseteq s \;\equiv\; [P \Rightarrow s.Q \wedge s.\langle y \rangle]$
by proving the implication in either direction.

$(\Rightarrow)$

$(i) \qquad \{P\} x :\!- Q \sqsubseteq s$

$\Rightarrow \qquad$ "definition $\sqsubseteq$"

$\qquad [\{P\} x :\!- Q.Q \Rightarrow s.Q]$

$= \qquad$ "semantics"

$\qquad [P \wedge (\mathbf{A}x :: Q \Rightarrow Q) \Rightarrow s.Q]$

$= \qquad$ "calculus"

$^{\scriptscriptstyle |} \qquad [P \Rightarrow s.Q]$

$(ii) \qquad \{P\} :\!- Q \sqsubseteq s$

$\Rightarrow \qquad$ "definition of $\sqsubseteq$"

$\qquad (\mathbf{A}i :: [\{P\} x :\!- Q.(i = y) \Rightarrow s.(i = y)])$

$= \qquad$ "semantics"

$\qquad (\mathbf{A}i :: [P \wedge (\mathbf{A}x :: Q \Rightarrow i = y) \Rightarrow s.(i = y)])$

$= \qquad$ "calculus, x and y disjoint"

$\qquad (\mathbf{A}i :: [P \wedge ((\mathbf{A}x :: \neg Q) \vee i = y) \Rightarrow s.(i = y)])$

$\Rightarrow \qquad$ "calculus"

$$(\mathbf{A}\,i:: [P \wedge i = y \Rightarrow s.(i = y)])$$

=   "calculus"

$$(\mathbf{A}\,i:: [P \Rightarrow (i = y \Rightarrow s.(i = y))])$$

=   "calculus"

$$[P \Rightarrow (\mathbf{A}\,i:: i = y \Rightarrow s.(i = y))]$$

$\Rightarrow$ "definition"

$$[P \Rightarrow s.\langle y\rangle] \,.$$

Hence

$$\{P\}\, x :- Q \sqsubseteq s$$

$\Rightarrow$ "(i), (ii)"

$$[P \Rightarrow s.Q] \wedge [P \Rightarrow s.\langle y\rangle]$$

=   "calculus"

$$[P \Rightarrow s.Q \wedge s.\langle y\rangle]$$

$(\Leftarrow)$

$$\{P\}\, x :- Q \sqsubseteq s$$

=   "definition $\sqsubseteq$, X arbitrary, semantics"

$$[P \wedge (\mathbf{A}\,x:: Q \Rightarrow X) \Rightarrow s.X]$$

$\Leftarrow$ "given $[P \Rightarrow s.Q \wedge s.\langle y\rangle]$"

$$[s.Q \wedge s.\langle y\rangle \wedge (\mathbf{A}\,x:: Q \Rightarrow X) \Rightarrow s.X]$$

$\Leftarrow$ "Lemma 6.2 with $P := (\mathbf{A}\,x:: Q \Rightarrow X)$, $R := X$"

$$[Q \wedge (\mathbf{A}\,x:: Q \Rightarrow X) \Rightarrow X]$$

=   "calculus"

$$[(\mathbf{A}\,x:: Q \Rightarrow X) \Rightarrow (Q \Rightarrow X)]$$

=   "calculus"

true .   □

Corollary 6.0

If s assigns at most to x then

$$\{P\}\, x :- Q \sqsubseteq s \quad \equiv \quad [P \Rightarrow s.Q] \,.$$

Proof   Exercise.   □

Corollary 6.0 will also be referred to in proofs as the "prescription theorem";
this naming convention will hold for subsequent corollaries also.

Theorem 6.1 ("extended prescription theorem")
Let y be a list of the program variables not occurring in x; then

$$\{P\}\, x\langle e\rangle :-Q \sqsubseteq s \;\equiv\; [P \Rightarrow s.Q \wedge s.\langle y\rangle \wedge s.\langle e\rangle]\,.$$

Proof Exercise. □

The preceding theorem guarantees that any implementation of $\{P\}\, x\langle e\rangle :-Q$ derived according to the rules does indeed preserve the value of e. We now present a collection of theorems concerned with refining prescriptions.

Theorem 6.2 ("**skip** theorem")

$$\{P\}\, x :-Q \sqsubseteq \textbf{skip} \;\equiv\; [P \Rightarrow Q]\,.$$

Proof Apply Corollary 6.0. □

Theorem 6.3 ("assignment theorem")

$$\{P\}\, x :-Q \sqsubseteq x := e \;\equiv\; [P \Rightarrow (\textbf{E}\,i::\, i = e) \wedge Q(x/e)]\,.$$

Proof Apply Corollary 6.0. □

Theorem 6.4 ("postcondition theorem")

$$\{P\}\, x :-Q \sqsubseteq x :-R \;\equiv\; [(\textbf{A}\,x'::\, P \wedge R(x, x'/x', x) \Rightarrow Q(x, x'/x', x))]\,,$$

(Note: We are admitting x' in Q and R).

Proof Exercise. □

Corollary 6.1

$$x :-Q \sqsubseteq x :-R \;\equiv\; [R \Rightarrow Q]\,.$$

Proof Apply Theorem 6.4. □

Corollary 6.2
If x does not occur free in P then

(i) $\{P\}\, x :-Q \sqsubseteq x :-R \;\equiv\; [P \wedge R \Rightarrow Q]$

(ii) $\{P \wedge PP\}\, x :-Q \sqsubseteq x :-R$ if $[P \wedge R \Rightarrow Q]$

(iii) $\{P\}\, x :-Q \wedge R \sqsubseteq x :-R$ if $[P \wedge R \Rightarrow Q]\,.$

Proof Apply Theorem 6.4. □

Corollary 6.3

If x does not occur free in Q then

$$\{P\}\, x :\!- Q \wedge R \ \sqsubseteq \ x :\!- R \quad \text{if } [P \Rightarrow Q]\,.$$

Proof   Apply Theorem 6.4.   □

For the purposes of an example, let Min.b denote the minimum of a bag b of integers (assuming b has a minimum) and let $\mathbf{B}(i, j, \dots)$ denote the bag containing $i, j, \dots$. Let $\varnothing = \mathbf{B}()$. For x a natural number, b a bag of natural numbers, and m a variable of type **Int**:

$$\{b \neq \varnothing \ \wedge \ m = \text{Min}.b\}\, m :\!- m = \text{Min}.(b \cup \mathbf{B}(x)) \ \wedge \ b \neq \varnothing$$

$\sqsubseteq$ "Corollary 6.3 (and Theorem 4.2(*iv*) to carry the context)"

$$\{b \neq \varnothing \ \wedge \ m = \text{Min}.b\}\, m :\!- m = \text{Min}.(b \cup \mathbf{B}(x))$$

$=$ "theory of minima"

$$\{b \neq \varnothing \ \wedge \ m = \text{Min}.b\}\, m :\!- m = \text{Min}.b \ \mathbf{min} \ \text{Min}.\mathbf{B}(x)$$

$=$ "theory of minima"

$$\{b \neq \varnothing \ \wedge \ m = \text{Min}.b\}\, m :\!- m = \text{Min}.b \ \mathbf{min} \ x$$

$\sqsubseteq$ "Theorem 6.4"

$$\{b \neq \varnothing \ \wedge \ m = \text{Min}.b\}\, m :\!- m = m' \ \mathbf{min} \ x$$

$\sqsubseteq$ "Theorem 7.1 below"

$$m := m \ \mathbf{min} \ x\,.$$

This concludes the example.

Theorem 6.5

$$x :\!- Q = x :\!- Q\{Q\}\,.$$

Proof   Exercise.   □

Theorem 6.6   ("dropping a variable")

$$x, y :\!- Q \ \sqsubseteq \ x :\!- Q(y'/y) \quad \text{where } x', y' \text{ may occur free in } Q.$$

Proof   Exercise.   □

Theorem 6.7

(i) $x\langle f.e\rangle :- Q \sqsubseteq x\langle e\rangle :- Q$

   if $f.e$ is a function of e satisfying $(f.e)(x/i) = f.(e(x/i))$ for all i.

(ii) $x\langle e\rangle :- Q \sqsubseteq x :- Q$ if x not free in e.

Proof   Routine exercises beginning with an application of Theorem 6.1.
□

   For an example of Theorem 6.7(i), let P stand for $(\mathbf{A}x: x \in d: 0 \le x < 100)$ for d an integer sequence; then $d\langle P\rangle :- Q \sqsubseteq d\langle bag.d\rangle :- Q$ for any Q because P can be written as a function of bag.d that does not otherwise depend on d.

Theorem 6.8 ("semicolon theorem")

   $x :- P \wedge Q \sqsubseteq x :- P; \; x\langle P\rangle :- Q$.

Proof   For arbitrary X

   $(x :- P; \; x\langle P\rangle :- Q).X$

=   "semantics, define $Y' = Y(x/x')$ for any Y"

   $(\mathbf{A}x:: P \Rightarrow (\mathbf{A}x:: Q \wedge P = P' \Rightarrow X)(x'/x))$

=   "rename dummy, substitution"

   $(\mathbf{A}x:: P \Rightarrow (\mathbf{A}x':: Q' \wedge P' = P \Rightarrow X'))$

=   "calculus"

   $(\mathbf{A}x:: (\mathbf{A}x':: P \Rightarrow (Q' \wedge P' = P \Rightarrow X')))$

=   "calculus"

   $(\mathbf{A}x:: (\mathbf{A}x':: P \wedge Q' \wedge P' = P \Rightarrow X'))$

⇐   "calculus"

   $(\mathbf{A}x:: (\mathbf{A}x':: P' \wedge Q' \Rightarrow X'))$

=   "rename dummy x', calculus"

   $(\mathbf{A}x:: P \wedge Q \Rightarrow X)$

=   "semantics"

   $x :- P \wedge Q.X$. □

Corollary 6.4

If P does not contain y free and Q does not contain x free, then

   $x, y :- P \wedge Q \sqsubseteq x :- P; \; y :- Q$.

Proof   Exercise.   □

Finally we present a lemma for the commonly occurring case of refining $d\langle \text{bag}.d \rangle :- Q$ for d a sequence. Let $d(i \circ j)$ for $i, j \in \text{dom}.d$ denote the sequence d with elements indexed by i and j interchanged; formally $\text{dom}.d(i \circ j) = \text{dom}.d$, $d(i \circ j).i = d.j$, $d(i \circ j).j = d.i$, and $d(i \circ j).k = d.k$ for $k \neq i$ and $k \neq j$.

Lemma 6.3 ("permutation lemma")
If all assignments to d in s are of the form $d := d(i \circ j)$ for $i, j \in \text{dom}.d$, and if $d :- Q \sqsubseteq s$, then $d\langle \text{bag}.d \rangle :- Q \sqsubseteq s$.

Proof   Use Theorems 6.0 and 6.1 to show $d\langle \text{bag}.d \rangle :- Q \sqsubseteq s \equiv [s.\langle \text{bag}.d \rangle]$, and then proceed by structural induction on s; the details are left to the reader.
□

7 Assignment

Theorem 7.0
If $[P \Rightarrow e0 = e1]$ then $\{P\}\, x := e0 \ \sqsubseteq\ x := e1$.

Proof   Exercise.   □

Theorem 7.1 ("second assignment theorem")
If $[P \Rightarrow (\mathbf{E}\, i:: i = e)]$, then $\{P\}\, x :- x = e' \sqsubseteq x := e$, where e' stands for $e(x/x')$.

Proof   Exercise.   □

For an application of Theorem 7.1, see the example following Corollary 6.3. The extension of Theorem 7.1 to cover concurrent assignment should be obvious.

8 Loops

A set C partially ordered with respect to $\leq$ is said to be "well founded" if, for any $S, S \subseteq C$,

$$S \neq \varnothing \equiv (\mathbf{E}\, k: k \in S: (\mathbf{A}\, i: i \in S: \neg\, i < k)).$$

The well-founded sets of greatest interest to us are the natural numbers with their usual ordering and, very occasionally, Cartesian products of natural numbers ordered lexicographically.

Theorem 8.0 ("invariance theorem")
Let D be a set partially ordered by $\leq$, and e be an expression such that $[e \in D]$.

Let C be a subset of D well founded with respect to $\leq$ such that for assertions P, Q and expression e,

$$[P \wedge \neg Q \Rightarrow e \in C] .\tag{0}$$

Then

$$x :- P \wedge Q \sqsubseteq x :- P;$$
$$\textbf{do } \neg Q \rightarrow$$
$$\{P \wedge \neg Q\} x :- P \wedge e < e'$$
$$\textbf{od} ,$$

where e' stands for $e(x/x')$.

Proof   Let s stand for $\{P \wedge \neg Q\} x :- P \wedge e < e'$ and **DO** stand for $\textbf{do } \neg Q \rightarrow s \textbf{ od}$. First we rewrite the demonstrandum:

$$x :- P \wedge Q \sqsubseteq x :- P; \textbf{ do } \neg Q \rightarrow \{P \wedge \neg Q\} x :- P \wedge e < e' \textbf{ od}$$

$=$ "**DO**, s"

$$x :- P \wedge Q \sqsubseteq x :- P; \textbf{ DO}$$

$=$ "prescription theorem"

$$[x :- P; \textbf{ DO}.(P \wedge Q)]$$

$=$ "semantics"

$$[(\mathbf{A} x :: P \Rightarrow \textbf{DO}.(P \wedge Q))]$$

$=$ "$[\ldots]$"

$$[P \Rightarrow \textbf{DO}.(P \wedge Q)] .\tag{1}$$

Next we show that for all k, $k \in C$,

$$[P \wedge \neg Q \wedge e = k \Rightarrow s.(P \wedge e < k)] :\tag{2}$$

$$\{P \wedge \neg Q\} x :- P \wedge e < e' = s$$

$\Rightarrow$ "$=$"

$$[\{P \wedge \neg Q\} x :- P \wedge e < e'.(P \wedge e < k) \Rightarrow s.(P \wedge e < k)]$$

$=$ "semantics; let X' denote $X(x/x')$ for any X"

$$[P \wedge \neg Q \wedge (\mathbf{A} x :: P \wedge e < e' \Rightarrow P \wedge e < k)' \Rightarrow s.(P \wedge e < k)]$$

$=$ "calculus"

$$[P \wedge \neg Q \wedge (\mathbf{A} x' :: P' \wedge e' < e \Rightarrow P' \wedge e' < k) \Rightarrow s.(P \wedge e < k)]$$

$\Rightarrow$ "calculus"

$$[P \wedge \neg Q \wedge (\mathbf{A} x' :: e' < e \Rightarrow e' < k) \Rightarrow s.(P \wedge e < k)]$$

$\Rightarrow$ "calculus"

$[P \wedge \neg Q \wedge e = k \Rightarrow s.(P \wedge e < k)]$.

So it remains to infer (1) from (0) and (2), which is just the version of the invariance theorem proved in [7]. $\Box$

In the invariance theorem, P is called the "invariant" and e the "variant". Appeals to the theorem in program derivations will be signalled by hints such as "invariant P, variant e". We have been assuming throughout that the Q in $x :- Q$ does not contain x' free, but now the invariance theorem has introduced such a Q. So we need some rules for refining the bodies of loops. First we define

$s \textbf{ decs } e \; = \; (\textbf{A}k: k = e: s.(e < k))$

$s \textbf{ incs } e \; = \; (\textbf{A}k: k = e: s.(e > k))$.

(We continue to assume that assertions do not contain free primed variables unless the contrary is explicitly indicated.)

Theorem 8.1 ("**decs** theorem")

If $[P \Rightarrow s \textbf{ decs } e]$ (0)

and $\{P\}x :- Q \sqsubseteq s$ (1)

then $\{P\}x :- Q \wedge e < e' \sqsubseteq s$

where e' stands for $e(x/x')$.

Proof   Let x, y be a list of the program variables. Then for arbitrary k

$[P \wedge e = k \Rightarrow s.(Q \wedge e < k) \wedge s.\langle y \rangle]$ (2)

$=$ "s conjunctive"

$[P \wedge e = k \Rightarrow s.Q \wedge s.(e < k) \wedge s.\langle y \rangle]$

$\Leftarrow$ "calculus"

$[P \Rightarrow s.Q \wedge s.\langle y \rangle] \; \wedge \; [P \wedge e = k \Rightarrow s.(e < k)]$

$=$ "prescription theorem, calculus"

$\{P\}x :- Q \sqsubseteq s \; \wedge \; [P \Rightarrow (e = k \Rightarrow s.(e < k))]$

$\Leftarrow$ "(1), **decs**"

$[P \Rightarrow s \textbf{ decs } e]$

$=$ "(0)"

true .

With the truth of (2) established, the proof is:

$$\{P\}x:-Q \land e < e' \sqsubseteq s$$

$=$　"$\sqsubseteq$, X arbitrary"

$$[P \land (\mathbf{A}x:: Q \land e < e' \Rightarrow X)_x^{x'} \Rightarrow s.X]$$

$=$　"calculus; let Y' stand for $Y(x/x')$ for any Y"

$$[P \land (\mathbf{A}x':: Q' \land e' < e \Rightarrow X') \Rightarrow s.X]$$

$=$　"1-point"

$$[(\mathbf{A}k: k = e: P \land (\mathbf{A}x':: Q' \land e' < k \Rightarrow X') \Rightarrow s.X)]$$

$=$　"calculus"

$$(\mathbf{A}k:: [P \land k = e \land (\mathbf{A}x':: Q' \land e' < k \Rightarrow X') \Rightarrow s.X])$$

$=$　"generalize over k; rename dummy x'"

$$[P \land k = e \land (\mathbf{A}x:: Q \land e < k \Rightarrow X) \Rightarrow s.X]$$

$\Leftarrow$　"(2)"

$$[s.(Q \land e < k) \land s.\langle y \rangle \land (\mathbf{A}x:: Q \land e < k \Rightarrow X) \Rightarrow s.X]$$

$\Leftarrow$　"Lemma 6.2 with $Q := Q \land e < k$, $P := (\mathbf{A}x:: Q \land e < k \Rightarrow X)$, $R := X$"

$$[Q \land e < k \land (\mathbf{A}x:: Q \land e < k \Rightarrow X) \Rightarrow X]$$

$=$　"calculus"

$$[(\mathbf{A}x:: Q \land e < k \Rightarrow X) \Rightarrow (Q \land e < k \Rightarrow X)]$$

$=$　"calculus"

true .　□

In making a loop we may introduce $x:-P \land (e1-e) < (e1-e)'$ where $e1$ does not contain x free, which we immediately refine (by Theorem 6.4) to $x:-P \land e > e'$. Then the following may be useful:

Theorem 8.2 ("**incs** theorem")
If $[P \Rightarrow s \textbf{ incs } e]$ and $\{P\}x:-Q \sqsubseteq s$ then $P\}x:-Q \land e > e' \sqsubseteq s$.

Proof　Similar to that of Theorem 8.1.　□

Theorem 8.3 ("step first")
Let f be a function with inverse f^{-1}; then

(i)　　$\{Q\}x, k:-P \land k < k' \sqsubseteq k := f.k;\ \{Q(k/f^{-1}.k)\}x:-P$
　　　if for all k　$[Q \Rightarrow f.k < k]$, and

(ii)　　$\{Q\}x, k:-P \land k > k' \sqsubseteq k := f.k;\ \{Q(k/f^{-1}.k)\}x:-P$
　　　if for all k　$[Q \Rightarrow f.k > k]$.

Proof　Apply Theorems 8.1 and 8.2.　□

Theorem 8.4 ("step last")
Let f be a function. Then

(i) $\{Q\}\,x, k :\!- P \wedge k < k' \sqsubseteq x :\!- P(k/f.k); \ k := f.k$
         if $[Q \Rightarrow f.k < k]$, and

(ii) $\{Q\}\,x, k :\!- P \wedge k > k' \sqsubseteq x :\!- P(k/f.k); \ k := f.k$
         if $[Q \Rightarrow f.k > k]$.

Proof   Apply Theorems 8.1 and 8.2. $\square$

An example illustrating some of the theorems of this section follows. For n and t integer variables:

$$n :\!- n \geq 0 \wedge n^2 \geq t$$

$\sqsubseteq$ "invariant $n \geq 0$, variant $t - n^2$, Theorem 6.4"

$$n :\!- n \geq 0;$$

do $\neg\, n^2 \geq t \rightarrow \{n \geq 0 \wedge n^2 < t\}\, n :\!- n \geq 0 \wedge n > n'$ **od**

$\sqsubseteq$ "postcondition theorem for $n :\!- n \geq 0$, assertions theorem"

$$n :\!- n = 0;$$

do $\neg\, n^2 \geq t \rightarrow \{n \geq 0\}\, n :\!- n \geq 0 \wedge n > n'$ **od**

$\sqsubseteq$ "second assignment theorem, step last theorem"

$$n := 0;$$

do $\neg\, n^2 \geq t \rightarrow \{n \geq 0\}\, n :\!- n + 1 \geq 0; n := n + 1$ **od**

$\sqsubseteq$ "**skip** theorem, **skip** a left identity of semicolon"

$$n := 0;$$

do $\neg\, n^2 \geq t \rightarrow n := n + 1$ **od**.

9 *Minor Miracles*

Theorem 9.0 ("miracle theorem")
If s assigns at most to the variable(s) x, then

$$\{P\}\,x :\!- R \sqsubseteq (Q \rightarrow s) \equiv [P \wedge Q \Rightarrow s.R].$$

Proof

$$\{P\}\,x :\!- R \sqsubseteq (Q \rightarrow s)$$

$=$ "prescription theorem"

$$[P \Rightarrow (Q \rightarrow s).R]$$

=   "semantics"

$[P \Rightarrow (Q \Rightarrow s.R)]$

=   "calculus"

$[P \wedge Q \Rightarrow s.R]$.   □

Theorem 9.1 ("delete guard")

$\{P\} (Q \rightarrow s) \sqsubseteq s$ if $[P \Rightarrow Q]$.

Theorem 9.2 ("miracle distribution")

$(Q \rightarrow s); t = (Q \rightarrow s; t)$.

Theorem 9.3

$(Q \rightarrow s) = (Q \rightarrow \{Q\} s)$.

Theorem 9.4 ("miracle introduction")

$\{P\} s \sqsubseteq (Q \rightarrow \{P \wedge Q\} s)$.

Proofs (Theorems 9.1 to 9.4)   Exercise.   □

10 *Blocks*

Theorem 10.0 ("variable introduction")

(i) $\{P\} x :- Q \sqsubseteq [\![y: Ty; \; x, y :- Q]\!]$

(ii) $\{P\} s \sqsubseteq [\![y: Ty; \; y :- Q; \; \{P \wedge Q\} s]\!]$,

where in each case y is a fresh name.

Proof   Exercise.   □

Theorem 10.1 ("unnesting blocks")
If x and y are distinct, and y does not occur free in s or u, then

$[\![x: Tx; \; s; \; [\![y: Ty; \; t]\!]; \; u]\!] \sqsubseteq [\![x: Tx; \; y: Ty; \; s; \; t; \; u]\!]$.

Proof   Exercise.   □

Theorem 10.2

$[\![x: Tx; \; y: Ty; \; s]\!] = [\![y: Ty; \; x: Tx; \; s]\!]$.

Proof   Exercise.   □

11 *Example*

Our purpose in doing an example here is to illustrate the rules of programming developed above. As a consequence we will be more formal and explicit than is perhaps necessary in solving the problem, and at the same time we will not bother too much with heuristics (which in any case will be quite standard). We address the problem of counting the number of essentially different ways in which a natural number can be written as the sum of two squares. Formally, we are to derive an implementation of

$\{t \in \mathbf{nat}\}$

$[\![k \colon \mathbf{int} \, ;$

$\qquad\qquad k \coloneq (\mathbf{N}i, j \colon 0 \le i \le j \colon i^2 + j^2 = t) = k;$

$\qquad\qquad \text{write}.k$

$]\!]$.

Here $\mathbf{N}$ is the "counting quantifier": $(\mathbf{N}i \colon P \colon Q) = \#\{i \colon P \wedge Q\}$, and similarly for more than one dummy variable. For notational convenience (and with an eye on a likely invariant) we introduce function $f \colon \mathbf{int} \rightarrow \mathbf{int} \cup \{\infty\} \rightarrow \mathbf{nat}$ defined by

$\qquad f.m.n = (\mathbf{N}i, j \colon m \le i \le j \le n \colon i^2 + j^2 = t) \, .$

The assignment to k in the specification can now be written as $k \coloneq f.0.\infty = k$.
    We take it as evident that f enjoys for integers m, n

(*i*) $m > n \Rightarrow f.m.n = 0$

(*ii*) $n \ge 0 \wedge n^2 \ge t \Rightarrow f.0.n = f.0.\infty$.

We propose, with integer variables m and n, to employ as invariant

$\qquad P.m.n \colon \ f.0.\infty = k + f.m.n \wedge m \ge 0 \, ,$

and so

$\qquad\quad k \coloneq f.0.\infty = k$

$\quad \sqsubseteq \qquad\qquad$ "variable introduction"

$\qquad [\![m, n \colon \mathbf{int} \, ;$
$\qquad\qquad k, m, n \coloneq f.0.\infty = k$
$\qquad]\!]$

$\quad \sqsubseteq \qquad\qquad$ "postcondition theorem, (*i*)"

$\qquad [\![m, n \colon \mathbf{int} \, ;$
$\qquad\qquad k, m, n \coloneq P.m.n \wedge m > n$
$\qquad]\!]$

⊑   "invariant $P.m.n$, variant $n - m$"

$[\![m, n:$ **int** ;

    $k, m, n :\!\!-P.m.n;$

    do $\neg\, m > n \rightarrow \{P.m.n \,\wedge\, m \leq n\}$

             $k, m, n :\!\!-P.m.n \,\wedge\, n - m < (n - m)\,'$

    od

$]\!]$.

For the loop initialization

    $k, m, n :\!\!-P.m.n$

⊑   "postcondition theorem, (*ii*)"

    $k, m, n :\!\!-k = 0 \,\wedge\, m = 0 \,\wedge\, n \geq 0 \,\wedge\, n^2 \geq t$

⊑   "semicolon theorem"

    $k, m :\!\!-k = 0 \,\wedge\, m = 0;\ n :\!\!-n \geq 0 \,\wedge\, n^2 \geq t$

⊑   "second assignment theorem; example of section 8"

    $k, m := 0, 0;\ n := 0;$

    do $\neg\, n^2 \geq t \rightarrow n := n + 1$ **od** .

For the body of the main loop we can decrease the variant by decreasing n or increasing m.

Consider decreasing n:

    $k, m, n :\!\!-P.m.n \,\wedge\, n - m < (n - m)\,'$

⊑   "drop m"

    $k, n :\!\!-P.m.n \,\wedge\, n - m < n' - m$

⊑   "postcondition theorem"

    $k, n :\!\!-P.m.n \,\wedge\, n < n'$

⊑   "step last"

    $k :\!\!-P.m.(n - 1);\ n := n - 1$.

It remains to refine $\{P.m.n \wedge m \leq n\}\ k :\!\!-P.m.(n-1)$. Comparing the precondition and postcondition invites us to consider the relationship between $f.m.n$ and $f.m.(n - 1)$.

    $f.m.n$

$=$ "definition"

$$(\mathbf{N}i, j: \ m \le i \le j \le n: \ i^2 + j^2 = t)$$

=   "split range to introduce $n-1$"

$$(\mathbf{N}i, j: \ m \le i \le j \le n-1: \ i^2 + j^2 = t)$$

$$+(\mathbf{N}i, j: \ m \le i \le j = n: \ i^2 + j^2 = t)$$

=   "definition, calculus"

$$f.m.(n-1) + (\mathbf{N}i: \ m \le i \le n: \ i^2 + n^2 = t).$$

We take it as evident that for all m, n

(*iii*) $m \ge 0 \ \wedge \ m^2 + n^2 > t \ \Rightarrow \ (\mathbf{N}i: \ m \le i \le n: \ i^2 + n^2 = t) = 0$,

and so we have established, for all m, n, that

$$m \ge 0 \ \wedge \ m^2 + n^2 > t \ \Rightarrow \ f.m.n = f.m.(n-1),$$

and so

$$[P.m.n \ \wedge \ m^2 + n^2 > t \ \Rightarrow \ P.m.(n-1)].\tag{0}$$

Hence

$$\{P.m.n \ \wedge \ m \le n\} \ k :\!- P.m.(n-1)$$

⊑   "miracle introduction"

$$(m^2 + n^2 > t \rightarrow \{P.m.n \ \wedge \ m \le n \ \wedge \ m^2 + n^2 > t\} \ k :\!- P.m.(n-1))$$

⊑   "assertions theorems, (0)"

$$(m^2 + n^2 > t \rightarrow \{P.m.(n-1)\} \ k :\!- P.m.(n-1))$$

⊑   "**skip** theorem"

$$(m^2 + n^2 > t \rightarrow \mathbf{skip}).$$

In summary, we have shown that the loop body is refined by

$$(m^2 + n^2 > t \rightarrow \mathbf{skip}); \ n := n-1$$

=   "miracle distribution; identity element of composition"

$$(m^2 + n^2 > t \rightarrow n := n-1).$$

Considering the case $m^2 + n^2 = t$ (and $m \ge 0$)

$$f.m.n$$

=   "as above"

$$f.m.(n-1) + (\mathbf{N}i: \ m \le i \le n: \ i^2 + n^2 = t)$$

=   "range splitting; $m^2 + n^2 = t$"

$$f.m.(n-1)+1+(\mathbf{N}i\colon m+1 \le i \le n\colon i^2+n^2 = t)$$
$$= \quad \text{``}(m+1)^2 + n^2 > t;\ (iii)\text{''}$$
$$f.m.(n-1)+1$$

and so we have established, for all m, n that

$$m \ge 0 \ \wedge \ m^2 + n^2 = t \ \Rightarrow \ f.m.n = f.m.(n-1)+1 \,. \qquad (1)$$

Hence

$$P.m.n \ \wedge \ m^2 + n^2 = t$$
$$= \quad \text{``definition''}$$
$$f.0.\infty = k + f.m.n \ \wedge \ m \ge 0 \ \wedge \ m^2 + n^2 = t$$
$$\Rightarrow \quad \text{``(1)''}$$
$$f.0.\infty = k + 1 + f.m.(n-1) \ \wedge \ m \ge 0$$
$$= \quad \text{``assignment''}$$
$$k := k+1.(f.0.\infty = k + f.m.(n-1) \ \wedge \ m \ge 0)$$
$$= \quad \text{``definition''}$$
$$k := k+1.(P.m.(n-1)) \,.$$

And so we have established

$$[P.m.n \ \wedge \ m^2 + n^2 = t \ \Rightarrow \ k := k+1.(P.m.(n-1))]\,,$$

which by the miracle theorem is equivalent to

$$\{P.m.n\}\, k :- P.m.(n-1) \sqsubseteq (m^2 + n^2 = t \rightarrow k := k+1)\,.$$

In summary, we have shown that the loop body is also refined by

$$(m^2 + n^2 = t \rightarrow k := k+1);\ n := n-1$$
$$= \quad \text{``miracle distribution''}$$
$$(m^2 + n^2 = t \rightarrow k := k+1;\ n := n-1)\,.$$

Reasoning similarly, the reader may show that the loop body is also refined by

$$(m^2 + n^2 < t \rightarrow m := m+1)\,.$$

We can combine the three minor miracles using the choice theorem —the disjunction of the three guards is true— and with block unnesting and a minor rewriting of expressions the implementation is

```
⟦k: int ; m, n: int

    k, m := 0, 0;  n := 0;

    do ¬ n * n ≥ t → n := n + 1 od

    do ¬ m > n →   if m * m + n * n > t   →   n := n - 1

                   ▯ m * m + n * n = t   →   k := k + 1;  n := n - 1

                   ▯ m * m + n * n < t   →   m := m + 1

                   fi

    od;

    write.k

⟧ .
```

For other treatments of the problem, see [3, 4]; the invariant *P.m.n* is taken from [3]. Bear in mind that the style of programming above was chosen so as best to illustrate the formal rules and is not necessarily an exhortation to program normally in that style.

12 *Summary and Conclusion*

We began by extending the programming notation of guarded commands to the extent that we could use it to make specifications as well as programs. The extension is quite simple: We add the nondeterministic assignment, assert, and minor miracle statements, and admit fancy data operators such as logical quantifiers. This notation is good enough to describe in a couple of lines small programming problems such as those found in [3, 4, 8, 9]. The task we addressed is that of formulating a set of rules whereby one can transform a given specification into a program that preserves the intention, the transformation to proceed with mathematical rigor. A little more technically, one wants to impose on specifications (as semantic objects) a partial ordering $\sqsubseteq$ such that specifications (and hence programs) s and t satisfy $s \sqsubseteq t$ just when a customer asking for s would be willing to accept t; we defined such an ordering. The programming task is then viewed as one of, given a specification s, finding a program p such that $s \sqsubseteq p$. In fact, we have to construct a program rather than "find" one, and this involves generating a chain of specifications $s \sqsubseteq s_1 \sqsubseteq s_2 \sqsubseteq \cdots \sqsubseteq p$ beginning with the given specification and ending with a program. Ideally we would like each step from s_i to s_{i+1} to be small and to be justified by an appeal to one of a fairly small bag of laws. We have presented such a bag and demonstrated its use on a small programming problem.

Deriving elegant programs is by now a well-established game that has proceeded quite happily using semiformal methods [3, 4, 8, 9]. Moreover, much of the success of this game is due not simply to the judicious use of formal manipulations but also to the deployment of very effective heuristics, of which we have said nothing. So we must accept that the contribution to be made by formalizing the laws of programming in the way we have is limited. That said, the exercise is nevertheless a useful one. Firstly, there is a little comfort to be drawn from the knowledge that our methods are mathematically sound. Secondly, a formalization of program construction is a necessary prelude to employing machine assistance in programming, should we deem that necessary. Thirdly, there is indeed some practical benefit because experience (albeit limited) suggests that the laws of refinement, and the notations we introduced to express them, lead to a smoother and logically tighter development of the program in many cases: We can make explicit what freedom we have in assigning to variables. We can employ minor miracles to minimize our commitments at each step, such as committing ourselves to the guards of an if-statement we intend to construct. We can use the laws to reduce the need to calculate weakest preconditions during programming. The $\sqsubseteq$-notation allows a better integration of the laws of the programming calculus and the predicate calculus. In short, formalizing the laws of programming allows us to be a little more formal when it suits our purposes.

Nevertheless the calculus we have described falls short of being a universal medium of program construction. Even with small programs we can find ourselves entwined in unwieldy proofs, often of rather shallow theorems; in particular, assignments to arrays are cumbersome formally. Furthermore, while we greatly value a property such as monotonic replacement that allows us to work on components of a specification in isolation, there are good programming techniques that are not so localized and consequently don't sit comfortably in the formal calculus. Among these is the technique of "strengthening an invariant", which entails replacing an invariant P with a stronger invariant $P \wedge Q$ at a stage when the loop has already taken shape. This technique is not local in that earlier text must now be reworked to accommodate the new component of the invariant, and to do that formally may ask for more writing than we care for. Other gaps in the theory are the omission of many programming notions such as procedures, modules, and concurrency, and the fact that no evidence has been offered that the formalities scale up to larger problems. It remains to formalize much of programming in a way that helps us to program better.

Acknowledgments

Weakest preconditions and the programming calculus based on them are due to Dijkstra [4]. His methods have been further developed and explicated in [3, 8, 9]. The idea of enlarging the notation of guarded commands to admit specifications is due to Back [1, 2]; it was he who first introduced the nondeterministic assignment and the assert statements and described the underlying mathematics of stepwise refinement in terms similar to ours. The minor miracle as a statement in its own right I borrowed from [10]. The style of predicate calculus used is due to Dijkstra as is the treatment of loops using least fixpoints, and in particular the guts of Lemma 3.0.

References

[1] Back, R. J. R. "On the correctness of refinement steps in program development". Report A-1978-4, Dept. of Com. Sci., University of Helsinki, 1978.

[2] Back, R. J. R. "Correctness preserving program refinements: proof theory and applications". Mathematical Centre Tracts 131, Mathematisch Centrum, Amsterdam, 1980.

[3] Backhouse, R. C. *Program Construction and Verification.* Prentice-Hall, Englewood Cliffs, N. J., 1986.

[4] Dijkstra, E. W. *A Discipline of Programming.* Prentice-Hall, Englewood Cliffs, N. J., 1976.

[5] Dijkstra, E. W. "The equivalence of bounded nondeterminacy and continuity". *Selected Writings on Computing: A Personal Perspective,* E. W. Dijkstra, pp. 358–359. Springer-Verlag, New York, 1982.

[6] Dijkstra, E. W. and Feijen, W. H. J. *Een Methode van Programmeren.* Academic Service, Den Haag, 1984.

[7] Dijkstra, E. W. and van Gasteren, A. J. M. "A simple fixpoint argument without the restriction to continuity". *Acta Informatica* 23 (1986), pp. 1–7.

[8] Gries, D. *The Science of Programming.* Springer-Verlag, New York, 1981.

[9] Hehner, E. C. R. *The Logic of Programming.* Prentice-Hall, Englewood Cliffs, N. J., 1984.

[10] Morgan, C. "Data refinement by miracles". *Information Processing Letters,* to appear.

[11] Morris, J. M. "Piecewise data refinement". This volume.

[12] Tarski, A. "A lattice theoretical fixpoint theorem and its applications". *Pacific J. Math. 5* (1955), pp. 285–309.

Piecewise Data Refinement

10

Joseph M. Morris
University of Glasgow

1 *Introduction*

We take the view that a specification language is a programming language
with added fancy constructs and notions that admit ease of expression but
may be expensive or even impossible to implement. The programming task
is to make a specification and then, step by step, to eliminate the fancy constructs with correctness-preserving transformations, or refinements, until, all
going well, we arrive at a program. Among the added notions of specification
languages are a richer set of data types —sets, bags, mappings, unbounded
sequences, etc.— than we are used to seeing in programming languages; their
replacement with simpler types during program development is called "data
refinement". To be useful, data refinement must proceed piecewise. That is
to say, we want to refine the constituent pieces of a specification more or less
independently of one another so that the refinement of the whole specification is not much more than the composition of its refined constituents. We
give a new formal definition of data refinement, prove that it's good, and use

it to derive some basic laws of piecewise data refinement.

A great deal of work has been done in recent years on the making of specifications [4, 7], but the business of formally deriving programs from specifications using some "programming calculus" is less well developed. We are here contributing to this goal. Our underlying philosophy is that no semantic distinction is to be made between specifications and programs. Programs are specifications—albeit somewhat special in that we know how to extract automatically a computation from them. The programming language is the implementable subset of the specification language. We view programming as constructing a sequence of specifications, the first one being supplied by the customer and thereafter each one being a "more algorithmic" derivative of its predecessor. The final members of the sequence are programs; we don't necessarily finish when a program first emerges for we may wish to continue development to satisfy efficiency obligations. A specification notation is richer than its constituent programming language in two regards: It has more exotic statements and fancier data types. Procedural refinement is the business of reducing the exotic statements to executable ones; data refinement is concerned with replacing the fancy data types with data types of the programming language. It is obviously highly desirable that both these refinement techniques should coexist harmoniously within the one developmental framework. The laws of procedural refinement have been described in outline in [1, 8, 10]; here we are incorporating data refinement into the theory.

2 *Specifications and Refinement*

We take as the programming language that of guarded commands [2] augmented by blocks of the form

   |[*var*1 : *T*1; *var*2 : *T*2; ... statement]| .

The specification language is the programming language plus three extensions. Firstly, we allow arbitrary assertions as guards in if-statements and loops. Secondly, we admit the generalized assignment statement. This has the form $x :\!- P$ for x any variable(s) and P an assertion; it asks for the establishment of P without changing the values of variables other than x. Thirdly, we regard assertions in chain brackets not as comments but as formal statements; we call these "assert statements". Of course we also admit a richer set of data types, but we don't have to be more specific about what these types are.

We let capital letters stand for assertions, and the small letters $p, q, \ldots$ stand for specifications. Type names are Tx, Ty, etc. T and F are the assertions satisfied by all states and by no state, respectively. [X] stands for assertion X universally quantified over its free specification variables. $X(x/e)$ stands for

X with each free occurrence of variable *x* replaced by expression *e*. An infix period is used for function application. We do not distinguish notationally between specifications as syntactic and semantic objects, preferring to write the more compact *s.X* instead of the familiar *wp(s,X)* to denote the weakest precondition for *s* to establish *X*. The predicate transformer semantics of programs is given in Fig. 1. **A** and **E** denote universal and existential quantification, respectively. In the semantic rules it is assumed that the names of local variables are chosen so that they do not conflict with the names in surrounding blocks. We also do not bother to specify the number of guarded commands in an if-statement, writing $(\mathbf{E}\,i:P_i)$ instead of the more complete $(\mathbf{E}\,i(0 \le i < n):P_i)$ where *n* denotes the number of guarded commands.

Following convention we may omit the connecting semicolon before or after {*P*}. The expression $(\mu Y\!:f.Y)$ denotes the least fixpoint of function *f* and will be elaborated on later. We add that our notation is not intended to be a general specification language, but rather one suited to the purpose at hand.

The operators used, grouped in order of decreasing precedence, are

.	function application,
¬	negation,
∧ ∨	conjunction and disjunction,
⇒	implication, and
=	equality.

Figure 1.   Predicate-transformer semantics of programs.

$s.X =$

- *s* is **skip** : *X*

- *s* is $x := e$: $X(x/e)$

- *s* is $x :- P$: $(\mathbf{A}\,x: P \Rightarrow X)$

- *s* is {*P*} : $P \wedge X$

- *s* is $p;q$: $p.(q.X)$

- *s* is $|[x:Tx;\ y:Ty;\ \ldots t]|$: $(\mathbf{A}\,x,y(x \in Tx,\ y \in Ty, \ldots): t.X)$

- *s* is **if** $(\![P_i \rightarrow t_i)$**fi**: $(\mathbf{E}\,i: P_i) \wedge (\mathbf{A}\,i: P_i \Rightarrow t_i.X)$

- *s* is **do** $P \rightarrow t$ **od**: $(\mu Y\!: (P \Rightarrow t.Y) \wedge (\neg P \Rightarrow X))$

Specifications enjoy two important properties. They are conjunctive, i.e.,

$$[s.X \land s.Y = s.(X \land Y)],$$

and monotonic, i.e.,

$$[X \Rightarrow Y] \Rightarrow [s.X \Rightarrow s.Y]$$

for all assertions X, Y. These properties are proved by structural induction; we omit the proofs.

We briefly review procedural refinement. Programming consists in making a sequence of specifications starting from an initially given specification. At each step we make the current specification s "more algorithmic" —for example, by replacing a generalized assignment by a sequence of simpler assignments— producing a new specification t that will be the subject of the next step. We say that specification t is a "refinement" of specification s and denote the relationship by $s \leq t$, defined by

$$s \leq t = (\mathbf{A}X: [s.X \Rightarrow t.X]).$$

Procedural refinement is the process of eliminating, in such small steps, the quantifiers in guards and the generalized assignment statements. Stepwise procedural refinement is possible because of two properties of $\leq$. The first is that of "monotonic replacement":

$$u \leq v \Rightarrow s(w/u) \leq s(w/v)$$

for all specifications u, v, and s, where $s(w/u)$ denotes s with each occurrence of component w in s replaced by u, and similarly for $s(w/v)$. Monotonic replacement permits refinement of a specification by refinement of one of its components. Also, $\leq$ is transitive. Together with monotonic replacement the transitivity of $\leq$ allows us to refine a specification in small steps such that the derived specification is always a refinement of the original. See [8, 10] for a discussion and proofs of these properties and for the laws of stepwise procedural refinement in general. Note that an implementation can ignore assert statements because, as is easily seen, $\{X\} \leq$ **skip** for any assertion X.

3 *Data Refinement*

In the context set out above, data refinement is a special instance of refining a block. More specifically, given $|[b:Tb;\ s]|$ we are to produce $|[v:Tv;\ t]|$ such that

$$|[b:Tb;\ s]| \leq |[v:Tv;\ t]|.$$

In essence, we are to replace variable b and operations on it with variable v and corresponding operations on v. The given block is called the "abstract specification", and the derived block is called the "concrete specification". By extension we talk of "abstract statements" and "concrete statements", and so on. Variable b is the "abstract variable" and v the "concrete variable". In general there may be more than one abstract and more than one concrete variable, but it contributes nothing to the general argument to make this explicit. It is not excluded that s and t refer to common variables declared in surrounding blocks; we call these the "common variables".

We intend to construct the concrete specification so that it has the same structure as the abstract specification and so that each primitive concrete statement is the translation of the corresponding abstract statement, according to a uniform rule. Central to this strategy is the introduction of a relationship between the concrete and abstract variables via a so-called "abstraction invariant". Throughout, I will stand for the abstraction invariant, b (of type Tb) for the abstract variable, and v (of type Tv) for the concrete variable. Only b and v may occur free in I. We assume of course that I respects types, and so we have

$$[I \;\Rightarrow\; b \in Tb] \text{ and } [I \;\Rightarrow\; v \in Tv].$$

There are no other requirements on I other than that it enables the translation to go through, as will become evident later.

We denote "abstract statement s on abstract variable b is data refined by concrete statement t under the abstraction invariant I" by $s \ll_{I,b} t$; the subscript I, b is fixed for our presentation and so we omit it hereafter. We propose the definition

$$s \ll t = (\mathbf{A} X: [(\mathbf{E} b: I \wedge s.X) \;\Rightarrow\; t.(\mathbf{E} b: I \wedge X)]).$$

This definition is chosen for two reasons. First, it allows data refinement of any construct to be distributed over its component pieces, each piece being data refined independently of the others; it will be part of our task to show this. Second, we can supply a body of theorems that allow us to evaluate $s \ll t$ for primitive statements with ease; this will be the second part of our task. In the definition of $s \ll t$ it is not made explicit what the range of the universally quantified X is. It is to be understood that the X's are predicates on the abstract domain; i.e., we do not require the implication to hold for X containing free concrete variables. Note that $t.(\mathbf{E} b: I \wedge X)$ does not contain b free; we will be appealing to this fact in proofs. We have chosen to apply the epithet "piecewise", rather than "stepwise", to data refinement because the steps in data refinement proceed more in parallel than in series; formally, $\ll$ does not enjoy the transitivity and monotonic replacement properties of $\leq$.

If in refining $|[b: Tb; s]|$ with concrete variable v we construct t satisfying $s \ll t$, then, apart from a requirement to initialize v, we will have solved the original problem:

Theorem 1

If $s \ll t$, then $\|[b:Tb;\ s]\| \leq \|[v:Tv;\ v :- (\mathbf{E}b:I);\ t]\|$.

Proof   (See the note on proofs below.) First, for any X not containing b we show

$$s \ll t \Rightarrow [(\mathbf{E}b:I \wedge s.X) \Rightarrow t.X] :\tag{*}$$

$\qquad s \ll t$

$= \qquad \{\ll\}$

$\qquad [(\mathbf{E}b:I \wedge s.X) \Rightarrow t.(\mathbf{E}b:I \wedge X)]$

$= \qquad \{b \text{ not in } X\}$

$\qquad [(\mathbf{E}b:I \wedge s.X) \Rightarrow t.((\mathbf{E}b:I) \wedge X)]$

$\Rightarrow \qquad \{t \text{ monotonic}\}$

$\qquad [(\mathbf{E}b:I \wedge s.X) \Rightarrow t.X]$.

For the body of the proof:

$\qquad \|[b:Tb;\ s]\| \leq \|[v:Tv;\ v :- (\mathbf{E}b:I);\ t]\|$

$= \qquad \{\leq, \text{ semantics, } X \text{ arbitrary (assumed not to contain } b \text{ or } v \text{ free})\}$

$\qquad [(\mathbf{A}b(b \in Tb): s.X) \Rightarrow (\mathbf{A}v(v \in Tv): (\mathbf{A}v: (\mathbf{E}b:I) \Rightarrow t.X))]$

$\Leftarrow \qquad \{\text{calculus}\}$

$\qquad [(\mathbf{A}b(b \in Tb): s.X) \Rightarrow (\mathbf{A}v: (\mathbf{E}b:I) \Rightarrow t.X)]$

$= \qquad \{\text{absorption}— v \text{ not in antecedent}\}$

$\qquad [(\mathbf{A}b(b \in Tb): s.X) \Rightarrow ((\mathbf{E}b:I) \Rightarrow t.X)]$

$= \qquad \{\text{importation}\}$

$\qquad [(\mathbf{A}b(b \in Tb): s.X) \wedge (\mathbf{E}b:I) \Rightarrow t.X]$

$= \qquad \{\text{range elimination}\}$

$\qquad [(\mathbf{A}b: b \in Tb \Rightarrow s.X) \wedge (\mathbf{E}b:I) \Rightarrow t.X]$

$\Leftarrow \qquad \{\text{calculus}\}$

$\qquad [(\mathbf{E}b:I \wedge (b \in Tb \Rightarrow s.X)) \Rightarrow t.X]$

$= \qquad \{[I \Rightarrow b \in Tb]\}$

$\qquad [(\mathbf{E}b:I \wedge s.X)) \Rightarrow t.X]$

$= \qquad \{(*)— b \text{ is not in } X\}$

$\qquad \text{true}$. $\square$

The initialization requirement is best met by choosing I such that $[\mathbf{E}b:I]$ holds, in which case $v :- (\mathbf{E}b:I)$ can be omitted in the foregoing theorem, as may easily be verified. We will see in Sections 7 and 8 that the use of so-called "minor miracles" makes this strategy practical.

Note on proofs   Hints for the justification of proof steps are written within chain brackets. Proofs usually proceed by reducing the demonstrandum to "true", some steps using $\Leftarrow$, pronounced "follows from": $A \Leftarrow B$ is the same as $B \Rightarrow A$. These steps often appeal to the rule

$$[A \Rightarrow D] \Leftarrow [A \Rightarrow B] \wedge [B \Rightarrow D].$$

For example,

$$[A \Rightarrow D]$$

$\Leftarrow$ {hint why $[A \Rightarrow B]$}

$$[B \Rightarrow D]$$

$\Leftarrow$ {hint why $[C \Rightarrow D]$}

$$[B \Rightarrow C]$$

$=$ {hint why $[B \Rightarrow C]$}

true .

Some rules are specifically named in proofs, viz.,

importation/exportation: $[(A \wedge B \Rightarrow C) = (A \Rightarrow (B \Rightarrow C))]$;

absorption: for x a specification variable and Q not containing x,

$$[P] = [\mathbf{A}x:P],$$

$$[P \Rightarrow Q] = [(\mathbf{E}x:P) \Rightarrow Q], \text{ and}$$

$$[Q \Rightarrow P] = [Q \Rightarrow (\mathbf{A}x:P)] ;$$

1-point: $[(\mathbf{E}x: x = y \wedge P) = P(x/y)]$ and

$$[(\mathbf{A}x: x = y \Rightarrow P) = P(x/y)] .$$

We frequently use

$$[(\mathbf{E}x:P) \wedge (\mathbf{A}x:Q) \Rightarrow (\mathbf{E}x:P \wedge Q)] .$$

The hint "calculus" records an appeal to rules of predicate calculus that are presumed to be familiar; "substitution" hints at the elementary laws of substitution of variables; and "semantics" hints at the predicate transformer semantics of specifications. By "x does not occur in P" we mean that it does not occur free.

4 *Data Refinement of Compositions*

We proceed to show that the structure of the abstract specification carries over to the concrete specification. To begin with, data refinement distributes over sequential composition.

Theorem 2

$p; q \ll s; t$ follows from $p \ll s$ and $q \ll t$.

Proof   We are given, for any X

(*i*) $[(\mathbf{E}\, b: I \wedge p.X) \Rightarrow s.(\mathbf{E}\, b: I \wedge X)]$

(*ii*) $[(\mathbf{E}\, b: I \wedge q.X) \Rightarrow t.(\mathbf{E}\, b: I \wedge X)]$

$\quad\quad\quad p; q \ll s; t$

$\quad = \quad \{\ll, \text{semantics}, X \text{ arbitrary}\}$

$\quad\quad\quad [(\mathbf{E}\, b: I \wedge p.(q.X)) \Rightarrow s.(t.(\mathbf{E}\, b: I \wedge X))]$

$\quad \Leftarrow \quad \{(ii), \text{monotonicity of } s\}$

$\quad\quad\quad [(\mathbf{E}\, b: I \wedge p.(q.X)) \Rightarrow s.(\mathbf{E}\, b: I \wedge q.X)]$

$\quad = \quad \{(i) \text{ with } X := q.X\}$

$\quad\quad\quad \text{true} . \quad \square$

The primary role of the assert statement is to supply a context for refinement. $\{G\}\, s \leq t$ amounts to saying that t may replace s in a state in which G holds, but not necessarily otherwise. Such a G is called the context of the refinement. One may easily show that $\{T\}\, s \leq t$ equals $s \leq t$, and so no generality is lost by assuming that statements are refined in some arbitrary context; we make this assumption. Similar remarks hold for $\{G\}\, s \ll t$.

Local blocks may be carried over to the concrete specification:

Theorem 3

$|[k:Tk;\ s]| \ll |[k:Tk;\ t]|$ follows from $s \leq t$.

Proof   Exercise. $\square$

The choice of invariant I becomes significant when we come to translate guards. If I is too weak then the translation may not be possible. It turns out that a good translation of abstract guard P_i to concrete guard Q_i is to take $(\mathbf{A}\, b: I \wedge G \Rightarrow P_i)$ for Q_i where G denotes the context of the refinement. I is then good enough if it satisfies an adequacy condition, viz.,

$$[(\mathbf{E}\, b: I \wedge G \wedge (\mathbf{E}\, i: P_i)) \Rightarrow (\mathbf{E}\, i: Q_i)] .$$

Theorem 4

Let Q_i be $(\mathbf{A}\,b:I \wedge G \;\Rightarrow\; P_i)$ for each i. Then

$$\{G\}\,\mathbf{if}\;(\![]P_i \to s_i)\;\mathbf{fi} \;\;\ll\;\; \mathbf{if}\;(\![]Q_i \to t_i)\;\mathbf{fi}$$

follows from

$$\{G \wedge P_i\}\,s_i \ll t_i$$

for each i, and

$$[(\mathbf{E}\,b:I \wedge G \wedge (\mathbf{E}\,i:P_i)) \;\Rightarrow\; (\mathbf{E}\,i:Q_i)]\,.$$

Proof   The proof is similar in style to that of Theorem 5. We will tackle the harder proof, leaving the present one to the reader. $\square$

We will see in Section 6 that the adequacy condition is always met by the commonly occurring forms of abstraction invariant.

   An adequacy condition also manifests itself in the transformation of loops. There is in addition the requirement that the initial assertion of the loop be a loop invariant:

Theorem 5

Let $Q = (\mathbf{A}\,b:I \wedge G \;\Rightarrow\; P)$, and let $Q\tilde{} = (\mathbf{A}\,b:I \wedge G \;\Rightarrow\; \neg P)$. Then

$$\{G\}\,\mathbf{do}\;P \to s\;\mathbf{od} \;\;\ll\;\; \mathbf{do}\;Q \to t\;\mathbf{od}$$

follows from

(i) $\{G \wedge P\}\,s \ll t\,,$

(ii) $[G \wedge P \;\Rightarrow\; s.G]\,,$ and

(iii) $[(\mathbf{E}\,b:I \wedge G) \;\Rightarrow\; Q \vee Q\tilde{}\,]\,.$

Proof   We introduce some abbreviations. For fixed X on the abstract domain let

$$f.Y = (P \;\Rightarrow\; s.Y) \wedge (\neg P \;\Rightarrow\; X)\,,$$

$$g.Y = (Q \;\Rightarrow\; t.Y) \wedge (\neg Q \;\Rightarrow\; (\mathbf{E}\,b:I \wedge X))\,,\;\text{and}$$

$$Z = (\mu Y\!:g.Y)\,.$$

Then

$$\mathbf{do}\;P \to s\;\mathbf{od}.X = (\mu Y\!:f.Y)$$

and

$$\mathbf{do}\;Q \to t\;\mathbf{od}.\,(\mathbf{E}\,b:I \wedge X) = Z\,.$$

It is shown in [10] that assertions partially ordered by [... ⇒ ...] are embedded in a complete lattice, and as *f.Y* and *g.Y* are easily shown to be monotonic it follows that the two least fixpoints of interest exist [11]. We will be using the least-fixpoint property,

$$[h.X \Rightarrow X] \Rightarrow [(\mu Y{:}\,h.Y) \Rightarrow X] \text{ for monotonic } h \text{ and any } X.$$

Now

$$\{G\}\, \textbf{do}\, P \to s\, \textbf{od} \Rightarrow \textbf{do}\, Q \to t\, \textbf{od}$$

$=$ 　　{≪, semantics, *X* arbitrary}

$$[(\textbf{E}b{:}\,I \wedge G \wedge (\mu Y{:}f.Y)) \Rightarrow Z]$$

$=$ 　　{absorption— *b* not in consequent}

$$[I \wedge G \wedge (\mu Y{:}f.Y) \Rightarrow Z]$$

$=$ 　　{exportation}

$$[(\mu Y{:}f.Y) \Rightarrow (I \wedge G \Rightarrow Z)]$$

$=$ 　　{absorption— *v* not in antecedent; we are here translating the consequent to an assertion on the abstract domain in anticipation of applying the least-fixpoint property}

$$[(\mu Y{:}f.Y) \Rightarrow (\textbf{A}v{:}\,I \wedge G \Rightarrow Z)]$$

$=$ 　　{let $W := (\textbf{A}v{:}\,I \wedge G \Rightarrow Z)$}

$$[(\mu Y{:}f.Y) \Rightarrow W]$$

$\Leftarrow$ 　　{least fixpoint property}

$$[f.W \Rightarrow W]$$

$=$ 　　{*W*, absorption}

$$[f.W \Rightarrow (I \wedge G \Rightarrow Z)]$$

$=$ 　　{importation}

$$[I \wedge G \wedge f.W \Rightarrow Z]$$

$=$ 　　{*Z* a fixpoint}

$$[I \wedge G \wedge f.W \Rightarrow g.Z]$$

$=$ 　　{*f, g*}

$$[I \wedge G \wedge (P \Rightarrow s.W) \wedge (\neg P \Rightarrow X) \Rightarrow$$
$$(Q \Rightarrow t.Z) \wedge (\neg Q \Rightarrow (\textbf{E}b{:}\,I \wedge X))]$$

$\Leftarrow$ 　　{calculus}

$$[I \wedge G \wedge (P \Rightarrow s.W) \Rightarrow (Q \Rightarrow t.Z)] \qquad \wedge$$
$$[I \wedge G \wedge (\neg P \Rightarrow X) \Rightarrow (\neg Q \Rightarrow (\textbf{E}b{:}\,I \wedge X))]$$

and we prove each conjunct separately.

$$[I \wedge G \wedge (P \Rightarrow s.W) \Rightarrow (Q \Rightarrow t.Z)]$$

$=$ {absorption— consequent does not contain b}

$$[(\mathbf{E}b : I \wedge G \wedge (P \Rightarrow s.W)) \Rightarrow (Q \Rightarrow t.Z)]$$

$=$ {importation, Q}

$$[(\mathbf{E}b : I \wedge G \wedge (P \Rightarrow s.W)) \wedge (\mathbf{A}b : I \wedge G \Rightarrow P) \Rightarrow t.Z]$$

$\Leftarrow$ {calculus}

$$[(\mathbf{E}b : I \wedge G \wedge (P \Rightarrow s.W) \wedge (I \wedge G \Rightarrow P)) \Rightarrow t.Z]$$

$=$ {calculus}

$$[(\mathbf{E}b : I \wedge G \wedge P \wedge s.W) \Rightarrow t.Z]$$

$=$ {(ii), s conjunctive}

$$[(\mathbf{E}b : I \wedge G \wedge P \wedge s.(G \wedge W)) \Rightarrow t.Z]$$

$\Leftarrow$ {(i)}

$$[t.(\mathbf{E}b : I \wedge G \wedge W) \Rightarrow t.Z]$$

$\Leftarrow$ {t monotonic}

$$[(\mathbf{E}b : I \wedge G \wedge W) \Rightarrow Z]$$

$=$ {absorption—Z does not contain b}

$$[I \wedge G \wedge W \Rightarrow Z]$$

$=$ {exportation}

$$[W \Rightarrow (I \wedge G \Rightarrow Z)]$$

$=$ {W, calculus}

true .

To complete the proof,

$$[I \wedge G \wedge (\neg P \Rightarrow X) \Rightarrow (\neg Q \Rightarrow (\mathbf{E}b : I \wedge X))]$$

$=$ {absorption—consequent does not contain b}

$$[(\mathbf{E}b : I \wedge G \wedge (\neg P \Rightarrow X)) \Rightarrow (\neg Q \Rightarrow (\mathbf{E}b : I \wedge X))]$$

$=$ {importation}

$$[(\mathbf{E}b : I \wedge G \wedge (\neg P \Rightarrow X)) \wedge \neg Q \Rightarrow (\mathbf{E}b : I \wedge X)]$$

$=$ {calculus}

$$[(\mathbf{E}b : I \wedge G) \wedge (\mathbf{E}b : I \wedge G \wedge (\neg P \Rightarrow X)) \wedge \neg Q \Rightarrow (\mathbf{E}b : I \wedge X)]$$

$\Leftarrow$ {(iii)}

$$[(Q \vee Q\tilde{\ }) \wedge (\mathbf{E}b : I \wedge G \wedge (\neg P \Rightarrow X)) \wedge \neg Q \Rightarrow (\mathbf{E}b : I \wedge X)]$$

$\Leftarrow$ {calculus, $Q\tilde{\ }$}

$$[(\mathbf{A}b : I \wedge G \Rightarrow \neg P) \wedge (\mathbf{E}b : I \wedge G \wedge (\neg P \Rightarrow X)) \Rightarrow (\mathbf{E}b : I \wedge X)]$$

$\Leftarrow$ {calculus}

   $[(\mathbf{E}\,b:I \wedge G \wedge (\neg P \Rightarrow X) \wedge (I \wedge G \Rightarrow \neg P)) \Rightarrow (\mathbf{E}\,b:I \wedge X)]$

=   {calculus}

   $[(\mathbf{E}\,b:I \wedge G \wedge \neg P \wedge X) \Rightarrow (\mathbf{E}\,b:I \wedge X)]$

=   {calculus}

   true . $\square$

If we do not need to exploit context in the data refinement of a loop, as is often the case, then the following corollary suffices.

Corollary 1

   do $P \rightarrow s$ **od** $\ll$ **do** $(\mathbf{A}\,b:I \Rightarrow P) \rightarrow t$ **od**

follows from

   $\{P\}\,s \ll t$ and $[(\mathbf{E}\,b:I) \Rightarrow (\mathbf{A}\,b:I \Rightarrow P) \vee (\mathbf{A}\,b:I \Rightarrow \neg P)]$.

Proof   Similar to the preceding proof. $\square$

It will turn out that the adequacy conditions in Theorem 5 and Corollary 6 are always met by the common forms of abstraction invariants.

To summarize this section: If the abstraction invariant is strong enough to allow the translation of guards, then the structure of the abstract specification carries over to the concrete specification. Data refinement is then reduced to refining the primitive statements.

5 *Data Refinement of Primitives*

First we show that for statements s on the abstract domain that do not refer to abstract variables, data refinement is no more than procedural refinement (bear in mind that typically there are variables common to the abstract and concrete specifications). In particular, because $s \leq s$, such statements are their own translation to concrete form.

Theorem 6

If s and t refer to no abstract variables, then $s \ll t$ follows from $s \leq t$.

Proof   By a routine structural induction left to the reader. $\square$

Proving $s \ll t$ from first principles may be hard work because of the universal quantification over assertions in its definition. We therefore construct a body of theorems that obviate this difficulty for the elementary statements. The following will be useful:

Lemma 1

If s assigns to no variables occurring in G, then $[G \wedge s.X \Rightarrow s.Y]$ follows from $[G \wedge X \Rightarrow Y]$.

Proof   One may show by structural induction that $[G \wedge s.T \Rightarrow s.G]$; we leave the proof of this obvious fact to the reader. Then

$$[G \wedge s.X \Rightarrow s.Y]$$

$=$ $\{s \text{ conjunctive}\}$

$$[G \wedge s.T \wedge s.X \Rightarrow s.Y]$$

$\Leftarrow$ $\{[G \wedge s.T \Rightarrow s.G]\}$

$$[s.G \wedge s.X \Rightarrow s.Y]$$

$=$ $\{s \text{ conjunctive}\}$

$$[s.(G \wedge X) \Rightarrow s.Y]$$

$\Leftarrow$ $\{s \text{ monotonic}\}$

$$[G \wedge X \Rightarrow Y] .\ \ \square$$

In some of the theorems, we will want to make explicit that there may be more than one abstract variable. We will let c, d be a partitioning of the abstract variables b; i.e., $b = c, d$.

The construct $\{G\} x :- P$ is a particularly important specification device. It says: Given an initial state satisfying G, establish the postcondition P while changing only the values of variable(s) x. It is the mechanism through which many small programs are specified, and is essentially the "specification statement" of [8] and the "prescription" of [10]. Its semantics, derived from Fig. 1, is

$$(\{G\} x :- P).X = G \wedge (\mathbf{A} x : P \Rightarrow X) .$$

Theorem 7

If t assigns to no common variables, then $\{G\} c :- Q \ll t$ follows from $[(\mathbf{E} c : I \wedge G) \Rightarrow t.(\mathbf{E} c : I \wedge Q)]$.

Proof

$$\{G\} c :- Q \ll t$$

$=$ $\{\ll, \text{ semantics, } X \text{ arbitrary}\}$

$$[(\mathbf{E} c,d : I \wedge G \wedge (\mathbf{A} c : Q \Rightarrow X)) \Rightarrow t.(\mathbf{E} c,d : I \wedge X)]$$

$=$ $\{\text{let } Z := (\mathbf{E} c,d : I \wedge X)\}$

$$[(\mathbf{E} c,d : I \wedge G \wedge (\mathbf{A} c : Q \Rightarrow X)) \Rightarrow t.Z]$$

$=$ $\{\text{absorption—consequent does not contain } d\}$

$\qquad [(\mathbf{E}c: I \wedge G) \wedge (\mathbf{A}c: Q \Rightarrow X)) \Rightarrow t.Z]$

$\Leftarrow \qquad \{[(\mathbf{E}c: I \wedge G) \Rightarrow t.(\mathbf{E}c: I \wedge Q)]\}$

$\qquad [t.(\mathbf{E}c: I \wedge Q) \wedge (\mathbf{A}c: Q \Rightarrow X)) \Rightarrow t.Z]$

$\Leftarrow \qquad \{\text{Lemma 1 with } G := (\mathbf{A}c: Q \Rightarrow X), X := (\mathbf{E}c: I \wedge Q), Y := Z, s := t\}$

$\qquad [(\mathbf{E}c: I \wedge Q) \wedge (\mathbf{A}c: Q \Rightarrow X)) \Rightarrow Z]$

$\Leftarrow \qquad \{\text{calculus}\}$

$\qquad [(\mathbf{E}c: I \wedge Q \wedge (Q \Rightarrow X)) \Rightarrow Z]$

$= \qquad \{\text{calculus}\}$

$\qquad [(\mathbf{E}c: I \wedge Q \wedge X) \Rightarrow Z]$

$= \qquad \{Z, \text{calculus}\}$

$\qquad$ true . $\square$

Corollary 2

If t assigns to no common variables, then $\{G\}\, b :\!- Q \ll t$ follows from $[(\mathbf{E}b : I \wedge G) \Rightarrow t.(\mathbf{E}b: I \wedge Q)]$.

Proof   Let d be empty in Theorem 7. $\square$

Theorem 8

Let e be an expression on the abstract domain. If t assigns to no common variables, then $\{G\}\, c := e \ll t$ follows from $[I \wedge G \Rightarrow t.(I(c/e))]$.

Proof   The proof proceeds much as for Theorem 7 and is left as an exercise. $\square$

Simple assignments to common variables are more problematic; they are considered in the next section.

Theorem 9

Let m be a variable common to the abstract and concrete domains, and let t be a concrete specification that assigns to m and concrete variables only. Then

$\qquad \{G\}\, m :\!- Q \ll t$ follows from $[I \wedge G \Rightarrow t.(\mathbf{E}b: I \wedge Q)]$.

Proof   Exercise. $\square$

6 *Functional Invariants*

When the abstract variable(s) b and concrete variable(s) v are related by $b = e$ for e an expression in the concrete variables, then life becomes simpler because data refinement becomes not much more than substitution. When this is the case we say that the abstract variables are functional in v. This is commonly, even usually, the case. The functionality requirement is formulated as $[I \wedge G \Rightarrow b = e]$ where G is the context of the refinement. We consider three cases where the simplification is most beneficial—assignments to a common variable, if-statements, and loops. In this section e will always stand for an expression in the concrete variables.

Theorem 10

Let m be a variable common to the abstract and common domains, let f be an expression possibly containing abstract variables, and let $f^\sim$ stand for f with e substituted for b. Then $\{G\}\, m := f \ll m := f^\sim$ if $[I \wedge G \Rightarrow b = e]$.

Proof

$$\{G\}\, m := f \ll m := f^\sim$$

$= \quad \{\ll, \text{semantics, } X \text{ arbitrary, substitution}\}$

$$[(\mathbf{E}\, b : I \wedge G \wedge X(m/f)) \Rightarrow (\mathbf{E}\, b : I \wedge X(m/f^\sim))]$$

$= \quad \{\text{let } Z := (\mathbf{E}\, b : I \wedge X(m/f^\sim))\}$

$$[(\mathbf{E}\, b : I \wedge G \wedge X(m/f)) \Rightarrow Z]$$

$\Leftarrow \quad \{[I \wedge G \Rightarrow b = e]\}$

$$[(\mathbf{E}\, b : b = e \wedge I \wedge X(m/f)) \Rightarrow Z]$$

$= \quad \{\text{1-point}\}$

$$[(I \wedge X(m/f))(b/e) \Rightarrow Z]$$

$= \quad \{\text{substitution— } e \text{ does not contain } b\}$

$$[(I \wedge X(m/f^\sim))(b/e) \Rightarrow Z]$$

$= \quad \{Z, \text{ calculus}\}$

$\text{true} \,.\ \ \square$

The adequacy condition on I for the translation of guards is now automatically met.

Theorem 11

$$\{G\}\ \mathbf{if}\ (\llbracket P_i \to s_i)\mathbf{fi} \ll \mathbf{if}\ (\llbracket P_i(b/e) \to t_i)\mathbf{fi}$$

follows from $\{G \wedge P_i\}\, s_i \ll t_i$, for each i, and $[I \wedge G \Rightarrow b = e]$.

Proof   Exercise. $\square$

Theorem 12

$\{G\}\,\textbf{do}\;P \rightarrow s\,\textbf{od}\;\ll\;\textbf{do}\;P(b/e) \rightarrow s\,\textbf{od}$

follows from $\{G \wedge P\}\,s \ll t$, $[G \wedge P \Rightarrow s.G]$, and $[I \wedge G \Rightarrow b = e]$.

Proof   Similar to that of Theorem 5. $\square$

Corollary 3

$\textbf{do}\;P \rightarrow s\,\textbf{od} \ll \textbf{do}\;P(b/e) \rightarrow s\,\textbf{od}$ follows from $\{P\}\,s \ll t$ and $[I \Rightarrow b = e]$.

Proof   Similar to that of Theorem 5. $\square$

7 *Minor Miracles*

We add a further statement to the specification language. This is the minor miracle with form $(P \rightarrow s)$ and semantics $(P \rightarrow s).X = (P \Rightarrow s.X)$. It satisfies the conjunctivity and monotonicity laws. The minor miracle plays a somewhat special role: It is used not so much to make specifications as to play a mediating role in refining them. They were introduced into data refinement by Morgan [9]. The primary concern here is to show how to eliminate them using assert statements.

We refine a minor miracle by supplying an appropriate context:

Lemma 2

$\{G\}\,(P \rightarrow s) \leq s$ follows from $[G \Rightarrow P]$.

Proof   Routine. $\square$

To exploit Lemma 2 we may need to add assert statements to specifications. There are no surprises in doing this:

Lemma 3

$\{G\}\,\textbf{if}\;(\llbracket P_i \rightarrow s_i)\textbf{fi}\;=\;\{G\}\,\textbf{if}\;(\llbracket P_i \rightarrow \{G \wedge P_i\}\,s_i)\textbf{fi}$.

Lemma 4

If G is an invariant of the loop,

$\{G\}\,\textbf{do}\;P \rightarrow s\,\textbf{od}\;=\;\{G\}\,\textbf{do}\;P \rightarrow \{G \wedge P\}\,s\,\textbf{od}$.

Lemma 5

$\{G\}\,s = \{G\}\,s\,\{Q\}$ if $[G \Rightarrow s.Q]$.

Proofs of Lemmas 3, 4, 5   Exercise. $\square$

One may easily show $(s \leq (P \to t)) = (\{P\}\, s \leq t)$. It follows that minor miracles are a device for associating context with the refined specification rather than with the source specification. This is useful in data refinement where the context may be in terms of the concrete variables. Minor miracles will be used in the next section.

8 *Example*

We present an example of refining a specification on bags of integers to one using a sequence of integers. The specification, which sums the elements in a bag, is taken from [9] and is shown in Fig. 2. (It may well be the case that in the program of Fig. 2 procedural refinement has run too far ahead of the data refinement step, but that doesn't matter for the purposes of the example.) The abstract variables are b, d. The concrete variables will be

x : **sequence of integer**; n : **integer**

and variables h and e will be common to the abstract and common specifications. The following notation for bags and sequences is used:

$\#x$	length of sequence x
$x.n$	element n of sequence x, $0 \leq n < \#x$
bag.x	the bag containing precisely the elements of sequence x
$x{\downarrow}n$	the initial segment of length n of sequence x, $0 \leq n \leq \#x$
$\varnothing$	the empty bag
$\langle e \rangle$	the bag containing integer e only
$+, -$	bag addition and subtraction
$\in$	bag membership.

Figure 2.   Original specification.

$\lVert\quad b$: **bag of integer**; d: **bag of integer**;

$\quad h$: **integer**; e: **integer**;

$\quad d := \varnothing;\ h := 0;$

$\quad$**do** $d \neq b \to$

$\qquad\qquad e :- e \in b - d; d := d + \langle e \rangle;\ h := h + e$

$\quad$**od**

$\rrbracket$

The precedence of operators is now

.

$-, +$

$\downarrow$

$\in$

followed by the logical operators as before. We will appeal to the following laws of "bag theory":

$B1$: $(\text{bag}.(x{\downarrow}n) = \emptyset) = (n = 0)$

$B2$: $(\text{bag}.(x{\downarrow}n) = \text{bag}.x) = (n = \#x)$

$B3$: $0 \le n < \#x \;\Rightarrow\; x.n \in \text{bag}.x - \text{bag}.(x{\downarrow}n)$

$B4$: $0 \le n < \#x \;\Rightarrow\; (\text{bag}.(x{\downarrow}n) + \langle x.n\rangle = \text{bag}.(x{\downarrow}n + 1))$.

The abstraction invariant is

I: $b = \text{bag}.x \;\wedge\; d = \text{bag}.(x{\downarrow}n)$.

Because $[\mathbf{E}\,b,d:I]$ there is no requirement to initialize I. Because I has a functional form we may appeal to the results of Section 6.
    We refine the primitives in turn.

- $d := \emptyset \ll n := 0$

$\Leftarrow$ {Theorem 8 with $G := T$}

    $[I \;\Rightarrow\; (n := 0.(I(d/\emptyset))]$

$=$ {substitution}

    $[I \;\Rightarrow\; (b = \text{bag}.x \;\wedge\; \emptyset = \text{bag}.(x{\downarrow}0))]$

$=$ {I, $B1$}

    true

- $e :- e \in b - d \ll (0 \le n < \#x \to e := x.n)$

$\Leftarrow$ {Theorem 9 with $G := T$}

    $[I \wedge T \;\Rightarrow\; (0 \le n < \#x \to e := x.n).(\mathbf{E}\,b,d : I \wedge e \in b - d)]$

$=$ {1-point}

    $[I \;\Rightarrow\; (0 \le n < \#x \to e := x.n).(e \in \text{bag}.x - \text{bag}.(x{\downarrow}n))]$

$=$ {semantics}

    $[I \;\Rightarrow\; (0 \le n < \#x \;\Rightarrow\; x.n \in \text{bag}.x - \text{bag}.(x{\downarrow}n))]$

$=$ {$B3$}

true

- $d := d + \langle e \rangle \ll (0 \le n < \#x \ \land \ e = x.n \rightarrow n := n + 1)$

  Exercise

- $(d \ne b)(b,d/\text{bag}.x, \ \text{bag}.(x \downarrow n))$

= {substitution}

  $\text{bag}.(x \downarrow n) \ne \text{bag}.x$

= {*B2*}

  $n \ne \#x$.

Appealing to Theorem 2 (for sequential composition), Theorem 6 (for the common statements), Corollary 3 (for the loop), Theorem 1 (for the whole), and the foregoing, we refine to the specification of Fig. 3.

Data refinement takes us no further; from here progress is made through procedural refinement. By Lemma 2 the guard P of each minor miracle can be eliminated if we can prefix the minor miracle with $\{P\}$. The first minor miracle in Fig. 3 can be prefixed with $\{0 \le n < \#x\}$ because we easily show $0 \le n \le \#x$ is an invariant of the loop that is initially true, and we then appeal to Lemma 4. The legitimacy of $\{0 \le n < \#x \ \land \ e = x.n\}$ before the second minor miracle follows from an application of Lemma 5. The final program is shown in Fig. 4.

Figure 3. Refined specification.

$\lVert \quad x :$ **sequence of integer**; $n :$ **integer**;

$\quad h :$ **integer**; $e :$ **integer**;

$\quad n := 0; \ h := 0;$

$\quad$ **do** $n \ne \#x \rightarrow$

$\qquad\qquad (0 \le n < \#x \rightarrow e := x.n);$

$\qquad\qquad (0 \le n < \#x \ \land \ e = x.n \rightarrow n := n + 1);$

$\qquad\qquad h := h + e$

$\quad$ **od**

$\rVert$

---

9 *Conclusion*

Although data refinement is a well-established technique —it was popular-
ized in [5] and has been central to VDM[7]— there has been renewed interest
in it recently [3, 6, 9] stemming from our better understanding of the mathematics of programming. A previous treatment based on predicate transform-
ers is [3]; this takes $[l \wedge s.T \Rightarrow t.(\neg s.(\neg l))]$ for the definition of $s \ll t$, as does
[9]. We have not proceeded from this definition for two reasons. The first is
that it does not appear to accommodate comfortably variables common to
the abstract and common domains. A naive application of the definition, for
example, would suggest that $m := 1$ is data refined by $m := 2$ where m is a
common variable; [3] uses a renaming device to overcome this difficulty. The
second reason is that the earlier definition does not seem to lend itself as
readily to formal manipulation; [3] does not make a formal justification of
the definition. None of this is to question the legitimacy of the definition in
[3]. The contribution of the present work has been to propose a definition
of data refinement that admits of its formal justification, and that places it
squarely beside procedural refinement in the one specification and developmental framework. Back has earlier presented, in [1], a theory combining
procedural and data refinement that is similar in many respects. En route we
have introduced the assert statement as a device for eliminating the minor
miracles that arise in formal program development. Data refinement is also
applicable to the construction of modules or packages. There should be no
essential added difficulty in this; we have preferred to present the theory in
the setting of blocks because that presents fewer extraneous details.

Figure 4. The final program.

```
|[  x: sequence of integer; n: integer;
    h: integer; e: integer;
    n := 0;  h := 0;
    do n ≠ #x →
            e := x.n;  n := n + 1;  h := h + e
    od
]|
```

References

[1] Back, R. J. R. "Correctness preserving program refinements: Proof theory and applications". Mathematical Center Tracts 131. Mathematisch Centrum, Amsterdam, 1980.

[2] Dijkstra, E. W. *A Discipline of Programming.* Prentice-Hall, Englewood Cliffs, N. J., 1976.

[3] Gries, D. and Prins, J. A. "A new notion of encapsulation". Proceedings of Symposium on Language Issues in Programming Environments. *ACM SIGPLAN Notices 20* (1985), pp. 131–139.

[4] Hayes, I. (ed). *Specification Case Studies.* Prentice-Hall, Englewood Cliffs, N. J., 1987.

[5] Hoare, C. A. R. "Proofs of correctness of data representations". *Acta Informatica 1* (1972), pp. 271–281.

[6] Hoare, C. A. R., He, J. F., and Sanders, J. W. "Prespecification in data refinement". *Information Processing Letters 25* (1987).

[7] Jones, C. B. *Systematic Software Development using VDM.* Prentice-Hall, Englewood Cliffs, N. J., 1986.

[8] Morgan, C. "The specification statement". Submitted for publication.

[9] Morgan, C. "Data refinement by miracles". Submitted for publication.

[10] Morris, J. M. "A theoretical basis for stepwise refinement and the programming calculus". *Science of Computer Programming*, to appear.

[11] Tarski, A. "A lattice theoretical fixpoint theorem and its applications". *Pacific J. Mathematics 5* (1955), pp. 285–309.

Exercises
in
Formula
Manipulation

11

W. H. J. Feijen
Eindhoven University of Technology[0]
Lex Bijlsma[1]
Eindhoven University of Technology

This is a very technical, yet shallow, paper. It is very technical in that there are formulae all over the place, and it is shallow (the opposite of "deep— difficult to penetrate or to comprehend") in that it tries to manipulate these formulae in steps so small that nowhere should there be much doubt about correctness. As such this may be the kind of paper that some mathematicians do not like, because it may contain only a few logical gaps and perhaps even no mistakes, so that nothing remains to be done. Other mathematicians may even dislike it, because of the danger that the calculational is prevailing over the conceptual, thus killing the spirit of mathematics. Sadly true as this may be, we decide it to be none of our business now: The design of programs has demanded such a style.

---

0. Department of Computer Sciences, The University of Texas at Austin (for the academic year 1987-1988).
1. co-author of Section 4.

Using a number of disconnected examples, we will try to show how a nearly uninterpreted manipulation of formulae can do the work, and how sometimes the work is done more concisely, more rigorously, and with less intellectual investment on our part than would have been the case otherwise. We also hope to show how the mere decision not to interpret formulae, but to focus on their shape and on the manipulative freedom they offer, can provide strong heuristic guidance.

The five sections in this paper are mostly self-contained and can be read more or less independently (though perhaps a little less so for the last section). The scopes of formulae and names never extend beyond a section. As for the self-containedness, we will not explain the rules of arithmetic or of high-school algebra, nor the elements of the predicate calculus, nor the proof rules and notations for programs, nor even the mutual exclusion problem. We believe them to belong to the standard formalisms and notions of our profession.

0   *Touching a Little Calculus*

The main purpose of this section is to transmit some of the flavor of uninterpreted formula manipulation. We have chosen to deal with a little calculus that centers around the maximum of two numbers, not in order to convey any new information about this (though we may) but because it provides about the simplest setting that can meet our purpose.

Before we start off, we mention a fairly general theorem about numbers:

$$[x = y \equiv (\mathbf{A}z :: z \geq x \equiv z \geq y)] ; \qquad (0)$$

here and in the remainder of this section, square brackets denote universal quantification over the (free) variables in the enclosed expression. The typical use we will make of the theorem is to demonstrate the equality of two numbers x and y by demonstrating that, for any z, the expressions $z \geq x$ and $z \geq y$ —which do not contain an equality sign— are equivalent.

We denote the maximum of x and y by $x \uparrow y$ (pronounced "x up y"). By postulate, it satisfies

$$[z \geq x \uparrow y \equiv z \geq x \wedge z \geq y] . \qquad (1)$$

We show how all sorts of familiar properties of the maximum follow from (1).

Property   For instance we can now derive that operator $\uparrow$ is idempotent, i.e.

$$[x \uparrow x = x] ,$$

and that it is symmetric, i.e.

$$[x \uparrow y = y \uparrow x] , \qquad (2)$$

and associative, i.e.

$$[(x \uparrow y) \uparrow z = x \uparrow (y \uparrow z)] \, .$$

Let us derive (2), the symmetry. Because (2) contains an equality sign there is nothing we can do except to instantiate (0) properly. With the instantiation $x, y := x \uparrow y, y \uparrow x$, we find

$$[x \uparrow y = y \uparrow x \ \equiv \ (\mathbf{A} z :: z \geq x \uparrow y \ \equiv \ z \geq y \uparrow x)] \, ,$$

and hence we can conclude (2) whenever we can derive

$$[(\mathbf{A} z :: z \geq x \uparrow y \ \equiv \ z \geq y \uparrow x)] \, .$$

The latter follows from the following calculation:

$$z \geq x \uparrow y$$
$$= \quad \{(1)\}$$
$$z \geq x \ \wedge \ z \geq y$$
$$= \quad \{\wedge \text{ is symmetric}\}$$
$$z \geq y \ \wedge \ z \geq x$$
$$= \quad \{(1) \text{ with } x, y := y, x\}$$
$$z \geq y \uparrow x \, .$$

Property   Next, we expect the maximum of two numbers to be at least as big as either of these numbers. We can formulate this as

$$[x \uparrow y \geq x \ \wedge \ x \uparrow y \geq y] \, . \tag{3}$$

Can it follow from postulate (1)? It is an instantiation of (1)'s right-hand side for $z := x \uparrow y$. Therefore we are invited to consider

$$x \uparrow y \geq x \ \wedge \ x \uparrow y \geq y$$
$$= \quad \{(1) \text{ with } z := x \uparrow y\}$$
$$x \uparrow y \geq x \uparrow y$$
$$= \quad \{\geq \text{ is reflexive}\}$$
$$\text{true} \, ,$$

and this establishes (3).

Property   Also, we expect the maximum of two numbers to be equal to at least one of them. We can formulate this as

$$[x \uparrow y = x \ \vee \ x \uparrow y = y] \, . \tag{4}$$

Can it follow from postulate (1)? It is not simply the case that (4) is an instantiation of (1) or of any of its subexpressions. Formula (1) does not even mention an equality sign. Therefore we investigate how (4) can be massaged all by itself. In view of the symmetry of $\uparrow$, we investigate one of its disjuncts only:

$$x \uparrow y = x$$

= {We have to eliminate symbol $=$; one opportunity is offered by (0), but the simplest choice we can think of is this.}

$$x \uparrow y \geq x \land x \geq x \uparrow y$$

= {by (3), the first conjunct is true}

$$\text{true} \land x \geq x \uparrow y$$

= {true is the identity element of $\land$}

$$x \geq x \uparrow y$$

= {(1) with $z := x$}

$$x \geq x \land x \geq y$$

= {reflexivity of $\geq$, and predicate calculus}

$$x \geq y .$$

Having thus established the equivalence of the two extreme lines of the above calculation, we conclude that for numbers x and y, (4) is as valid as

$$[x \geq y \lor y \geq x] .$$

Property   There are a few more properties for the maximum in isolation, but in combination with other operators there are many more. One of them is —as everyone knows— that addition distributes over the maximum; i.e.,

$$[c + (x \uparrow y) = (c + x) \uparrow (c + y)] . \tag{5}$$

(Here I would very much like to admit that, if I knew this property at all, it was not in the front of my mind, not even at a time when I was already supposed to be a professional mathematician.) Using (0), we can show (5) by showing that for any z,

$$[z \geq c + (x \uparrow y) \equiv z \geq (c + x) \uparrow (c + y)] ,$$

as follows:

$$z \geq c + (x \uparrow y)$$

= {algebra}

$$z - c \geq x \uparrow y$$

= {(1) with $z := z - c$}

$$z - c \geq x \ \wedge \ z - c \geq y$$

=   {algebra, twice}

$$z \geq c + x \ \wedge \ z \geq c + y$$

=   {(1) with $x, y := c + x, c + y$}

$$z \geq (c + x) \uparrow (c + y) \ .$$

This settles (5).

Property   What about the triangular inequality

$$[\ |x + y| \leq |x| + |y| \ ] \ ?$$ (6)

This has nothing to do with the foregoing until we realize that by definition

$$[\ |x| = x \uparrow -x \ ] \ .$$ (7)

Now we can prove (6) as follows:

$$|x| + |y|$$

=   {(7), twice}

$$(x \uparrow -x) + (y \uparrow -y)$$

=   {+ distributes over $\uparrow$, i.e. using (5) many times}

$$(x + y) \uparrow (-x + y) \uparrow (x - y) \uparrow (-x - y)$$

$\geq$ {using (3), symmetry, and associativity of $\uparrow$ }

$$(x + y) \uparrow (-x - y)$$

=   {(7)}

$$|x + y| \ .$$

Property   And so on.

So much for the touch of a little calculus.

Many of us have been introduced to the maximum in a different way, some-what along the lines of

$$\max(a, b) = \begin{cases} a & \text{if } a \geq b \\ b & \text{otherwise.} \end{cases}$$

Small though the difference may seem, we have found that such introductions cause a lifelong inconvenience, minor perhaps, but an inconvenience never-theless. The problem with the above formula is that it is hardly susceptible to manipulation. (The reader should try to use it in proving the associativity of max.) By its very unmanipulability the formula invites interpretation and the drawing of pictures. Moreover, by its shape it invites case-analysis. Its "if" hides an equivalence, and its "otherwise" a symmetry. It was the notice-able inefficiency with which some professional mathematicians would prove a theorem like

$$a + b \geq \max(a, b) \equiv a \geq 0 \wedge b \geq 0$$

that inspired our little calculus.

1 *A Calculation with Predicates*

In this section we shall describe the design of a calculational proof of the following theorem, which was communicated by Edsger W. Dijkstra.

Theorem
For any bag V of predicates,

$$[V \neq \varnothing \equiv (\mathbf{E}x\colon x \in V\colon x \equiv (\mathbf{A}y\colon y \in V\colon y))] . \tag{0}$$

To fully explain the square brackets falls outside the scope of this section, and also outside the scope of our current concern. The reader may be reas-sured to learn that the only property of square brackets we will be using is that from $[A \equiv B]$ and $[B \equiv C]$ we are entitled to conclude $[A \equiv C]$. This reasoning will be rendered as

    A

=   {hint why $[A \equiv B]$}

    B

=   {hint why $[B \equiv C]$}

    C .

The theorem itself is of mild interest, and so is its proof. There are many theorems from predicate logic, and their proofs are developed along the same lines as the one in our current example. The only peculiar observation related to the theorem above was that people who tried to convince themselves of its correctness by interpreting the formula all got confused. The reason for their confusion becomes apparent when the theorem is reformulated in set notation. It then assumes a shape so vast and massive and inhomogeneous that all of our interest in it fades away. One of the reasons for the blow-up is that set theory offers no smooth analogues for the square brackets and the equivalence. (Whereas mathematics has introduced the notion of symmetric set difference, I have never found an answer to the question why mathematics has failed or even refused to introduce the much nicer notion of symmetric set equality, even in the presence of a universe.)

Next we construct a calculational proof of the theorem. We will carry out the calculation in very small steps, partly for the convenience of the reader who is not too familiar with the rewrite rules of predicate calculus, and partly to show how the "anatomy" of the formulae can guide one in taking the next step.

Proof   Formula (0) is an equivalence, which we could prove by mutual implication. We could also carry out a case-analysis, which is made possible by the left-hand side of (0) being a boolean scalar. We consider it as our current game, however, not to follow either suggestion.

The first thing to do about (0) is to provide a definition of $V \neq \emptyset$. We propose

$$[V \neq \emptyset \ \equiv \ (\mathbf{E}x\colon x \in V\colon \text{true})] \ .$$

Now we can prove (0) by showing

$$[(\mathbf{E}x\colon x \in V\colon \text{true}) \ \equiv \ (\mathbf{E}x\colon x \in V\colon x \ \equiv \ (\mathbf{A}y\colon y \in V\colon y))] \ , \tag{1}$$

which is our new demonstrandum.

It would be easiest to show equivalence (1) by showing that the existentially quantified expressions are termwise equivalent, but this is too much to hope for: One of the terms has a ubiquitous occurrence of x and the other one none at all. Therefore we should be prepared to massage an entire quantified expression. Which one, then? Here we stick to the rule of thumb that we start massaging the more complicated side, which in our case definitely is (1)'s right-hand side. For reasons of brevity we omit the ranges of the dummies.

$$(\mathbf{E}x\colon\colon x \ \equiv \ (\mathbf{A}y\colon\colon y))$$

=   {There is no nice rewrite rule for an existential quantification with an equivalence as its term. Therefore we rewrite the term. Among all the possibilities we have for rewriting an equivalence, we choose mutual implication ... }

$$(\mathbf{E}x\colon\colon (x \ \Rightarrow \ (\mathbf{A}y\colon\colon y)) \ \wedge \ (x \ \Leftarrow \ (\mathbf{A}y\colon\colon y)))$$

=   {..., anticipating that for any x we have $[x \ \Leftarrow \ (\mathbf{A}y\colon\colon y)]$, which is the Rule of Instantiation.}

$$(\mathbf{E}x\colon\colon x \ \Rightarrow \ (\mathbf{A}y\colon\colon y))$$

=   {Neither is there a nice rewrite rule for an existential quantification in case the term is an implication. Therefore we rewrite the implication, but without reintroducing an equivalence.}

$$(\mathbf{E}x\colon\colon \neg x \ \vee \ (\mathbf{A}y\colon\colon y))$$

=   {This is of the type "there is only one thing you can do."}

$$(\mathbf{E}x\colon\colon \neg x) \ \vee \ (\mathbf{E}x\colon\colon (\mathbf{A}y\colon\colon y))$$

= 　　{Not much can be done about the first disjunct. The second one is an existential quantification with a constant term that can be taken outside the quantification whenever we can write the term as a conjunction. The simplest possibility is ...}

$(\mathbf{E}x:: \neg x) \lor (\mathbf{E}x:: \text{true} \land (\mathbf{A}y:: y))$

= 　　{$\land$ distributes over $\mathbf{E}$.}

$(\mathbf{E}x:: \neg x) \lor ((\mathbf{E}x:: \text{true}) \land (\mathbf{A}y:: y))$

= 　　{The target expression has popped up. With the observation that $(\mathbf{E}x:: \neg x)$ and $(\mathbf{A}y:: y)$ are each other's negation, we can use the Rule of Complement: $[P \lor (Q \land \neg P) \equiv P \lor Q]$.}

$(\mathbf{E}x:: \neg x) \lor (\mathbf{E}x:: \text{true})$

= 　　{joining the terms}

$(\mathbf{E}x:: \neg x \lor \text{true})$

= 　　{simplification}

$(\mathbf{E}x:: \text{true})$. □

The above calculation takes less than a dozen very small steps, and each of the individual steps appeals to only one or two rewrite rules drawn from a very modestly sized repertoire of such rules. It is quite conceivable that with a different step here or there, or with a somewhat different repertoire, different calculations would emerge, a little bit longer or a little bit shorter. But that is not our point. More important is that without hesitation we could design a reasonably short and precise proof for such a (seemingly strange) theorem, and that at each step of the calculation we were almost always exclusively concerned with that particular step, almost opportunistically so. But it is precisely that continuing small scope of concern that makes calculational proofs so attractive, in the sense of doing justice to the limited scope of our minds. As for the potential opportunism, experience is creating more and more evidence that all the time it is the shape of the formulae and the manipulative possibilities at hand that chiefly dictate the next step.

However, we do not end without saying that if calculational techniques are to play a more important role in everyday mathematics, the arts of designing useful notations and of organizing calculations may require more of our attention.

2 *Gries's Saddleback Search*

David Gries's Saddleback Search is one of the nicest little programs that emerged during the 80's. In its most rudimentary form, the programming problem can be phrased as follows.

Given integer value F and integer function $f.(i, j : 0 \leq i \wedge 0 \leq j)$ satisfying

$$(\mathbf{E}\, i, j:\ 0 \leq i \wedge 0 \leq j:\ f.i.j = F)\ ;$$

function f is ascending in its first argument; i.e., for any p, q, and j within range we have

$$p \leq q\ \Rightarrow\ f.p.j \leq f.q.j\ ;\ \text{and}$$

function f is descending in its second argument; i.e., for any p, q, and i within range we have

$$p \leq q\ \Rightarrow\ f.i.p \geq f.i.q\ .$$

Now, we can define X and Y satisfying each of the conditions

$$0 \leq X \wedge 0 \leq Y\ ;\tag{0}$$

$$f.X.Y = F\ ;\tag{1}$$

$$(\mathbf{A}\, i, j:\ 0 \leq i \wedge 0 \leq j \wedge f.i.j = F:\ X \leq i \wedge Y \leq j)\ .\tag{2}$$

(We wish to delegate to the reader the task of constructing an argument why the above conditions define X and Y. In the combination of (1) and (2) the monotonicity properties of f do play a role.)

Program Saddleback Search has to establish, for integer variables x and y, relation

$$R:\ x = X \wedge y = Y\ .$$

We will develop a program by doing justice to each of the conditions (0), (1), and (2) one at a time.

Approximation 0   We can establish R without any reference to (0), (1), or (2) simply by the program

$$x, y := X, Y\ .$$

This would do it, if only we could compute X and Y analytically (as we could for $F = 3$ and $f = 3$). But since nothing specific is given about F or f, we will have to resort to a different algorithm.

Approximation 1   The next simplest algorithm that establishes R is

$\{(0)\}$

    $x, y := 0, 0$

$\{$invariant $P\}$

    ; **do** $x < X \rightarrow x := x + 1$

      $[\!]$ $y < Y \rightarrow y := y + 1$

    od

$\{R\}$.

Its repetition maintains

$$P:\ \ 0 \leq x \wedge x \leq X \wedge 0 \leq y \wedge y \leq Y,$$

and it terminates in precisely $X + Y$ steps. Property (0) is used and needed to establish P initially.

This would be it, if it were not for the occurrences in the program text of the unknown constants X and Y. But the situation is different from that in approximation 0, in that not X and Y but the guards $x < X$ and $y < Y$ have to be eliminated, which in general is less demanding.

Approximation 2   In eliminating these guards we have to bear in mind that strengthening them is harmless to termination and to the already established invariance of P. (Weakening them is not.) We also have to bear in mind that their strengthening should not be too vigorous, lest their negation become too weak to allow for any useful conclusion upon termination.

As for the elimination of guard $x < X$, we observe

    $x < X$

$\Leftarrow$ $\{f$ is ascending in its first argument$\}$

    $f.x.y < f.X.y$

$\Leftarrow$ $\{$heading for the use of (1)$\}$

    $f.x.y < f.X.Y \wedge f.X.Y \leq f.X.y$

$=$ $\{$the second conjunct is true: by invariant P we have $y \leq Y$, and by f's descendingness in the second argument we therefore have $f.X.Y \leq f.X.y\}$

    $f.x.y < f.X.Y$

$=$ $\{$using (1)$\}$

    $f.x.y < F$.

By symmetry, analogy, or what have you,

    $y < Y \Leftarrow f.x.y > F$.

With these strengthenings our program becomes

$$x, y := 0, 0$$
$$; \textbf{do } f.x.y < F \rightarrow x := x + 1$$
$$\quad \text{[]} \quad f.x.y > F \rightarrow y := y + 1$$
$$\textbf{od}$$
$$\{P \wedge f.x.y = F\}.$$

Regrettably, the postcondition no longer mentions R. But we haven't used property (2) about X and Y yet. Using it, R can still be concluded upon termination, as follows from

$$x = X \wedge y = Y$$
$$= \quad \{\text{from } P, x \leq X \wedge y \leq Y\}$$
$$X \leq x \wedge Y \leq y$$
$$\Leftarrow \quad \{\text{from (2) with the instantiation } i, j := x, y\}$$
$$0 \leq x \wedge 0 \leq y \wedge f.x.y = F$$
$$= \quad \{\text{by the actual postcondition}\}$$
$$\text{true .}$$

On many occasions when I had explained the foregoing derivation, I encountered people who would construct an example and then manually execute the program in order to find out how it would "really" work. On this occasion I cordially invite any reader who feels that temptation to resist it.

3 *The Safe Sluice and Peterson's Little Mutual Exclusion Algorithm*

In this section we study a very simple mutual exclusion algorithm for two programs, which is known as the Safe Sluice. The algorithm suffers from the danger of deadlock, but we ask the reader not to be bothered by this. Our purpose is to design a proof of the (partial) correctness of the algorithm, but subject to the condition that *nowhere* in our argument is a reference to a computational model allowed to occur, and *nowhere* an operational thought, not even a trace of one. The history of computing science has created abundant evidence that operational reasoning about multiprograms is far beyond what we can intellectually grasp. Hence this experiment, and hence such a small example as the Safe Sluice to start with.

The other reason why we have chosen the Safe Sluice is that from the design of our correctness proof emerges G. L. Peterson's mutual exclusion algorithm for two programs, which is an algorithm that no longer suffers from the dangers of deadlock or starvation. Furthermore, among such algorithms Peterson's is about the most succinct and beautiful one we can think of. Therefore it deserves our attention (and we think it ought to belong to the body of knowledge of any modern computing scientist).

In order to abandon operational thought, we had better use a formalism. For the sake of simplicity we propose to use the theory of Owicki and Gries, or a mild variation thereof. The theory deals with partial correctness only ("Safety Properties" in the jargon). We can explain the theory briefly as follows.

There is a system of sequential programs and we are allowed to place assertions in each of these programs. For each assertion we then have to prove that it holds both locally and globally. For an assertion to hold locally we have to prove that it is correct local to the program in which it occurs. Here we can use the proof techniques for sequential programs. For an assertion to be globally correct we have to prove that it is not falsified by any atomic statement from a different program of the system. (This implies that under all circumstances we have to make clear which statements are atomic.)

The Safe Sluice is as follows. Two programs p and q share two boolean variables, $x.p$ and $x.q$, which are false initially. Program p is a repetition of

> $x.p :=$ true
> ; **if** $\neg x.q \rightarrow$ skip **fi**
> $\{R.p.q\}$
> ; $CS.p$
> ; $x.p :=$ false .

Program q is Program p with p and q interchanged. Each line of code is an atomic statement. Statement **if** $B \rightarrow$ skip **fi** is a synonym of **do** $\neg B \rightarrow$ skip **od** .

We can appreciate the above algorithm as a correct mutual exclusion algorithm whenever R satisfies both (0) and (1), given by

$$R.p.q \wedge R.q.p \Rightarrow p = q , \tag{0}$$

the assertions R hold. $\tag{1}$

(This is one way of formally stating the mutual exclusion problem.) Now the design of a correctness proof for the Safe Sluice has been rephrased as the design of a predicate R satisfying requirements (0) and (1).

If it were only for requirement (0), false would do for R, but this choice would not agree with (1). If it were only for (1), true would do for R, but this would be no good for (0). So here is a dilemma.

Apology   The previous three sentences display in a nutshell the dilemmas and the problems called forth by not deriving multiprograms but giving a posteriori proofs instead. Had we derived the algorithm from scratch, (0) would have been our functional specification and the first thing we would do is to choose R so as to satisfy (0). With this choice for R we would have derived the program that would comply with requirement (1). And there would have been no dilemma. Here, where the program is given, we are not free to choose any R we like, but we have to resort to the program text first in order to make a first *guess* for what R might be. From a methodological point of view this is very unsatisfactory; hence the apology. Although for our current example it is easy to give a formal derivation, formally deriving multiprograms does not belong to the state of the art yet, though it may very well be in the air.

Our first approximation for $R.p.q$ is $x.p \wedge \neg x.q$. The choice is inspired by the requirement in (1) that assertion $R.p.q$ be correct locally to Program p. The choice is no good globally, however, because Program q falsifies the second conjunct by the assignment $x.q :=$ true (and in no other statement). Therefore we weaken that conjunct, and our next approximation for $R.p.q$ becomes

$$R.p.q :\ x.p \ \wedge \ (\neg x.q \ \vee \ H.p.q).$$

In order that this choice satisfy (1), we require that

$$x.q := \text{true}\quad \text{truthify}\quad H.p.q.\tag{2}$$

As for (0), we observe

$$R.p.q \ \wedge \ R.q.p$$

$=\quad$ {our choice for R}

$$x.p \ \wedge \ (\neg x.q \ \vee \ H.p.q) \ \wedge \ x.q \ \wedge \ (\neg x.p \ \vee \ H.q.p)$$

$=\quad$ {predicate calculus}

$$x.p \ \wedge \ x.q \ \wedge \ H.p.q \ \wedge \ H.q.p$$

$\Rightarrow\quad$ {on account of (3) below}

$$p = q \ ,$$

so that (0) is satisfied whenever we require H to satisfy

$$H.p.q \ \wedge \ H.q.p \ \Rightarrow \ p = q \ .\tag{3}$$

Now we have dispensed with requirements (0) and (1) about R, provided we adhere to requirements (2) and (3) about H. When comparing (0) and (3) though, it seems as if we have put the cart before the horse, but this is not the case: Whereas R is an assertion in the program, H is not, and therefore we are less restricted in dealing with H.

One of the simplest choices for H such that (3) is met definitely is

$$H.p.q :\ v = q \ ,$$

for a fresh variable v. With this choice we can satisfy (2) by replacing statement $x.q :=$ true with $x.q, v :=$ true, q .

This, as such, completes our correctness proof for the Safe Sluice. But there is a little bit more to it. Let us reconsider the program text and the assertion we derived. Program p is

$x.p, v := \text{true}, p$
$; \textbf{if} \; \neg x.q \rightarrow \text{skip} \; \textbf{fi}$
$\{x.p \wedge (\neg x.q \vee v = q)\}$
$; CS.p$
$; x.p := \text{false} .$

The assertion is not falsified by the other program, and it remains correct locally when we replace the guard $\neg x.q$ with the weaker $\neg x.q \vee v = q$. (For the sake of progress we should do so.) The price we pay for this replacement is that variable v flips from thought variable to genuine program variable, but by the investment we remove from the algorithm the dangers of deadlock and starvation (without proof here). In fact we have arrived at Peterson's Little Mutual Exclusion Algorithm.

Postscript   The transformation of the above program into one in which the atomic multiple assignment no longer occurs can be effected as follows. We introduce a fresh shared variable y that will take over the role of x. Because partial correctness is preserved by strengthening a guard, we require y to satisfy $\neg y \Rightarrow \neg x$ or —equivalently— $x \Rightarrow y$. This leaves us no choice for the relative order of the assignments $x := \text{true}$ and $y := \text{true}$. For Program p we obtain

$y.p := \text{true}$
$; x.p, v := \text{true}, p$
$; \textbf{if} \; \neg y.p \vee v = q \rightarrow \text{skip} \; \textbf{fi}$
$; CS.p$
$; y.p, x.p := \text{false}, \text{false} ,$

from which thought-variable x can now be removed.

4 A Mathematical Treatment of Peterson's General Mutual Exclusion Algorithm

From an engineering point of view, Peterson's general mutual exclusion algorithm is not too attractive. In the absence of any competition (jargon) it takes $O(N^2)$ memory accesses for a program to enter its critical section, in a system with N programs. Nevertheless, we were interested in the algorithm, albeit for different reasons.

Mutual exclusion algorithms, not excluding Peterson's, tend to come without proofs of correctness. At best, some sort of operational argument is provided. Understandable as this may be from a historical perspective, scientifically this state of affairs is very unsatisfactory. Peterson's general algorithm, in its capacity of being a generalization of the extremely elegant algorithm for two programs, thus presented itself as a serious candidate for being supplied with a formal proof of correctness. This was one of the reasons for our interest in the algorithm.

   Our other interest in the algorithm was directly related to our reinvestigation of the usefulness of the simplest formalism we knew of for proving the (partial) correctness of multiprograms, to wit, the theory of Owicki and Gries. So here, the potential simplicity of Peterson's algorithm offered a nice ground for our experiments in using the theory.

4.0   *Choosing a Strategy*

Peterson's algorithm manipulates a state space which is as large as the square of the number of programs in the system. One of the traps one can fall into when applying the Owicki-Gries theory is to introduce equally many predicates, or even more. The resulting formulae then will presumably display an overwhelming number of indices, many nested quantified expressions, and a multitude of absolutely irrelevant detail which has to be dragged along. A different possibility is to concentrate on the algorithm's global structure and formulate its relevant mathematical properties. In the subsequent analysis we follow this pattern and concentrate on the heart of the algorithm first.

4.1 *The Algorithm*

The heart of Peterson's algorithm can be characterized as follows. A system of programs cooperates via shared variables v and boolean function x. Initially,

$$(\mathbf{A}q:: \neg x.q) \wedge (\mathbf{E}q:: v = q)$$

(dummies range over program names). Program p is a repetition with body *prog.p*,

$$
\begin{aligned}
prog.p: \quad & x.p, v := \text{true}, p \\
& ; \textbf{if } v \neq p \vee (\mathbf{A}q: q \neq p: \neg x.q) \rightarrow \text{skip } \textbf{fi} \\
& ; section.p \\
& ; x.p := \text{false} .
\end{aligned}
$$

Each line of code is an atomic statement, and *section.p* is a skip for variables v and x.

   Now we use, for once and for all, an operational interpretation of the above program text so as to formalize what we want to prove about the algorithm. Given that an alternative construct is a conditional blocking mechanism and given the perfect symmetry of the programs, nothing can be of importance other than the number of programs engaged in their *prog* and the number of them that have passed the alternative construct. Therefore we introduce two fresh integer variables f and g to record these numbers. Initially,

$f = 0 \land g = 0$.

The programs are modified as follows:

prog.p :

$\{\neg x.p\}$ $f, x.p, v := f + 1, \text{true}, p$

$\quad\{g < f\}$; **if** $v \neq p \lor (\mathbf{A}q: q \neq p: \neg x.q) \rightarrow$ skip **fi**

$\quad\{g < f\}$; $g := g + 1$

$\{H.p\}$; *section.p*

$\{H.p\}$; $g, f, x.p := g - 1, f - 1, \text{false}$

$\{\neg x.p\}$.

Our goal is to express what these programs maintain of the new variables f and g. We have plugged in a number of assertions to be used below, but we address their correctness first. The assertions $g < f$ hold by the pattern of operations on f and g. (This is a little theorem from this field of programming which we mention without proof.) The assertions $\neg x.p$ pertain to a local variable of program p and are obviously valid. For the assertions $H.p$ we will have to make a choice. Inspired by the guard, we choose

$\quad v \neq p \lor (\mathbf{A}q: q \neq p: \neg x.q)$,

which is correct local to program p. However, one of the troubles with this choice is that now our assertions do not provide a link between the program's (f, g) coordinates and its (x, v) coordinates. The other trouble is that the choice yields a formula which is one order of magnitude more complicated than the formulae in the other assertions and thus threatens potential simplicity. Both the link and the simplification are provided by the obvious invariance of

$\quad f = (\mathbf{N}q:: x.q)$.

(This is another little theorem from the field which we mention without proof.) Using this invariant we can simplify our choice for $H.p$ by weakening its second disjunct to $f \leq 1$:

$\quad H.p: \quad v \neq p \lor f \leq 1$.

By the weakening, its local correctness remains guaranteed. As for its global correctness, decrements of f do not falsify it, and an increment of f in program $r, r \neq p$, is accompanied by $v := r$, which truthifies the first disjunct of $H.p$. So much for the assertions and their correctness.

4.2 *Proving that* P0 *is Maintained*

Now we are ready to design a proof of the theorem stating that this system of programs maintains relation *P*0, which is given by

$$PO: \quad g < f \vee f \le 1.$$

After we have done so we will show how PO is used in conducting our discussion of Peterson's mutual exclusion algorithm.

Proof From the assertions in the program text we conclude the invariance of

$$(\mathbf{A}p:: \neg x.p \vee g < f \vee H.p),$$

or —equivalently, by predicate calculus—

$$g < f \vee (\mathbf{A}p:: \neg x.p \vee H.p).$$

When we compare this with PO, it can hardly escape our attention that the simplest way to ensure the invariance of PO is then to insist on the invariance of

$$(\mathbf{A}p:: \neg x.p \vee H.p) \Rightarrow f \le 1. \tag{0}$$

So let us insist on it, for simplicity's sake.

   Now the only task left is to demonstrate the invariance of (0). In view of its complicated shape, the best thing we can do first is to try to simplify it. For its antecedent we have

$$(\mathbf{A}p:: \neg x.p \vee H.p)$$

=   {definition of $H.p$}

$$(\mathbf{A}p:: \neg x.p \vee v \ne p \vee f \le 1)$$

=   {predicate calculus, viz., trading}

$$(\mathbf{A}p: v = p: \neg x.p \vee f \le 1)$$

=   {predicate calculus, viz., the one-point rule}

$$\neg x.v \vee f \le 1.$$

Hence (0) can be rewritten as

$$\neg x.v \vee f \le 1 \Rightarrow f \le 1,$$

or —equivalently— as the still simpler

$$x.v \vee f \le 1. \tag{1}$$

Now (1) { $\equiv$ (0)} has a shape which is no longer amenable to manipulation. So now and only now the time has come to see whether we can prove the invariance of (1) using the program text.

   Initially (1) holds, because initially $f = 0$ holds. Increments of f can falsify (1)'s second disjunct, but they are accompanied by $x.p, v := \text{true}, p$, truthifying the first disjunct. Decrements of f do not falsify (1). The only critical statement left is $x.v := \text{false}$, in Program v. Its precondition implies $H.v$ {see the annotated program text} or, equivalently {see definition of $H.v$}, $f \leq 1$. Therefore we are done whenever we can show {see (1) and program text for *prog.v*}

$\{f \leq 1\}$

$g, f, x.v := g - 1, f - 1, \text{false}$

$\{x.v \lor f \leq 1\}$.

By the axiom of assignment this is as valid as $f \leq 1 \Rightarrow f \leq 2$.   □

Invariant *P0* describes what the system of programs maintains of the variables f and g. From now onward we had better forget about the implementational details with which *P0* is achieved. With $[f := f+1]$ as an ad hoc shorthand for the construction

$f, x.p, v := f + 1, \text{true}, p$

; **if** $v \neq p \lor (\mathbf{A} q: q \neq p: \neg x.q) \rightarrow \text{skip } \mathbf{fi}$,

and $[f := f - 1]$ for

$f, x.p := f - 1, \text{false}$,

we can summarize all the foregoing by saying that the system given by

Initially: $f = 0 \land g = 0$

prog.p : $[f := f + 1]$

              ; $g := g + 1$

              ; *section.p*

              ; $g := g - 1, [f := f - 1]$

maintains relations *P0* and *P1* given by

P0 : $g < f \lor f \leq 1$

P1 : $g \leq f \land 0 \leq g$

(*P1* on account of "the topology of the programs").

4.3 *Discussion*

Now we are ready to explain Peterson's algorithm. With the interpretation of f as the number of programs "heading for" their sections, and g as the number of programs "in" their sections, the validity of $g < f$ for $f \geq 2$, as expressed by *P0*, suggests that we repeat the trick we played on the (f, g) pair on the pair (g, h) : i.e., for a fresh variable h we replace the text fragment

$$g := g + 1; section.p; g := g - 1$$

with

$$[g := g + 1]$$
$$; h := h + 1$$
$$; section.p$$
$$; h := h - 1, [g := g - 1].$$

In fact we do repeat the trick, many times (as did Peterson). More precisely, we will introduce sequence $f.(i : 1 \leq i \leq N)$ of natural numbers and impose on it relations $Q0$ and $Q1$, given by

$Q0$: $(\mathbf{A}\, i\colon\; 1 < i \leq N\colon f.(i-1) < f.i \;\vee\; f.i \leq 1)$

$Q1$: $(\mathbf{A}\, i\colon\; 1 < i \leq N\colon f.(i-1) \leq f.i)$.

Then, with the interpretation of $f.N$ as the number of programs "heading for" their sections and $f.1$ as the number of programs "in" their sections, the theorem

R : $f.1 \leq 1 \;\vee\; f.N > N$

(to be shown below) tells us that the sections can be appreciated as critical sections whenever we can see to the falsity of R's second disjunct. This latter condition is fulfilled if, for instance, the number of programs in the system is at most N.

The validity of R follows from

$$f.1 > 1$$
$\Rightarrow$ {by $Q1$}
   $(\mathbf{A}\, i\colon\; 1 < i \leq N\colon f.i > 1) \;\wedge\; f.1 > 1$
$\Rightarrow$ {by $Q0$}
   $(\mathbf{A}\, i\colon\; 1 < i \leq N\colon f.(i-1) < f.i) \;\wedge\; f.1 > 1$
$\Rightarrow$ {f is a sequence of integers}
   $f.N > N$.

This completes our treatment of the algorithm.

4.4 *Concluding Remarks*

A few final remarks and observations are in order:

> Our discussion extended over two levels of concern. The interface between the levels is captured by the properties P. It is hard to envisage how the argument could be given without introducing such a separation of concerns.

The separation of concerns has worked out well by virtue of the simplicity of *P*.

At each level of concern we have played our game in essentially the same way. We have always used the predicate calculus as our main tool, mostly so as to mold expressions that would pop up into simpler ones.

It is a pleasure to use the Owicki–Gries theory after techniques of abstraction and the predicate calculus have done their simplifying work.

We could not have given the argument had we not disallowed ourselves any form of operational thinking.

We would have seriously hampered the construction of the argument had we not stuck to uninterpreted manipulation of formulae.

Our permanent desire to keep the formulae simple has been of heuristic importance.

We very much regret that we could not (yet) give a top-down development of the algorithm, since that would have made its treatment much simpler.

The backbone of our argument has been designed during a 17-minute car drive through a dark, rainy evening. Although we are in favor of postponing the use of pencil and paper as long as possible, we emphatically recommend other places for such exercises.

Acknowledgment

I am greatly indebted to the members of the Eindhoven Tuesday Afternoon Club, who over the past three and a half years {it is December 1987 as this is being written} have never stopped acting as a permanently present scientific forum.

Multiplication
and
Division
of
Polynomials

12

Martin Rem
Eindhoven University of Technology

---

1 Introduction

Multiplication and division of polynomials are computations that are often employed in such fields as coding theory and signal processing. We discuss the design of parallel programs for multiplying and dividing polynomials over $GF(2)$, i.e., polynomials of the form

$$q_0 X^{M-1} + q_1 X^{M-2} + \cdots + q_{M-2} X + q_{M-1},$$

where $q_i \in \{0, 1\}$. The formula above contains name X, which seems to be a parameter of it. The identity of X, however, is irrelevant: It is merely a way of coding the relative weights of the coefficients q_i. As an exercise in manipulating polynomials we shall, therefore, consider polynomials to be nonempty finite sequences. The elements of such sequences are indexed from 0 upward, and the length of sequence q is denoted by $l(q)$: For the polynomial above $l(q) = M$, its first element is $q(0)$, and its last one is $q(M-1)$.

Two remarks are in order: Why do we exclude the empty sequence, and what do we do with leading zeroes? In the next section we shall define the

159

product $q * r$ of sequences q and r. We want $l(q * r)$ to be a function of $l(q)$ and $l(r)$ only, and not of their elements. We shall define, as one would expect of polynomial multiplication, $l(q * r)$ to be equal to $l(q) + l(r) - 1$. But this is obviously impossible if $l(q) = 0$ and $l(r) = 0$. Hence our decision to allow nonempty sequences only.

Sequences q and q' with $l(q) \leq l(q')$ and

$$q'(i) = \begin{cases} 0 & \text{if } 0 \leq i < l(q') - l(q) \\ q(l(q) - l(q') + i) & \text{if } l(q') - l(q) \leq i < l(q') \end{cases}$$

are equivalent in the sense that they represent the same polynomial. We could choose one canonical sequence among the equivalent ones and adopt the rule to use canonical sequences only. A choice that observes our restriction $l(q) \geq 1$ would then be to require (canonical) sequences to have exactly one leading zero: $q(1) = 1$ if $l(q) \geq 2$ and $q(0) = 0$. But again, this would violate $l(q * r) = l(q) + l(r) - 1$: Multiplying a —or rather the— sequence of length 1 by any other sequence yields the former, irrespective of the length of the latter. Hence our decision to allow arbitrarily many leading zeroes.

2 *Multiplication*

The product of sequences p and q is sequence $p * q$, defined by

$$l(p * q) = l(p) + l(q) - 1$$

and, for $0 \leq i < l(p * q)$,

$$(p * q)(i) = (\mathbf{S} \, j, k \colon \, 0 \leq j < l(p) \wedge 0 \leq k < l(q) \wedge j + k = i \colon \, p(j) * q(k)) \tag{1}$$

where $\mathbf{S}$ denotes summation modulo 2.

We design a parallel program $MUL(q, N)$ that multiplies a given sequence q by a sequence of length N. Its input is the latter sequence, its output is a sequence of length $N + l(q) - 1$. The program establishes a relation between the input sequence and the output sequence. We call the input sequence a and the output sequence b; the program should establish the relation $a * q = b$. This is often called the *input/output* (or simply *i/o*) relation.

We are, however, aiming at a program text in which all communications of the individual elements of sequences are made explicit. Therefore, the specification of the program should also state the order in which the communications take place. We wish to perform each output communication as soon as all elements of sequence a on which its value depends have been received. According to (1), element $(a * q)(i)$ depends on values $a(j)$ for $0 \leq j \leq i$ (and, of course, $0 \leq j < N$). Consequently, for $0 \leq i < N$ element $b(i)$ is to be produced immediately after $a(i)$ has been received. The elements $b(i)$ for $N \leq i < N + l(q) - 1$ are produced after all elements of sequence a have been received. Thus, the order of communications of $MUL(q, N)$ is specified to be

$(a ; b)^N ; b^{l(q)-1}$

The expression above is often called the *communication behavior*. Notice that in this case the communication behavior is independent of the values communicated. Such computations are called *data independent* [5]. Data independence is typical for so-called systolic computations [3]. All computations in this paper are data independent.

We aim at CSP-like [2] programs. In such programs input communications are denoted by $a?x$, which results in assigning to variable x the value of the next element of sequence a. Output communications are denoted by $b!E$, which results in extending sequence b with the value of E. We call such programs *components*.

Let for $1 \le m \le l(q)$ sequence $q{\downarrow}m$ consist of the last m elements of q:

$l(q{\downarrow}m) = m$

and, for $0 \le i < m$,

$(q{\downarrow}m)(i) = q(l(q) - m + i)$.   (2)

We design components MUL$(q{\downarrow}m, N)$ for $1 \le m \le l(q)$. For $m = l(q)$ we then have MUL(q, N) , i.e., the one we are heading for. Component MUL$(q{\downarrow}m, N)$ is to have

$a * (q{\downarrow}m) = b$ (3)

as its i/o relation and

$(a; b)^N ; b^{m-1}$ (4)

as its communication behavior.

We have, for $0 \le i < N + m - 1$,

$b(i)$

$=$ $\{(3)\}$

$(a * (q{\downarrow}m))(i)$

$=$ $\{(1), l(a) = N, l(q{\downarrow}m) = m\}$

$(\mathbf{S}\, j, k:\ 0 \le j < N \wedge 0 \le k < m \wedge j + k = i:\ a(j) * (q{\downarrow}m)(k))$

$=$ $\{(2)\}$

$(\mathbf{S}\, j, k:\ 0 \le j < N \wedge 0 \le k < m \wedge j + k = i:\ a(j) * q(l(q) - m + k))$.   (5)

We first consider the case $m = 1$. We derive, for $0 \le i < N$,

$b(i)$

$=$ $\{(5), m = 1\}$

$(\mathbf{S}\, j:\ 0 \le j < N \wedge j = i:\ a(j) * q(l(q) - 1))$

$=$ $\{0 \le i < N,\ \text{calc.}\}$

$a(i) * q(l(q) - 1)$.

Observing communication behavior (4), we find for $m = 1$ the following component:

com $\text{MUL}(q{\downarrow}1, N)(a?\{0, 1\}, b!\{0, 1\})$:

$\|[x : \{0, 1\}; (a?x ; b!(x * q(l(q) - 1)))^N]\|$

moc .

After the name, $\text{MUL}(q{\downarrow}1, N)$, of the component we list the names of the input and output sequences, each postfixed by its direction (? or !) and its type. (The type of a sequence is the type of its elements.) The block, delineated by $\|[$ and $]\|$, contains a declaration of variable x and a repetition that is executed N times. As expected, the component depends on $q(l(q) - 1)$, the last element of sequence q.

Next we turn to the design of $\text{MUL}(q{\downarrow}m, N)$ for $2 \leq m \leq l(q)$. According to (5), we have

$$b(0) = a(0) * q(l(q) - m) . \tag{6}$$

To compute $b(i)$ for $1 \leq i < N + m - 1$ we employ a subcomponent p of type $\text{MUL}(q{\downarrow}(m - 1), N)$. We denote the input and output sequences of p by $p.a$ and $p.b$, respectively. Hence, p has i/o relation

$$p.a. * q{\downarrow}(m - 1) = p.b \tag{7}$$

and communication behavior

$$(p.a ; p.b)^N ; p.b^{m-2} \tag{8}$$

Sequence a is input to p; i.e., $p.a. = a$. Then, for $1 \leq i < N + m - 1$, we have

$b(i)$

$=$ $\{(5)\}$

$(\mathbf{S}\, j, k:\ 0 \leq j < N \wedge 0 \leq k < m \wedge j + k = i: a(j) * q(l(q) - m + k))$

$=$ $\{\text{separate } k = 0, \text{ calc.}\}$

$(\mathbf{S}\, j, k:\ 0 \leq j < N \wedge 0 \leq k < m - 1 \wedge j + k = i - 1$
$\qquad : a(j) * q(l(q) - m + 1 + k))$
$\oplus (\mathbf{S}\, j:\ 0 \leq j < N \wedge j = i:\ a(j) * q(l(q) - m))$

$=$ $\{(5)\}$

$(a * q{\downarrow}(m - 1))(i - 1) \oplus (\mathbf{S}\, j:\ 0 \leq j < N \wedge j = i:\ a(j) * q(l(q) - m))$

$=$ $\{(7), p.a = a\}$

$$p.b(i - 1) \oplus \begin{cases} a(i) * q(l(q) - m)) & \text{if } 1 \leq i < N \\ 0 & \text{if } N \leq i < N + m - 1 \end{cases} \tag{9}$$

where ⊕ denotes addition modulo 2.

Equations (6) and (9) show how sequence b can be computed. We merge communication behaviors (4) and (8) into

> $a\,;\,p.a,b$
>
> $;\ (a,\ p.b\,;\ p.a,b)^{N-1}$
>
> $;\ (p.b\,;\ b)^{m-1}\,.$

(The comma expresses no order and takes priority over the semicolon.) Then $b(i)$ aways depends on the values last received from environment and sub-component. For $2 \le m \le l(q)$ we propose as our solution:

> **com** $MUL(q{\downarrow}m, N)(a?\{0, 1\}, b!\{0, 1\})$:
>
> **sub** p : $MUL(q{\downarrow}(m-1), N)$ **bus**
>
> $|[\quad x, y : int;$
>
> $\qquad a?x\,;\ p.a!x, b!(x * q(l(q) - m))$
>
> $;\quad (a?x, p.b?y\,;\ p.a!x, b!(y \oplus x * q(l(q) - m)))^{N-1}$
>
> $;\quad (p.b?y\,;\ b!y)^{m-1}$
>
> $]|$

moc .

3 *Division*

Dividing sequence p by sequence q yields two sequences: the quotient p/q of length $l(p) - l(q) + 1$, and the remainder $p//q$ of length $l(q) - 1$. In order to have these two sequences be nonempty, we require $2 \le l(q) \le l(p)$. We also require $q(0) = 1$. Then, with an appropriate definition for addition of sequences, the equation

$$p = (p/q) * q + p//q \tag{10}$$

has exactly one solution for p/q and $p//q$. We adopt (10), together with

> $l(p/q)\ = l(p) - l(q) + 1$
>
> $l(p//q) = l(q) - 1$

as the definition for division.

We define $p + q$ for the case $l(p) \ge l(q)$ only. This slightly simplifies its definition and suffices for the addition in (10):

> $l(p + q) = l(p)$

and

$$(p+q)(i)$$

$$= \ p(i) \oplus \begin{cases} 0 & \text{if } 0 \le i < l(p)-l(q) \\ q(l(q)-l(p)+i) & \text{if } l(p)-l(q) \le i < l(p). \end{cases} \tag{11}$$

We design component DIV (q,N) with input a, $l(a) = N$, and outputs b and c. It establishes i/o relation

$$a/q = b \tag{12}$$

$$a//q = c. \tag{13}$$

Sequence q satisfies $2 \le l(q) \le N$ and $q(0) = 1$.
We have, for $0 \le i < N$,

$$a(i)$$

$$= \quad \{(10)\}$$

$$((a/q) * q + a//q)(i)$$

$$= \quad \{(11), l((a/q) * q) = N, l(a//q) = l(q)-1\}$$

$$((a/q) * q)(i) \oplus \begin{cases} 0 & \text{if } 0 \le i < N-l(q)+1 \\ (a//q)(l(q)-1-N+i) & \text{if } N-l(q)+1 \le i < N. \end{cases} \tag{14}$$

Output $b(0)$ is relatively easy to compute:

$$a(0)$$

$$= \quad \{(14)\}$$

$$((a/q) * q)(0)$$

$$= \quad \{(1)\}$$

$$(a/q)(0) * q(0)$$

$$= \quad \{q(0) = 1, (12)\}$$

$$b(0).$$

To determine how to compute $b(i)$ for $1 \le i < N-l(q)+1$, we consider sequence $(a/q) * q'$, where $q' = q{\downarrow}(l(q)-1)$. For $1 \le i < N$ we have

$$((a/q) * q')(i-1)$$

$$= \quad \{(1), l(a/q) = N-l(q)+1, l(q') = l(q)-1\}$$

$$(\mathbf{S}\, j,k\colon 0 \le j < N-l(q)+1 \wedge 0 \le k < l(q)-1 \wedge j+k = i-1$$
$$: (a/q)(j) * q'(k))$$

$$= \quad \{q'(k) = q(k+1), \text{calc.}\}$$

$$(\mathbf{S}\, j,k\colon 0 \le j < N-l(q)+1 \wedge 1 \le k < l(q) \wedge j+k = i$$
$$: (a/q)(j) * q(k))$$

$=$ $\{(1)\}$

$((a/q) * q)(i) \oplus (\mathbf{S}\, j\colon\, 0 \leq j < N - l(q) + 1 \wedge j = i\colon (a/q)(j) * q(0))$

$=$ $\{q(0) = 1, \text{calc.}\}$

$((a/q) * q)(i) \oplus \begin{cases} (a/q)(i) & \text{if } 1 \leq i < N - l(q) + 1 \\ 0 & \text{if } N - l(q) + 1 \leq i < N \end{cases}$

$=$ $\{(14)\}$

$$a(i) \oplus \begin{cases} (a/q)(i) & \text{if } 1 \leq i < N - l(q) + 1 \\ (a/\!/q)(l(q) - 1 - N + i) & \text{if } N - l(q) + 1 \leq i < N. \end{cases} \qquad (15)$$

Hence, for $1 \leq i < N - l(q) + 1$,

$b(i)$

$=$ $\{(12)\}$

$(a/q)(i)$

$=$ $\{(15)\}$

$a(i) \oplus ((a/q) * q')(i - 1)$ (16)

and, for $0 \leq i < l(q) - 1$,

$c(i)$

$=$ $\{(13)\}$

$(a/\!/q)(i)$

$=$ $\{(15)\}$

$a(N - l(q) + 1 + i) \oplus ((a/q) * q')(N - l(q) + i) .$ (17)

In view of (16) and (17), we employ a subcomponent p of type MUL($q', N - l(q) + 1$) to compute $(a/q) * q'$. Hence, we feed a/q to p:

$p.a = a/q .$

Then

$p.b = (a/q) * q' .$

We now have

$b(0) = a(0) ,$

and for $1 \leq i < N - l(q) + 1$, by (16),

$b(i) = a(i) \oplus p.b(i - 1) ,$

and for $0 \leq i < l(q) - 1$, by (17),

$$c(i) = a(N - l(q) + 1 + i) \oplus p.b(N - l(q) + i).$$

According to (4), subcomponent p has communication behavior

$$(p.a \; ; \; p.b)^{N-l(q)+1} \; ; \; p.b^{l(q)-2}. \tag{18}$$

We propose

$$(a \; ; \; b)^{N-l(q)+1} \; ; \; (a \; ; \; c)^{l(q)-1} \tag{19}$$

as the communication behavior of component $\text{DIV}(q, N)$. Then again, just as for the component MUL, the output values are produced as soon as the elements of sequence a on which they depend have been received. By merging behaviors (18) and (19) into

$$a \; ; \; p.a, b$$

$$; \; (a, p.b \; ; \; p.a, b)^{N-l(q)}$$

$$; \; (a, p.b \; ; \; c)^{l(q)-1},$$

output values $b(i)$ and $c(i)$ depend only on the values last received from environment and subcomponent. The coding of our solution is now straightforward:

com $\text{DIV}(q, N)(a?\{0, 1\}, b!\{0, 1\}, c!\{0, 1\})$:

       sub p: $\text{MUL}(q \downarrow (l(q) - 1), N - l(q) + 1)$ **bus**

       $|[x, y: int;$

          $a?x \; ; \; p.a!x, b!x$

       $; \; (a?x, p.b?y \; ; \; p.a!(x \oplus y), b!(x \oplus y))^{N-l(q)}$

       $; \; (a?x, p.b?y \; ; \; c!(x \oplus y))^{l(q)-1}$

       $]|$

  moc .

4 Cyclic Encoding

Let sequence a, with $1 \leq l(a) = N$, be a message to be encoded using a cyclic code of which sequence q, with $l(q) \geq 2$ and $q(0) = 1$, represents the generator polynomial. According to standard coding theory [1], the encoded message is sequence $(a'/q) * q$, where a' is sequence a followed by $l(q) - 1$ zeroes. The encoded message is, consequently, a multiple of q.

We design a component $\text{CYC}(q, N)$ with input a and output b. The component should establish

$$(a'/q) * q = b, \tag{20}$$

where

$$l(a') = N + l(q) - 1$$

and

$$a'(i) = \begin{cases} a(i) & \text{if } 0 \le i < N \\ 0 & \text{if } N \le i < N + l(q) - 1 \,. \end{cases} \tag{21}$$

We derive, for $0 \le i < N + l(q) - 1$,

$$b(i)$$

$$= \quad \{(20)\}$$

$$((a'/q) * q)(i)$$

$$= \quad \{(14), l(a') = N + l(q) - 1\}$$

$$a'(i) \oplus \begin{cases} 0 & \text{if } 0 \le i < N \\ (a'//q)(i - N) & \text{if } N \le i < N + l(q) - 1 \end{cases}$$

$$= \quad \{(21)\}$$

$$\begin{cases} a(i) & \text{if } 0 \le i < N \\ (a'//q)(i - N) & \text{if } N \le i < N + l(q) - 1 \,. \end{cases} \tag{22}$$

Hence, b consists of the message a followed by sequence $a'//q$. The latter forms a sequence of $l(q) - 1$ "check bits". As one would expect, component $CYC(q, N)$ will have communication behavior

$$(a \,;\, b)^N \,;\, b^{l(q)-1} \,.$$

Component $CYC(q, N)$ differs in two respects from $DIV(q, N)$. First, subcomponent p should compute $a'//q$ rather than $a//q$, and is therefore of type $MUL(q \downarrow (l(q) - 1), N)$. Second, its output sequence should, according to (22), satisfy

$$b(i) = \begin{cases} a(i) & \text{if } 0 \le i < N \\ p.b(N - 1 + i) & \text{if } N \le i < N + l(q) - 1 \,. \end{cases}$$

We thus arrive at the following solution:

com $CYC(q, N)(a?\{0, 1\}, b!\{0, 1\})$:

sub p: $MUL(q\!\downarrow\!(l(q) - 1, N)$ **bus**

$|[x, y: int;$

     $a?x$; $p.a!x, b!x$

   ; $(a?x, p.b?y$; $p.a!(x \oplus y), b!x)^{N-1}$

   ; $(p.b?y$; $b!y)^{l(q)-1}$

   $]|$

moc .

5 *Conclusion*

We have designed parallel programs for multiplication and division of polynomials and for the related problem of cyclic encoding. We constructed them by first giving a functional specification of their relation between input and output sequences. Since we are interested in detailing the programs to the level of individual communications, we next chose an appropriate order for the input and output communications and for the communications with the subcomponent. The orders we chose were appropriate in two respects: They were compatible with the order in which the subcomponent performs its communications, and they were chosen such that each value computed depends on the last values received only.

The fact that the programs express the individual communications allows a detailed study of their dynamic behavior. We have not done so in this paper, but two remarks are in order. First, the programs have *constant response time* [5] in the sense that the communications can be scheduled in such a fashion that the period between two successive outputs is constant and thus independent of, for example, $l(q)$ or N. Second, each output is produced immediately after all inputs on which it depends have been received. In component DIV, for example, the bits of a/q and $a//q$ are produced while a is being input, and the last bit of $a//q$ is output immediately after the last bit of a has been received.

The reader will not find it difficult to generalize our solutions in such a way that they do not terminate and process one sequence after another. This leads to programs similar to those presented in [5].

The type of programs we have designed lend themselves very well to silicon compilation. Alain J. Martin shows in [4] how such programs with explicit communications can be converted into delay-insensitive VLSI circuits.

Acknowledgments

California Institute of Technology is acknowledged for giving me the opportunity to prepare this paper during my visit of the winter of 1987–88.

The research reported in this paper was in part sponsored by the Defense Advanced Research Projects Agency, DARPA order number 6202, and monitored by the Office of Naval Research under contract number N00014-87-K-0745.

References

[1] Berlekamp, E. R. *Algebraic Coding Theory*. McGraw-Hill, New York, 1968.

[2] Hoare, C. A. R. "Communicating sequential processes". *Comm. ACM 21* (1978), pp. 666–677.

[3] Kung, H. T. "Let's design algorithms for VLSI systems". Proceedings 1st Caltech Conference on VLSI, C. L. Seitz, ed., pp. 65–90. California Institute of Technology, Pasadena, 1979.

[4] Martin, A. J. "Compiling communicating processes into delay-insensitive VLSI circuits". *Distributed Computing 1* (1986), pp. 226–234.

[5] Rem, M. "Trace theory and systolic computations". *PARLE: Parallel Architectures and Languages Europe* (Vol. 1), J. W. de Bakker, A. J. Nijman, and P. C. Treleaven, eds., pp. 14–33. Lecture Notes in Computer Science, vol. 258. Springer-Verlag, Berlin, 1987.

A Parallel Program that Generates the Möbius Sequence

13

Tom Verhoeff
Martin Rem
Eindhoven University of Technology

0 *Introduction*

We start by defining the Möbius sequence and specifying, in the style of [1], a computation that generates this sequence. In the major section of this paper we derive a parallel program from that specification. We analyze the response time of the resulting program. We also indicate how the program can be generalized to generate other sequences. Finally, we summarize the design techniques that were applied.

For integer n, $n \geq 1$, let $\pi(n)$ denote the number of (distinct) prime divisors of n. Since 1 is not considered prime, we have $\pi(1) = 0$. For $n \geq 2$ we have $\pi(n) \geq 1$; for example, $\pi(2) = 1$, $\pi(4) = 1$, and $\pi(6) = 2$. The *Möbius function* μ is defined for positive integers by

$$\mu(n) = \begin{cases} 0 & \text{if } (\mathbf{E}\, m : m > 1 : m^2 \mid n) \\ (-1)^{\pi(n)} & \text{otherwise,} \end{cases}$$

where $m^2 \mid n$ means "m^2 is a positive divisor of n". For instance, we have

$\mu(1) = 1$, $\mu(2) = -1$, $\mu(4) = 0$, and $\mu(6) = 1$. The sequence $\mu(n : n \geq 1)$ is called the *Möbius sequence*.

We now give a specification for a program that generates the Möbius sequence. In the next section we shall derive a parallel program satisfying this specification.

The program *MobSeq* has one *external communication port*: an integer *output* port *b*. The *communication behavior* of the program *MobSeq* is specified by the regular expression

b^*.

That is, an unbounded sequence of communications along port *b* is possible. The value of the *i*th communication ($i \geq 0$) along port *b* is denoted by $b(i)$. The *input/output* (or i/o) *relation* of the program *MobSeq* is specified by the equation

$b(i) = \mu(i + 1)$ for $i \geq 0$.

The following trivial "solution" gives an idea of what our program texts look like:

```
com  TrivMobSeq(b !int) :
       |[x : int;
         x := 1 ; (b !μ(x) ; x := x + 1)*
       ]|
moc .
```

We aim at a program that has *constant response time* under the assumption that integer addition and comparison are unit-time operations. Roughly speaking, this means that there is a fixed amount of time between successive external communications. The amount of computation required to determine $\mu(n)$, however, increases with *n*. Our program, therefore, will activate more and more processes and distribute the computation among them. Constant response time is achieved because the processes work harmoniously in parallel. This cooperation resembles that of a *systolic array*.

1 Derivation

In this section we derive a parallel program from the above specification. The derivation goes through a number of refinement steps that isolate design decisions. In the concluding section we summarize, in more general terms, the design techniques that we applied. We start our derivation by recalling from number theory that for $n \geq 1$,

$(\mathbf{S}d : d \mid n : \mu(d)) = U(n)$,

where $U(1) = 1$ and $U(n) = 0$ for $n > 1$ (see Appendix for a proof). Since $n \mid n$, we now can write a recurrent relation for μ:

$$\mu(n) = U(n) - (\mathbf{S}d : d < n \wedge d \mid n : \mu(d)) .$$

Computing $U(n)$ is simple; it will be done in a subprocess, which is designed at the end of this section. The computation of the quantified sum is delegated to another subprocess, which will be our main concern in the rest of the derivation. Aiming at a program with constant response time, this subprocess should not do the entire summation sequentially, since the domain of the quantified sum increases with n. Therefore, we introduce a sequence of processes M_j, $j \geq 1$, where M_j has a subprocess of type M_{j+1}. We still have the freedom to specify processes M_j. For that purpose we generalize the quantified sum by replacing the first occurrence of the variable n by a new variable m:

$$G(m, n) = (\mathbf{S}d : d < m \wedge d \mid n : \mu(d)) \qquad \text{for } 1 \leq m \leq n .$$

Hence we have

$$\mu(n) = U(n) - G(n, n) \qquad \text{for } n \geq 1 ,$$
$$G(1, n) = 0 \qquad \text{for } n \geq 1 ,$$

and

$$G(m + 1, n) = G(m, n) + \textbf{if } m \mid n \textbf{ then } \mu(m) \textbf{ else } 0 \textbf{ fi} \qquad \text{for } 1 \leq m < n .$$

Process M_j, $j \geq 1$, is specified as follows. M_j has two external communication ports: an integer output port c and an integer input port d. Its communication behavior is

$$(c ; d)^* ,$$

that is, communications along ports c and d alternate, starting along c. The i/o relation for M_j is (for $i \geq 0$)

$$c(i) = G(i + 1, i + j)$$
$$d(i) = \mu(i + 1) .$$

When fed with the values of μ, process M_j will produce the indicated partial sums; M_1 produces the desired values $G(n, n)$ for $n \geq 1$.

We shall now derive the program for M_j, $j \geq 1$. Let p be its subprocess of type M_{j+1}. M_j has two *internal* communication ports to its subprocess p: one input port and one output port, denoted by $p.c$ and $p.d$, respectively. This means that values coming from $p.c$ can be used, but also that the proper values for $p.d$ must be supplied—all in accordance with p's specification, of course. We first deal with the external output c, distinguishing the first and succeeding occurrences:

$c(0)$

$=$ {i/o relation of M_j}

$G(1, j)$

$=$ {property of G}

$0\,,$

and for $i \geq 1$,

$c(i)$

$=$ {i/o relation of M_j}

$G(i+1,\ i+j)$

$=$ {property of G}

$G(i,\ i+j) +$ **if** $i\,|\,(i+j)$ **then** $\mu(i)$ **else** 0 **fi**

$=$ {property of divisibility and i/o relation of M_j}

$G(i,\ i+j) +$ **if** $i\,|\,j$ **then** $d(i-1)$ **else** 0 **fi**

$=$ {$p.c$ satisfies i/o relation of M_{j+1}; hence $p.c(i) =$ $G(i+1,\ i+j+1)$}

$p.c(i-1) +$ **if** $i\,|\,j$ **then** $d(i-1)$ **else** 0 **fi** .

For the internal output $p.d$ we have (for $i \geq 0$):

$p.d(i)$

$=$ {$p.d$ satisfies i/o relation of M_{j+1}}

$\mu(i+1)$

$=$ {i/o relation of M_j}

$d(i)$.

Summarizing these results we now have

$c(0) = 0$

$c(i) = p.c(i-1) +$ **if** $i\,|\,j$ **then** $d(i-1)$ **else** 0 **fi**   for $i \geq 1$

and

$p.d(i) = d(i)$ for $i \geq 0$.

Taking into account the desired communication behaviors of M_j and p, we thus get as program text for M_j:

com $M_j(c!int, d?int)$:

    sub $p : M_{j+1}$ **bus**

    $\|[i, x, y : int;$

      $i := 0 ; c!0$

     ; $(d?x ; p.c?y$

       $; p.d!x; \; i := i + 1; \; c!$**if** $i | j$ **then** $y + x$ **else** y **fi**

      $)^*$

    $]\|$

moc .

Restricted to ports c and d, this program exhibits the communication behavior required of M_j; restricted to ports $p.c$ and $p.d$, it adheres to the communication behavior of M_{j+1}. Notice that the communication actions in the program are ordered more restrictively than necessary: For example, $d\,?x$ and $p.c\,?y$ could be done concurrently without violating any of the specifications.

There are, however, two problems with the above program for M_j. For one thing the computation refers to j, and therefore the program is not a recursive program in the usual sense. This could be remedied by distributing the value of j as part of the computation (add local variable j, j: int, and initial communications $d\,?j ; p.d\,!(j + 1)$; of course, this derives from a properly changed specification for M_j). But this phenomenon also disappears when dealing with the second problem.

The second problem is that computing $i | j$ is not a unit-time operation. Defining a **mod** b by

$$(\mathbf{E}\,q :: a = qb + a \textbf{ mod } b) \wedge 0 \leq a \textbf{ mod } b < b,$$

we observe that

$$i | j \equiv j \textbf{ mod } i = 0.$$

Subprocess M_{j+1} of M_j is therefore interested in $(j + 1)$ **mod** i, which is easily computed from j **mod** i and i. Working with the less obvious but as useful value of $(-j)$ **mod** i turns out to give a slightly more compact program. Hence we introduce another external input port e (and internal output port $p.e$) to distribute the values of $(-j)$ **mod** i. Furthermore, to eliminate the local computation for variable i we introduce external input port f that distributes i.

The adapted specification for M_j is as follows. M_j, $j \geq 1$, has four external communication ports: integer output port c and integer input ports d, e, and f. Its communication behavior is given by the extended regular expression

$$(c ; d, e, f)^* ,$$

where the comma indicates arbitrary interleaving of the communications along ports d, e, and f (expressing the possibility of concurrency). The i/o relation is given by the equations

$$c(i) = G(i+1,\ i+j)$$
$$d(i) = \mu(i+1)$$
$$e(i) = (-j) \bmod (i+1)$$
$$f(i) = i+1$$

for $i \geq 0$. We can now refine the previous program for M_j. Regarding the external output c we have, for $i \geq 1$,

$\quad c(i)$

$=$ {see above derivation}

$\quad p.c(i-1) +$ **if** $i \mid j$ **then** $d(i-1)$ **else** 0 **fi**

$=$ {property of divisibility}

$\quad p.c(i-1) +$ **if** $(-j) \bmod i = 0$ **then** $d(i-1)$ **else** 0 **fi**

$=$ {i/o relation of M_j}

$\quad p.c(i-1) +$ **if** $e(i-1) = 0$ **then** $d(i-1)$ **else** 0 **fi** .

The internal output $p.d$ is computed as before. For the new internal output $p.e$ we derive, for $i \geq 0$,

$\quad p.e(i)$

$=$ {$p.e$ satisfies i/o relation of M_{j+1}}

$\quad (-j-1) \bmod (i+1)$

$=$ {property of **mod**}

$\quad$ **if** $(-j) \bmod (i+1) = 0$ **then** i **else** $(-j) \bmod (i+1) - 1$ **fi**

$=$ {i/o relation of M_j}

$\quad$ **if** $e(i) = 0$ **then** $f(i) - 1$ **else** $e(i) - 1$ **fi**

$=$ {distribution}

$\quad$ **if** $e(i) = 0$ **then** $f(i)$ **else** $e(i)$ **fi** $- 1$.

For the new internal ouput $p.f$ we derive, for $i \geq 0$,

$\quad p.f(i)$

$=$ {$p.f$ satisfies i/o relation of M_{j+1}}

$\quad i+1$

$=$ {i/o relation of M_j}

$\quad f(i)$.

Summarizing these results we now have, for $i \geq 0$,

$$c(0) \quad = 0$$
$$c(i+1) = p.c(i) + \textbf{if } e(i) = 0 \textbf{ then } d(i) \textbf{ else } 0 \textbf{ fi}$$

and

$$p.d(i) = d(i)$$
$$p.e(i) = \textbf{if } e(i) = 0 \textbf{ then } f(i) \textbf{ else } e(i) \textbf{ fi} - 1$$
$$p.f(i) = f(i) .$$

Taking into account the communication behaviors of M_j and p, we thus get, as program text for M_j,

```
com Mⱼ(c!int, d?int, e?int, f?int) :
        sub p : Mⱼ₊₁ bus
        |[w, x, y, z : int;
          c!0
        ; (d?w, e?x, f?y, p.c?z
          ; if x = 0 then x, z := y, z + w fi
          ; p.d!w, p.e!(x − 1), p.f!y, c!z
          )*
        ]|
moc .
```

The above program for M_j has as primitive operations only communication actions and integer comparison, addition, and subtraction. Notice also that the computation of M_j no longer refers to j. Hence the indices can be omitted (from M) and we have an ordinary recursive program. This program, therefore, satisfies for all $j \geq 1$ the specification of M_j (which does contain j). We are only interested in M_1, but to realize that specification we introduced the others.

Let us now deal with the simpler subprocess *USeq* of *MobSeq* that computes $U(n)$. We work from the following specification for *USeq*. *USeq* has one external integer output port a, communication behavior a^*, and i/o relation $a(i) = U(i + 1)$ for $i \geq 0$. The program then directly derives from the definition of U:

```
com USeq(a !int) : a !1 ; (a !0)* moc .
```

The program for *MobSeq* is now a matter of combining *USeq* and M_1. Let q be the subprocess of type *USeq*, and let r be the subprocess of type M_1. *MobSeq* must supply r with the proper input values in order to have it produce sequence $G(n, n)$. Denoting the internal output ports to r by $r.d$, $r.e$, and $r.f$, the obligation of *MobSeq* is obtained by instantiating the corresponding i/o relations of M_j with $j = 1$. For $i \geq 0$ this yields

$$r.d(i) = \mu(i+1)$$
$$r.e(i) = (-1) \bmod (i+1) = \{\text{property of } \mathbf{mod}\}\, i$$
$$r.f(i) = i+1 .$$

For *MobSeq*'s external output b we have for $i \geq 0$:

$$b(i) = \mu(i+1) = U(i+1) - G(i+1, i+1) = q.a(i) - r.c(i) .$$

Combining this knowledge with the required communication behaviors gives rise to the following program text for *MobSeq*:

```
com  MobSeq(b!int) :
     sub q : USeq, r : M₁ bus
     |[x, y, z : int;  x := 0
     ; (q.a?y, r.c?z ;  y := y − z
       ; b!y, r.d!y, r.e!x, r.f!(x + 1) ;  x := x + 1
       )*
     ]|
moc .
```

2 *Response Time*

The response time of the program for *MobSeq* is critically dependent only on the response time of the program for M_1. We analyze the response time of M_1 by giving a *sequence function* σ_j for M_j that indicates at what moments the communications could be scheduled, taking into account the ordering imposed by the program. The ith communication along port c of M_j is scheduled at "time" $\sigma_j(c, i)$.

Since the communications along ports d, e, and f can all take place "at the same time", due to concurrency, we consider only ports c, d, $p.c$, and $p.d$. For these ports the program of M_j imposes the ordering expressed by

$$c ; (d, p.c ; p.d, c)^* .$$

We therefore suggest the sequence function defined, for $j \geq 1$ and $i \geq 0$, by

$$\sigma_j(c, 0) = j - 1$$
$$\sigma_j(d, i) = \sigma_j(p.c, i) = 2i + j$$
$$\sigma_j(p.d, i) = \sigma_j(c, i+1) = 2i + j + 1 .$$

Because the communication actions along port $p.c$ of M_j coincide with those along port c of M_{j+1} , they must have been scheduled at the same time by σ (and similarly for ports $p.d$ and d). Thus we need to verify

$$\sigma_j(p.c, i) = 2i + j = \sigma_{j+1}(c, i)$$

and

$$\sigma_j(p.d, i) = 2i + j + 1 = \sigma_{j+1}(d, i)$$

in order for σ to be an admissible sequence function.

From this sequence function we can derive that M_1 produces $G(i + 1, i + 1)$ at moment $\sigma_1(c, i) = 2i$. Hence the interval between external outputs is constant, that is, M_1 has constant response time. Furthermore, we see that M_j is activated at moment $\sigma_j(c, 0) = j - 1$. Solving $2i = j - 1$ for j tells us that $2i + 1$ subprocesses have been activated when M_1 does its ith external output.

We should point out, however, that such a sequence function places only an upper bound on the response time complexity of the parallel program.

3 *Generalization*

Integer functions on the positive integers are *arithmetical functions*. The Möbius function is an example. For an introduction to the theory of arithmetical functions consult [2]. We treat only a very small part of it in this section.

The *(Dirichlet) convolution* of arithmetical functions f and g is defined by

$$(f^*g)(n) = (\mathbf{S}k, m : km = n : f(k)g(m)) \qquad \text{for } n \geq 1.$$

The result is again an arithmetical function. Convolving is associative and symmetric. The function U, defined at the beginning of Section 1, is the unit: $f^*U = f$.

If we define the arithmetical function E by $E(n) = 1$ for $n \geq 1$, then the Theorem of the Appendix can be succinctly expressed as $\mu^*E = U$; that is, μ and E are each other's inverse under convolution. The derivation in Section 1 shows how to solve μ from $\mu^*E = U$. It would equally apply to the problem of solving g from the equation $g^*E = f$ for arbitrary given arithmetical function f. Since the solution of this equation is $f^*\mu$ (convolve both sides with $E^{-1} = \mu$), we have a way of computing $f^*\mu$. For example, the *Euler* function ϕ satisfies the equation $\phi^*E = I$, where I is defined by $I(n) = n$ for $n \geq 1$.

A generalized specification for program *ConvMob* could be: integer input port a and integer output port b, communication behavior $(a \; ; b)^*$, and i/o relation $(i \geq 0)$:

$$a(i) = f(i + 1)$$
$$b(i) = (f^*\mu)(i + 1).$$

A solution could be

com *ConvMob*(*a*?int, *b*!int) :
   sub $r : M_1$ **bus**
   |[*x*, *y*, *z* : int; *x* := 0
   ; (*a*?*y*, *r.c*?*z*; *y* := *y* − *z*
    ; *b*!*y*, *r.d*!*y*, *r.e*!*x*, *r.f*!(*x* + 1) ; *x* := *x* + 1
)*
   ]|
moc .

A nice challenge is finding a parallel program with constant response time that computes the Dirichlet convolution of two arbitrary arithmetical functions.

4 *Conclusion*

We would like to conclude by summarizing the design techniques that have made their appearance in our derivation. In hindsight they very much resemble techniques familiar from sequential programming and functional programming.

The first technique is the introduction of subprocesses to isolate concerns. We have no general heuristics to obtain the specifications of the subprocesses from those of the original process. A second technique is the introduction of an infinite nested chain of subprocesses. Their specification can often be obtained by generalizing the original specification, for example, by the introduction of a new variable. This resembles the way in which invariants are derived from the postcondition when designing a repetition for a sequential program. In order to define the infinite nested chain by a recursive program it is necessary to find a suitably parameterized specification. Finally, we have seen that the introduction of additional ports can be helpful to improve the efficiency of a program. This resembles the introduction of auxiliary variables and the strengthening of an invariant for a sequential repetition, or the introduction of additional parameters in a recursive function of a functional program.

Formal methods are important in the design of good programs. This is even more true for the design of parallel programs, because any operational approach is bound to confuse the designer; our mind cannot cope with the operational complexity of concurrency. Although we do not claim to have presented the ultimate tools for the design of parallel programs, we do think that our approach gives further insight in the requirements of a useful formalism.

Acknowledgments

Rudolf Mak suggested the problem of writing a parallel program to generate the Möbius sequence from its recurrent relation. The members of the Eindhoven VLSI Club are acknowledged for critically examining earlier presentations of this material.

References

[1] Rem, M. "Trace theory and systolic computations". *PARLE: Parallel Architectures and Languages Europe*, Proceedings 1987, Vol. I, G. Goos and J. Hartmanis, eds., pp. 14–33. Lecture Notes in Computer Science, vol. 258. Springer-Verlag, Berlin, 1987.

[2] McCarthy, P. J. *Introduction to Arithmetical Functions*. Springer-Verlag, Berlin, 1986.

Appendix

The following three lemmas follow from the Fundamental Theorem of Arithmetic (unique prime factorization).

Lemma 0

$$d \mid n \Rightarrow \pi(d) \leq \pi(n).$$

Lemma 1

$\mu(d) \neq 0 \equiv d$ is the product of $\pi(d)$ distinct primes.

Lemma 2

$$(\mathbf{S}d : d \mid n \wedge \mu(d) \neq 0 \wedge \pi(d) = i : 1) = (\pi(n) \textbf{ choose } i).$$

Theorem

$$(\mathbf{S}d : d \mid n : \mu(d)) = U(n).$$

Proof   We derive

$$(\mathbf{S}d : d \mid n : \mu(d))$$

$=$ {algebra}

$$(\mathbf{S}d : d \mid n \wedge \mu(d) \neq 0 : \mu(d))$$

$=$ {term grouping according to $\pi(d)$, using Lemma 0}

$$(\mathbf{S}i : 0 \leq i \leq \pi(n) : (\mathbf{S}d : d \mid n \wedge \mu(d) \neq 0 \wedge \pi(d) = i : \mu(d)))$$

$=$ {definition of μ}

$$(\mathbf{S}i : 0 \leq i \leq \pi(n) : (\mathbf{S}d : d \mid n \wedge \mu(d) \neq 0 \wedge \pi(d) = i : (-1)^i))$$

=   {Lemma 2}

$(\mathbf{S}i : 0 \leq i \leq \pi(n) : (\pi(n) \textbf{ choose } i)(-1)^i)$

=   {Binomial Theorem}

$(1 - 1)^{\pi(n)}$

=   {definition of U}

$U(n)$.   □

Distribution

and

Inversion

of

Warshall's Algorithm

14

Jan L. A. van de Snepscheut

Groningen University

1 *Introduction*

Warshall's algorithm is an efficient algorithm for computing the transitive closure of a binary relation (cf. [8]). We use the terminology of directed graphs rather than binary relations.

The transitive closure of a directed graph is obtained by adding a directed edge wherever the original graph contains a path from the source to the destination node of the new edge. The graph thus obtained is called closed. The transitive closure may also be obtained in situ, i.e., without reference to the original graph, by adding an edge from node i to node j if the graph under construction has an edge from i to k and an edge from k to j. If this action is performed repeatedly for all triples $i, j,$ and k until no more edges are added, it terminates with the graph under construction being the transitive closure of the original graph. Warshall's algorithm amounts to prescribing an ordering of the triples such that, if the action is performed once for every triple in the prescribed order, the graph is closed. The order is a partial order, and

183

we use the partiality to derive a version in which the actions are distributed over a number of processors.

The transitive reduction of a graph is obtained by removing edges whose absence does not affect the transitive closure. A graph thus obtained is called *reduced*. The transitive reduction of a directed graph is uniquely determined if and only if the graph is acyclic (cf. [1]). When discussing transitive reduction we therefore restrict ourselves to acyclic graphs. Consider the action of removing an edge from node i to node j if the graph under construction has an edge from i to k and an edge from k to j. Repeatedly performing this action for all triples i, j, and k does not necessarily lead to the reduced graph. We propose an ordering of the triples i, j, and k such that if the action is performed once for every triple in the proposed order, the graph is reduced provided that the initial graph is closed. This yields an algorithm which is in some sense the inverse of Warshall's algorithm (cf. [2, pp. 351–354] and [3, pp. 265–274]). Finally, we obtain an algorithm for the transitive reduction of any acyclic graph.

We use the following notation. For expressions P and e and identifier x, $P(x :=
e)$ denotes P with all free occurrences of x replaced by e.

The graph contains N nodes numbered 0 onward. For nodes i and j and integer k, $0 \le k \le N$, the predicate $i \xrightarrow{\ge k} j$ denotes the presence in the initial graph of a path from i to j via one or more intermediate nodes, all of which have a number at least k; the predicate $i \xrightarrow{<k} j$ denotes the presence in the initial graph of a path from i to j via one or more intermediate nodes, all of which have a number less than k. In the sequel, we omit the ranges of i, j, and k.

The graph that is being modified is recorded in variable b as an adjacency matrix: $b.i.j$ is equivalent to the presence of the edge from i to j in the graph. The initial graph is recorded in constant a as an adjacency matrix: $a.i.j.$ is equivalent to the presence of the edge from i to j in the initial graph.

We list some properties of predicate $i \xrightarrow{<k} j$ and its "dual" $i \xrightarrow{\ge k} j$.

$$\forall(i,j :: b.i.j \equiv a.i.j \lor i \xrightarrow{<0} j) \equiv (b = a) ; \tag{0}$$

$$\forall(i,j :: b.i.j \equiv a.i.j \land \neg i \xrightarrow{\ge N} j) \equiv (b = a) ; \tag{1}$$

$$\forall(i,j :: b.i.j \equiv a.i.j \lor i \xrightarrow{<N} j) \equiv (b = \text{closure of } a) ; \tag{2}$$

$$\forall(i,j :: b.i.j \equiv a.i.j. \land \neg i \xrightarrow{\ge 0} j) \equiv (b = \text{reduction of } a) ; \tag{3}$$

$$i \xrightarrow{<k+1} j \equiv i \xrightarrow{<k} j \lor ((i \xrightarrow{<k} k \lor a.i.k) \land (k \xrightarrow{<k} j \lor a.k.j)) ; \tag{4}$$

$$i \xrightarrow{\ge k} j \equiv i \xrightarrow{\ge k+1} j \lor ((i \xrightarrow{\ge k+1} k \lor a.i.k) \land (k \xrightarrow{\ge k+1} j \lor a.k.j)) . \tag{5}$$

It may not be obvious why we have chosen $i \xrightarrow{\geq k} j$ to represent the presence in the initial graph of a particular path consisting of at least two edges. The choice, however, is essential in the case of the reduction algorithm. For the closure algorithm we could equally well live with a path in the graph under construction, or with a path of at least one edge, or both.

2 *Warshall's Algorithm for Computing Transitive Closure*

Warshall's algorithm is

$$TC : k := 0 \{ W \}$$
$$; \mathbf{do} \;\; k \neq N \rightarrow \mathbf{forall}(\, i, j : b.i.k \,\wedge\, b.k.j : b.i.j := true)$$
$$\{ W(k := k + 1) \}$$
$$; k := k + 1 \{ W \}$$
$$\mathbf{od} \; .$$

Its invariant W is

$$W : \;\; b.i.j \equiv a.i.j \,\vee\, i \xrightarrow{<k} j \, .$$

We have omitted the universal quantification over i and j, as well as the ranges of i, j, and k. Notice that the **forall** statement can also be written as

$$\mathbf{forall}(i, j :: b.i.j := b.i.j \,\vee\, (b.i.k \,\wedge\, b.k.j)) \, .$$

We prefer the latter form in our proofs and the original form in the program text. $W(k := 0)$ is true on account of (0) and the initial condition $b = a$. $W \wedge k = N$ implies, on account of (2), that b is the transitive closure of a. We must show the invariance of W over the loop body. We investigate the right-hand side of $W(k := k + 1)$:

$$a.i.j \,\vee\, i \xrightarrow{<k+1} j$$
$$= \quad \{ (4) \}$$
$$a.i.j \,\vee\, i \xrightarrow{<k} j \,\vee\, ((i \xrightarrow{<k} k \,\vee\, a.i.k) \,\wedge\, (k \xrightarrow{<k} j \,\vee\, a.k.j))$$
$$= \quad \{ W \}$$
$$b.i.j \,\vee\, (b.i.k \,\wedge\, b.k.j) \, .$$

It follows that simultaneous execution of the up-to-N^2 assignments to $b.i.j$ maintains W. The assignments may, however, also be executed in any order since the values $b.i.k$ and $b.k.j$ are not changed: For example, $b.i.k$ is assigned the value *true* if $b.i.k \wedge b.k.k$ holds, which implies that $b.i.k$ is already *true*.

The time complexity of Warshall's algorithm is $O(N^3)$. In the next section we distribute execution of this program over a network of N^2 cells in such a way that the time complexity is $O(N)$.

3 *A Distributed Implementation*

The network consists of N^2 cells, identified by pairs (i, j). Cells (i, j) and (m, n) are connected if and only if $|i - m| + |j - n| = 1$. Each cell contains one boolean variable. The N^2 elements of matrix b are distributed in such a way that the variable of cell (i, j) equals $b.i.j$. It is assumed that all cells perform steps in synchrony. Each step consists of

> receiving messages via zero or more connections
>
> ; zero or more local computations
>
> ; sending messages via zero or more connections.

A message can be transmitted from one cell to another if the two cells are connected. A message sent by one cell during some step is received by the other cell during the next step. We see to it that, between any two steps, each connection transmits at most one message.

We now concentrate on one execution of the **forall** statement in Warshall's algorithm, which, for any value of k, $0 \le k < N$, is referred to as phase k. During phase k each cell (i, j) performs

$$b.i.j := b.i.j \vee (b.i.k \wedge b.k.j).$$

For $i = k \vee j = k$ the assignment reduces to the empty assignment. We therefore focus on the case $i \neq k \wedge j \neq k$. Since the two values $b.i.k$ and $b.k.j$ are not located in cell (i, j), they have to be transmitted from (i, k) and (k, j) to (i, j) (see Fig. 1).

Notice that these values arrive $|k - j|$ and $|k - i|$ steps, respectively, after being sent. Since no variables are available to store these two boolean values, it

Figure 1. Transmission of $b.i.k$ and $b.k.j$ to cell (i, j).

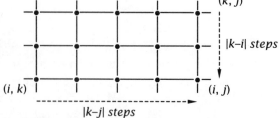

is required that the two values arrive simultaneously at cell (i, j). They may, therefore, have to be sent during distinct steps. In order to initiate transmission at the right steps we propose that (k, k) first sends a message to (i, k) and simultaneously one to (k, j); upon receipt of such an initiation message, each of these cells initiates transmission of the value of its boolean variable (see Fig. 2).

Since the two paths from (k, k) to (i, j) consist of the same number of connections, viz. $|k - j| + |k - i|$, the two boolean values arrive simultaneously at (i, j). The latter cell then performs the assignment. The "trick" to construct two paths of the same length constitutes the crux of our distributed solution.

In order to have all "off-k-line" cells (i, j), $i \neq k \wedge j \neq k$, perform the above assignment, each of them has to receive a value from two "on-k-line" cells (i, k) and (k, j). Hence, each off-k-line cell not only receives those two values but also propagates them. (Propagation means that a value received by (i, j) from $(i, j - 1)$ is sent to $(i, j + 1)$, and similarly for the other directions.) Sending via a nonexistent connection (at the border of the matrix) equals execution of the empty statement. Similarly, each on-k-line cell both propagates the initiation signal and transmits its boolean value in the two orthogonal directions. This corresponds to the following inventory of steps constituting phase k:

cell(k, k):

>   send initiation signals via all four connections.

cell(i, j), $(i = k \wedge j \neq k) \vee (i \neq k \wedge j = k)$:

>   receive an initiation signal via one connection

Figure 2.   Two initiation signals and the resulting value transmissions.

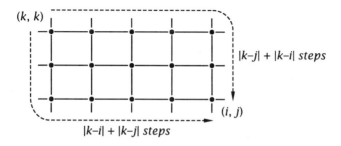

  ; propagate the initiation signal and send the value *b.i.j* via the
  remaining two connections.

cell(*i, j*), $i \neq k \wedge j \neq k$:

  receive the boolean values *b.i.k* and *b.k.j* via two connections

  ; perform the assignment *b.i.j* := *b.i.j* ∨ (*b.i.k* ∧ *b.k.j*)

  ; propagate *b.i.k* and *b.k.j* .

Notice that each connection transmits exactly one message during the entire
phase *k* (see Fig. 3).

  The three alternatives above are distinguished by the value of *k* and the
cell's identification. As it turns out, distinct alternatives are also distinguished
by the incoming signals. This allows the cell programs to be independent of
cell identifications and of *k*; i.e., all cells execute during each phase the same
program. A minor problem is the first alternative since it is distinguished by
the absence of incoming signals. We return to this later. So much for phase *k*.

Figure 3. Set of initiation signals and value transmissions.

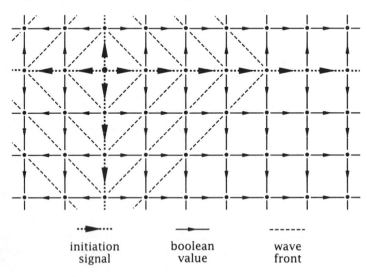

| initiation | boolean | wave |
| signal | value | front |

4 *Timing of Phases*

Next we concentrate on avoiding interference between consecutive phases. It is required that, between any two consecutive steps, each connection transmit at most one message. Notice that the (in time) first and last of the actions constituting phase k may be as much as $2(N-1)$ steps apart. One way of satisfying the requirement is, therefore, to start a phase $2N-1$ steps after starting the previous phase. Execution of N phases then results in a quadratic time-complexity, which is worse than we strive for. In order to devise a more refined strategy, we number consecutive steps with consecutive integer numbers, and we define, for $0 \le k < N$, $t.k$ as the number of the step during which (k, k) initiates phase k. Furthermore, we define $f.i.j.k$ as the number of the single step during which cell (i, j) performs its single action related to phase k. We show that there is no interference between consecutive phases; i.e., we show that in each step at most one message is transmitted per connection, if $f.i.j.k$ is a strictly increasing function of k. Since $f.i.j.k$ is the only step during which (i, j) receives a message related to phase k, interference of incoming messages to (i, j) of phases k and $k + 1$ is excluded if $f.i.j.k < f.i.j.(k + 1)$. Similarly, interference of outgoing messages is excluded if $f.i.j.k < f.i.j.(k + 1)$. It remains to show that no two adjacent cells send a message simultaneously via their common connection. We do so by contradiction. Since two such simultaneous messages belong to different phases, the two cells are involved in those two phases in opposite order, thereby contradicting $f.i.j.k < f.i.j.(k+1)$ in one of the two cells.

From $f.i.j.k = t.k + |k - i| + |k - j|$ we derive

$$f.i.j.k < f.i.j.(k + 1)$$

$=$ {def. of f}

$$t.k + |k - i| + |k - j| < t.(k + 1) + |k + 1 - i| + |k + 1 - j|$$

$=$ {calculus}

$$t.k + |k - i| - |k + 1 - i| + |k - j| - |k + 1 - j| < t.(k + 1)$$

$\Leftarrow$ $\{\, |x| - |x + 1| \le 1 \,\}$

$$t.k + 2 < t.(k + 1) .$$

Since 2 is independent of i, j, and k it turns out to be sufficient to start any phase 3 steps later than the preceding phase. The total number of steps is $5N - 4$ (see Fig. 4).

If so desired, messages may be routed through the network from (k, k) to $(k + 1, k + 1)$ to guarantee $t.k + 3 = t.(k + 1)$. For example, a message may be sent by (k, k) to $(k, k + 1)$ during step $t.k + 1$; it is received and then sent to $(k + 1, k + 1)$ during step $t.k + 2$; it is received during step $t.k + 3$, which causes $(k + 1, k + 1)$ to start phase $k + 1$. These two messages do not interfere with any other message of any phase.

The distributed implementation was obtained from Warshall's algorithm in two steps. First, the boolean matrix was distributed over a network of cells. Execution of one phase of the algorithm was made possible by routing the matrix elements involved through the network. Second, the proof obligation to avoid multiple messages on a connection led to the timing of successive phases. The resulting implementation is similar to, although an order of magnitude shorter than, the cellular automaton described in [6], and very different from the systolic array described in [5]. Both of them have the same time complexity as our version (cf. [7]).

5 *From Closed to Reduced Graph*

In this section we forget about distribution and focus on inversion of Warshall's algorithm to obtain an algorithm for transitive reduction. We do so for acyclic graphs only. The algorithm first appeared in [4].

Warshall's algorithm is an in situ algorithm that adds an edge from one

Figure 4. Wavefronts of three consecutive phases.

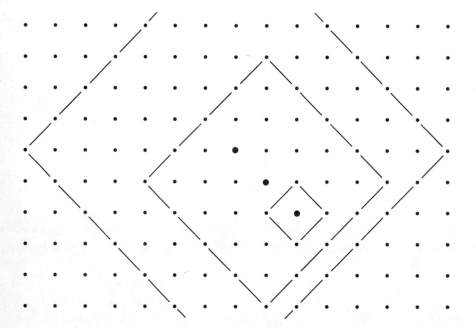

node to another if a path of two edges exists between those nodes. We aim at an inverse algorithm, i.e., an algorithm that removes an edge if a path of two edges exists between source and target. Such an algorithm does not exist in general, as is shown by the following example in which the redundant edge from 0 to 3 is not eliminated:

We therefore consider the case in which the initial graph a is closed. This case does not arise by accident: "The graph is closed" is the postcondition of the closure algorithm and, hence, the precondition of the inverted algorithm.

Informally, the invariant of Warshall's algorithm expresses that edges have been added between those nodes that are connected by a path all of whose intermediate nodes have a number less than k. A corresponding reduction algorithm will undo the actions of the closure algorithm: Edges will be deleted only between nodes that are connected by a path whose intermediate nodes are at least k. If we succeed in finding the exact "undoing", we have two algorithms with the same invariant. A problem arises if both $i \xrightarrow{<k} j$ and $i \xrightarrow{\geq k} j$ hold. In the (greedy) closure algorithm an edge from i to j is added as soon as $i \xrightarrow{<k} j$ is found to be true, even if $i \xrightarrow{\geq k} j$ is also true. In an equally greedy reduction algorithm the edge from i to j is removed as soon as $i \xrightarrow{\geq k} j$ is found to be true, even if $i \xrightarrow{<k} j$ is also true. Thus, we obtain two distinct invariants, W for the closure and G for the reduction algorithm; G is

$$G: \ b.i.j \equiv a.i.j \ \wedge \ \neg i \xrightarrow{\geq k} j \, .$$

$G(k := N)$ is true on account of (1) and the initial condition $b = a$. $G \wedge k = 0$ implies, on account of (3), that b is the transitive reduction of a. Our program is

$$TR: \ k := N \, \{\, G \,\}$$
$$; \textbf{do} \ \ k \neq 0 \to k := k - 1 \, \{\, G(k := k + 1) \,\}$$
$$; \textbf{forall}(i, j: b.i.k \wedge b.k.j: \ b.i.j := \text{false})\{\, G \,\}$$
$$\textbf{od} \, .$$

We check the invariance of G over the loop body of TR by manipulating the right-hand side of G while using the fact that a is closed.

$$a.i.j \wedge \neg i \xrightarrow{\geq k} j$$

$= \quad \{ (5) \}$

$$a.i.j \wedge \neg(i \xrightarrow{\geq k+1} j \vee ((i \xrightarrow{\geq k+1} k \vee a.i.k) \wedge (k \xrightarrow{\geq k+1} j \vee a.k.j)))$$

$= \quad$ {since a is closed, $i \xrightarrow{\geq k+1} k$ implies $a.i.k$}

$$a.i.j \wedge \neg(i \xrightarrow{\geq k+1} j \vee (a.i.k \wedge a.k.j))$$

$=$ {calculus}

$a.i.j \,\wedge\, \neg i \xrightarrow{\ \geq k+1\ } j \,\wedge\, \neg(a.i.k \,\wedge\, a.k.j)$

$=$ {on account of $G(k := k+1)$ we aim at terms of the form
$\quad a.i.j \,\wedge\, \neg i \xrightarrow{\ \geq k+1\ } j$ only}

$a.i.j \,\wedge\, \neg i \xrightarrow{\ \geq k+1\ } j \,\wedge$

$\neg((a.i.k \,\wedge\, \neg i \xrightarrow{\ \geq k+1\ } k \,\wedge\, a.k.j \,\wedge\, \neg k \xrightarrow{\ \geq k+1\ } j) \,\vee$

$(a.i.k \,\wedge\, a.k.j \,\wedge\, (i \xrightarrow{\ \geq k+1\ } k \,\vee\, k \xrightarrow{\ \geq k+1\ } j)))$

$=$ {since a is closed, $i \xrightarrow{\ \geq k+1\ } j$ is implied by
$\quad a.i.k \,\wedge\, a.k.j \,\wedge\, (i \xrightarrow{\ \geq k+1\ } k \,\vee\, k \xrightarrow{\ \geq k+1\ } j)$}

$a.i.j \,\wedge\, \neg i \xrightarrow{\ \geq k+1\ } j \,\wedge\, \neg(a.i.k \,\wedge\, \neg i \xrightarrow{\ \geq k+1\ } k \,\wedge\, a.k.j \,\wedge\, \neg k \xrightarrow{\ \geq k+1\ } j)$

$=$ $\{G(k := k+1)\}$

$b.i.j \,\wedge\, \neg(b.i.k \,\wedge\, b.k.j)\,.$

It follows that simultaneous execution of the up-to-N^2 assignments to $b.i.j$ maintains G. Again, the assignments may also be executed in any order: Whether an assignment is executed depends only on the values $b.i.k$ and $b.k.j$, and these are not changed since the acyclic nature of the graph enforces $b.k.k = false$.

6 *Transitive Reduction of Any Acyclic Graph*

Warshall's algorithm, TC, computes the transitive closure of any graph. The "inverse" of TC is TR, which reduces an initially closed, acyclic graph. We now look for an algorithm that reduces an arbitrary acyclic graph. The example given before shows that such an algorithm composed of simple reduction steps only does not exist. Fortunately there is a nice solution: Algorithm $(TC; TR)$ computes the transitive closure of an arbitrary acyclic graph and then reduces the closed graph, which has the same transitive reduction as the original graph.

$TC;\ TR:\quad k := 0$
$\quad ; \textbf{do } k \neq N \rightarrow \quad \textbf{forall}(i,j : b.i.k \,\wedge\, b.k.j : b.i.j := true)$
$\qquad\qquad\qquad\quad ; k := k+1$
$\quad \textbf{od}$
$\quad ; \textbf{do } k \neq 0 \rightarrow \quad k := k-1$
$\qquad\qquad\qquad\quad ; \textbf{forall}(i,j : b.i.k \,\wedge\, b.k.j : b.i.j := false)$
$\quad \textbf{od}\,.$

The time complexity of $(TC; TR)$ is $O(N^3)$. It is known (cf. [1]) that transitive closure and transitive reduction have equal time complexity.

Acknowledgments

The author is very grateful to David Gries for suggesting the idea of inverting Warshall's algorithm, to David Gries and Alain J. Martin for helping perform the inversion, and to Jan Tijmen Udding for invariant G, which is much simpler than the one we had proposed before.

References

[1] Aho, A. V., Garey, M. R., and Ullman, J. D. "The transitive reduction of a directed graph". *SIAM Journal of Computing 1*, 2 (June 1972), pp. 131–137.

[2] Dijkstra, E. W. *Selected Writings on Computing: A Personal Perspective.* Springer-Verlag, New York, 1982.

[3] Gries, D. *The Science of Programming.* Springer-Verlag, New York, 1981.

[4] Gries, D., Martin, A. J., and van de Snepscheut, J. L. A. "An algorithm for transitive reduction of an acyclic graph". *Science of Computer Programming* (to appear).

[5] Guibas, L. J., Kung, H. T., and Thompson, C. D. "Direct VLSI implementation of combinatorial algorithms". Proceedings of the Caltech Conference on VLSI (1979), pp. 509–525.

[6] Van Scoy, F. L. "The parallel recognition of classes of graphs". *IEEE Trans. Computers.* (1980), pp. 563–570.

[7] Van de Snepscheut, J. L. A. "A derivation of a distributed implementation of Warshall's algorithm". *Science of Computer Programming 7* (1986), pp. 55–60.

[8] Warshall, S. "A theorem on Boolean matrices". *Journal of the ACM 9* (1962), pp. 11–12.

A Distributed Algorithm for Mutual Exclusion

An Experiment in Presentation

15

Jan L. A. van de Snepscheut
Groningen University

This is a written version of a hands-in-the-pocket presentation, i.e., a presentation without the use of visual aids. It is an experiment in presentation since it denies the audience the possibility of looking (or listening) back and thereby requires, at any moment, an even thinner interface between past and present than usual. Because oral formula manipulation is virtually impossible, we have to restrict ourselves in the choice of algorithms to be presented in this way. The present algorithm was first described in [3].

We consider a finite set of processes that execute a program containing a critical section. At any moment at most one process may be in its critical section. To that end the processes communicate with each other. In [2], A. J. Martin provides three solutions for the case in which the communications network between the processes is a ring. First we describe those three solutions; next we consider the case in which the network is a tree; and then we extend the solution to the case in which the network is an arbitrary connected graph. Finally we show that our solution is fair.

Each of the solutions to the mutual exclusion problem that we consider relies on the presence of a unique "privilege" in the network. Before entering its critical section a process acquires the privilege, and it does not release the privilege before completing its critical section. Hence at any moment at most one process is in its critical section. The difference between the various algorithms is in the way in which the processes acquire the privilege. The first of the three algorithms given by Martin for the case of a ring network is called "perpetuum mobile". This algorithm is also listed in a paper by Le Lann (cf. [1]). In this solution the privilege perpetually rotates in a fixed direction along the ring. If a process is about to enter its critical section it is delayed until the privilege arrives at the process. Upon completion of the critical section the privilege is passed on to the next process in the ring. A nice property of this solution is that it is fair, by which we mean that for every process the number of times that other processes execute their critical sections while the process is awaiting the privilege is bounded. A not-so-nice property of this solution is that the number of message transmissions between the execution of two critical sections is unbounded. The other two ring algorithms bound this number. In all subsequent algorithms the bound is achieved by letting a process that is about to enter its critical section transmit a so-called request for the privilege, and by moving the privilege only in response to such a request.

The second solution for the case of a ring is called the "drifting privilege". In this solution the privilege and the requests move in the same direction along the ring. A process requests the privilege by transmitting a request in a fixed direction. The request travels along the ring until it hits the privilege. This causes the request to disappear and the privilege to start traveling along the ring in the same direction as the request did, until it reaches the requesting process, which thereupon executes its critical section. In an actual implementation of this algorithm we have to be careful in handling or avoiding the overtaking of messages, but we ignore this aspect here.

The third and last solution for the case of the ring is called the "reflecting privilege". In this solution the privilege and the requests move in opposite directions along the ring. As in the previous solution, a process requests the privilege by transmitting a request in a fixed direction. The request travels along the ring until it hits the privilege. This causes the request to disappear and the privilege to start traveling along the ring in the direction opposite to that of the request, until it reaches the requesting process, which thereupon executes its critical section. Again, in an actual implementation of this algorithm we have to be careful in handling or avoiding the overtaking of messages, and again we ignore this aspect here.

In both the second and the third algorithms, the number of messages transmitted between execution of two critical sections is bounded. The two algorithms' bounds are roughly the same, details depending on the actual implementation. An essential difference between the two algorithms is that the "drifting privilege" requires two disjoint paths between requesting and privileged process, whereas the "reflecting privilege" requires only one path. In graphs other than rings there may not be two disjoint paths, and our subsequent solutions are therefore based on the "reflecting privilege".

We now turn to the case in which the communications network between the processes is a tree. We develop an algorithm for this case while trying to retain as much as possible from the previous solution. Once again a process that is about to enter its critical section transmits a request, but now, because there may be many edges along which the request could be transmitted, we face a design decision. Since the network is a tree, the edges connect the process with subtrees that are not mutually connected. The choice to be made is between three alternatives: sending a single request to the subtree that is guaranteed to contain the privilege, sending requests to subtrees in some order until the privilege is encountered, or sending requests to all subtrees simultaneously. In general, the second alternative is the most time-consuming one, and the last alternative requires more messages to be transmitted while achieving the same time complexity as the first alternative.

For reasons of efficiency we opt for the first alternative. We record which subtree is the one that contains the privilege by assigning a direction to every edge. The directions are chosen such that each edge points toward the privileged process. The tree thereby becomes a rooted tree, which is rooted at the privileged process, and in which all edges point toward the root. Every nonprivileged process has exactly one outgoing edge. A process that is about to execute its critical section transmits a request on its outgoing edge. The request travels along a directed path until it hits the privilege. This causes the request to disappear and causes the privilege to start traveling along the same path but in the opposite direction, back to the requesting process. In order to maintain the representation of the location of the privilege, traversal of an edge by the privilege is accompanied by inversion of that edge's direction.

It is possible for a process to receive more than one request for the privilege on its incoming edges. In order to avoid unnecessary communications, it records all requests but transmits only one of them via its outgoing edge until it has received the privilege. Upon receiving the privilege, the process transmits it along one of the requesting incoming edges. If more incoming requests are pending, then a request for the privilege is transmitted along the same edge as the privilege, which causes the privilege to return in due time, and so on. As it stands, this algorithm is not fair. We ignore fairness for the moment and return to it when discussing the next algorithm.

We now address the case in which the communications network is an arbitrary connected graph. Again, we try to change as little as possible. Of course we could apply the previous algorithm to an arbitrary spanning tree of the graph, but we seek not to do so. We return to this option later.

An essential ingredient of the tree algorithm is that from each process there emerges a single finite path, which terminates in the process containing the privilege. In a general graph it is unavoidable that some processes have more than one outgoing edge and we therefore face another design decision: Should every outgoing path lead to the privileged process, or only some of them? For reasons of efficiency we choose the first option; i.e., we require that each directed path in the graph lead in a finite number of steps to the privileged process. We shall see to it that the finiteness requirement is fulfilled by avoiding directed cycles in the graph. Notice that it follows from this decision that the privileged process has no outgoing edge. Also notice that we have to impose two restrictions on the graph, viz., that it be connected (to allow for a path to the privileged process) and that each edge connect two distinct processes (to allow for the absence of cycles).

We observe that it is possible to assign directions to the edges of an arbitrary graph such that each directed path terminates in the privileged process. One such assignment can be obtained by using a depth-first search to construct, in the undirected graph, a palm tree whose root is the privileged process. (A palm tree consists of a spanning tree plus a number of so-called back edges that connect two processes, one of which is on the path in the spanning tree between the root and the other process.) All edges are then directed toward the root.

As before, a process that is about to execute its critical section transmits a request on its outgoing edge. The request travels along a directed path until it hits the privilege. This causes the request to disappear and the privilege to start traveling along the same path, but in the opposite direction, to the requesting process. Again, a process that receives more than one request on its incoming edges forwards only one request along one of its outgoing edges.

We now consider how to maintain the direction of the edges when the privilege traverses an edge between two processes. The process transmitting the privilege has no outgoing edges, and it has to have one after the privilege has departed on an (incoming) edge. Inverting that edge preserves the property that each directed path leads to the privileged process, but such a path need not terminate there. In fact, the inversion may introduce cycles. Notice that each path that terminated in the privilege-transmitting process is now extended with one edge to lead to the privilege-receiving process. Also notice that each path that passes through the privilege-receiving process still leads to the privilege, and that this property does not involve any of the receiving process's outgoing edges. Also notice that all other paths are unaffected.

We still have to worry about the existence of cycles because there may have been more than one path from the privilege-receiving process to the privilege-transmitting process. Cycles can have been introduced only through inversion of the edge traversed by the privilege. Hence every cycle contains this edge and, consequently, the newly privileged process. The cycles can be broken by reversing not only the one outgoing edge of the receiving process on which the privilege is received but all of its other outgoing edges as well. As noted before, those outgoing edges are not essential for preserving the requirement that each directed path lead to the privileged process. Does this reversal cause any problems with the decision that the privilege travel along the same path as the request but in the opposite direction, i.e., against the direction of the edges? No, it does not, because each process transmits only one request before obtaining the privilege, and therefore no request has been transmitted by the privilege-receiving process on those other outgoing edges. Their direction may freely be inverted.

Observe that the inversion of all of the privilege-receiving process's outgoing edges increases the number of paths to the privileged process and decreases their average length. It is this property that justifies our interest in developing the algorithm for the general graph rather than using the first algorithm on a suitable spanning tree.

As it stands the above algorithm does not guarantee fairness. It is not even guaranteed that a process that requests the privilege will eventually receive it. Assuming that each process is locally fair and that each critical section terminates, however, we now show that the whole algorithm is fair. A process is said to be locally fair if, for each incoming edge on which a request is pending, the number of times that the privilege is transmitted via one of the process's other edges is bounded.

A process that has requested the privilege but not yet received it has an outgoing path, along which requests have propagated, that leads from the process to the privileged process. With each edge in this path we associate a natural number, and thus obtain a finite sequence of natural numbers. The number associated with an edge is the maximum number of times that the privilege may still be transmitted via some other edge of the process to which it is an incoming edge. Let's see how the sequence of numbers changes as the privilege travels. The privilege either travels along the path toward the requesting process or it travels to another requesting process and thereby lengthens the path to the process that we are focusing on. In the first case the last number in the sequence is deleted. In the other case the last number of the sequence is decreased by one, due to the local fairness, and the sequence is extended with another natural number. In both cases the sequence is lexicographically decreased. Because the processes go on forever and because their critical sections terminate, the sequence is eventually decreased to its minimum, viz. the empty sequence, which corresponds to the requesting process receiving the privilege. Because of the local fairness, each of the numbers is bounded and therefore the number of steps taken to reduce the sequence to its minimum is also bounded.

References

[1] Le Lann, G. "Distributed systems: Towards a formal approach". *IFIP Congress* (Toronto, 1977), pp. 155–160.

[2] Martin, A. J. "Distributed mutual exclusion on a ring of processes". *Science of Computer Programming 5* (1985), pp. 265–276.

[3] Van de Snepscheut, J. L. A. "Fair mutual exclusion on a graph of processes". *Distributed Computing 2* (1987), pp. 113–115.

The Derivation of a Proof by J. C. S. P. van der Woude[0]

16

Edsger W. Dijkstra
The University of Texas at Austin

In the following

P and Q will be used to denote predicates on some space;

X and Y will be used to denote functions from the natural numbers to predicates on that space; accordingly, $X.i$ $(0 \leq i)$ and $Y.i$ $(0 \leq i)$ denote predicate sequences;

f will be used to denote a predicate transformer, i.e., a function from predicates to predicates;

square brackets will be used to denote universal quantification of the enclosed predicate over the space in question.

With the above notational conventions we give the following definitions:

---

0. Adapted, with permission, from Edsger W. Dijkstra and Carel S. Scholten, *Predicate Calculus and Program Semantics*, Springer-Verlag, Berlin, 1989.

"Sequence $X.i$ $(0 \le i)$ is monotonic" means

"sequence $X.i$ $(0 \le i)$ is weakening or strengthening".

"Sequence $X.i$ $(0 \le i)$ is weakening" means

$$(\mathbf{A}\,i,j\colon\ 0 \le i < j\colon [X.i\ \Rightarrow\ X.j])\,.$$

"Sequence $X.i$ $(0 \le i)$ is strengthening" means

$$(\mathbf{A}\,i,j\colon\ 0 \le i < j\colon [X.i\ \Leftarrow\ X.j])\,.$$

"Predicate transformer f is monotonic" means

$$[P\ \Rightarrow\ Q]\ \Rightarrow\ [f.P\ \Rightarrow\ f.Q]\ \text{for all}\ P,\ Q.$$

"Predicate transformer f is finitely conjunctive" means

$$[f.(P \wedge Q)\ \equiv\ f.P \wedge f.Q]\ \text{for all}\ P,\ Q.$$

"Predicate transformer f is *or*-continuous" means

$$[f.(\mathbf{E}\,i\colon\ 0 \le i\colon X.i)\ \equiv\ (\mathbf{E}\,i\colon\ 0 \le i\colon f.(X.i))]$$

for any monotonic sequence $X.i$ $(0 \le i)\,.$

"Predicate transformer f is *and*-continuous" means

$$[f.(\mathbf{A}\,i\colon\ 0 \le i\colon X.i)\ \equiv\ (\mathbf{A}\,i\colon\ 0 \le i\colon f.(X.i))]$$

for any monotonic sequence $X.i$ $(0 \le i)\,.$

We can now formulate the following theorem.

Theorem

For any predicate transformer f

$$(f \text{ is finitely conjunctive}) \wedge (f \text{ is } or\text{-continuous})\ \Rightarrow \qquad\qquad (0)$$

$$(f \text{ is } and\text{-continuous})\,.$$

Here we shall sketch the simple part of the proof and shall derive the exciting part (which we owe to J. C. S. P. van der Woude).

Proof   Under the truth of the antecedent of (0) we have to show for monotonic $X.i$ $(0 \le i)$

$$[f.(\mathbf{A}\,i\colon\ 0 \le i\colon X.i)\ \equiv\ (\mathbf{A}\,i\colon\ 0 \le i\colon f.(X.i))]\,. \qquad\qquad (1)$$

To begin with we recall —not proving it here— that because f is finitely conjunctive, f is monotonic. We now distinguish two cases.

0. $X.i$ $(0 \le i)$ *is weakening:* Because f is monotonic, the predicate sequence $f.(X.i)$ $(0 \le i)$ is also weakening; consequently —not shown here— both sides of (1) are equivalent to $f.(X.0)\,.$

1. *X.i* $(0 \le i)$ *is strengthening:* Because f is monotonic —not shown here— $LHS(1) \Rightarrow RHS(1)$, and we are left with the proof obligation

$$[f.(\mathbf{A}\, i:\ 0 \le i:\ X.i) \Leftarrow (\mathbf{A}\, i:\ 0 \le i:\ f.(X.i))] \qquad (2)$$

for strengthening *X.i* $(0 \le i)$ and an f that is finitely conjunctive and *or*-continuous.

Meeting the obligation of showing (2) is the exciting part of the proof. Reduced to its bare essentials, it consists of one definition and about a dozen simple steps. But in presenting just that irrefutable formal argument, we would pull several rabbits out of the magical hat. The proof is exciting because of the existence of heuristic considerations that quite effectively buffer these shocks of invention. For that reason, we shall develop this proof instead of just presenting it. To aid the reader in parsing the interleaved presentation of heuristic considerations and proof fragments, the latter will be indented. Here we go!

For the sake of brevity we shall omit from here on the ranges $0 \le i$ and $0 \le j$, which are to be understood. We begin with a general remark about the exploitation of *or*-continuity. The *or*-continuity of f states that

$$[f.(\mathbf{E}\, i::\ Y.i) \equiv (\mathbf{E}\, i::\ f.(Y.i))] \qquad (3)$$

for any monotonic sequence *Y.i* . For a strengthening sequence *Y.i* , just monotonicity of f suffices for (3) to hold, and for constant sequences *Y.i* , (3) holds for any f. The relevant conclusion from these observations is that, if f's *or*-continuity is going to be exploited —and it is a safe assumption that it has to be— a truly weakening sequence has to enter the picture.

Armed with this insight, we return to our demonstrandum (2). The simplest way of demonstrating an implication is to start at one side and then to repeatedly manipulate the expression (while either weakening or strengthening is allowed) until the other side is reached. So let us try that. That decision being taken, at which side should we start?

Both sides are built from the "familiar" universal quantification and the "unfamiliar" application of f, about which our knowledge is limited, the only difference being that, at the two sides, they occur in opposite order. In such a situation, the side with the "unfamilar" operation outermost counts as the more complicated one and is therefore the preferred starting point. In our case, it is the consequent

$$f.(\mathbf{A}\, i::\ X.i), \qquad (4)$$

so let us start from there. The formal challenge of manipulating (4) while exploiting what we know about f should provide the heuristic guidance as to the direction in which to proceed.

Rewriting (4) so as to exploit f's *or*-continuity would require rewriting its argument $(\mathbf{A}\, i::\ X.i)$ as an existential quantification over a truly weakening sequence, but how to do that —I tried in vain— is not clear at all. So let us try to exploit at this stage f's finite conjunctivity; i.e., let us introduce a P and Q such that

$$[(\mathbf{A}i::X.i) \equiv P \wedge Q].$$

For one of the conjuncts —say, P— we may choose any predicate that is implied by $(\mathbf{A}i::X.i)$; the law of instantiation tells us that any $X.j$ would do. (Note that this choice is less restrictive than it might seem: Because $X.i$ is a strengthening sequence, any finite conjunction of some $X.i$'s yields some $X.j$.) We could therefore consider for some j the introduction of a predicate Q constrained by

$$[(\mathbf{A}i::X.i) \equiv X.j \wedge Q].$$

But the introduction of one predicate Q for one specific j is unlikely to do the job: For one thing, the universal quantifications in the demonstrandum don't change their value if the range $0 \le i$ is replaced by $j < i$. This observation suggests, instead of the introduction of a single predicate Q, a predicate sequence $Y.j$, constrained by

$$(\mathbf{A}j::[(\mathbf{A}i::X.i) \equiv X.j \wedge Y.j]). \tag{5}$$

The introduction of the sequence $Y.j$ will turn out to be the major invention of the proof under design. For the time being, we don't define Y —as would be done immediately in a "bottom-up" proof— but only collect constraints on Y, of which (5) is the first one. We do so in the hope that, eventually, we can construct a Y that meets all the constraints.

A minor problem with the use of (5) as a rewrite rule is that it equates an expression not depending on j with one that formally does depend on j. The formal dependence on j that would thus be introduced can be eliminated by quantifying over j; because we are rewriting a consequent, we use existential quantification because that yields a formally weaker expression —the range being non-empty!— than universal quantification (and the weaker the consequent, the lighter the task ahead of us). In short, we propose to start our proof under design with

$$f.(\mathbf{A}i::X.i)$$
$$= \quad \{(5) \text{ and range of } j \text{ nonempty}\}$$
$$(\mathbf{E}j::f.(X.j \wedge Y.j))$$
$$= \quad \{f \text{ is finitely conjunctive}\}$$
$$(\mathbf{E}j::f.(X.j) \wedge f.(Y.j)). \tag{6}$$

So far, so good! We have not yet exploited f's *or*-continuity and we cannot do so before we have an existential quantification over a truly weakening sequence. In (6) we do have an existential quantification (albeit, as yet, over a constant sequence) and, with *X.i* a (truly) strengthening sequence, there is a fair chance that (5) permits a (truly) weakening sequence *Y.j* . So let us introduce the second constraint on Y,

$$\text{sequence } Y.j \ (0 \le j) \text{ is weakening,} \tag{7}$$

as a next step towards the use of *f*'s *or*-continuity, i.e., the use of (3) as a rewrite rule.

Comparison of the right-hand side of (3) with (6) shows that we can use (3) as a rewrite rule only after we have succeeded in removing in (6) the first conjunct *f.(X.j)* from the term. We cannot just omit it, as that would weaken the expression and, heading for an antecedent, we are not allowed to do that. We may strengthen it; in particular, strengthening it to something independent of *j* would allow us to take the constant conjunct outside the existential quantification of (6). In order to strengthen *f.(X.j)* to something that is independent of *j*, we propose to quantify universally over *j*. That is, at (6) we propose to continue our proof under design with

$$(\mathbf{E}\,j:: f.(X.j) \wedge f.(Y.j))$$

$\Leftarrow \qquad \{\text{instantiation, monotonicity of } \wedge, \mathbf{E}\}$

$$(\mathbf{E}\,j:: (\mathbf{A}\,i:: f.(X.i)) \wedge f.(Y.j))$$

$= \qquad \{\wedge \text{ distributes over } \mathbf{E}\}$

$$(\mathbf{A}\,i:: f.(X.i)) \wedge (\mathbf{E}\,j:: f.(Y.j))$$

$= \qquad \{(3) \text{ and } (7), \text{ i.e., the use of } or\text{-continuity}\}$

$$(\mathbf{A}\,i:: f.(X.i)) \wedge f.(\mathbf{E}\,j:: Y.j). \tag{8}$$

So far, so very good! Note that the left conjunct of (8) is the antecedent of (2) we are heading for! Again, we cannot just omit the second conjunct in (8) as that would weaken the expression; the second conjunct has to be subsumed —i.e. implied— by the first one. By the looks of it we can equate (8) with its first conjunct on just the monotonicity of *f* and some implicative relation between *X* and *Y* —which will emerge as our third and last constraint on Y. But be careful! If the range of *i* were empty, the first conjunct of (8) would yield true whereas (8) would yield *f.(**E**j:: Y.j)* , and there is no reason to assume these equivalent. Somewhere along the completion of our formal argument, we have to exploit the nonemptiness of *i*'s range. As we can do it immediately, let us do it immediately. In short, we propose to continue our proof under design at (8) with

$$(\mathbf{A}\,i:: f.(X.i)) \wedge f.(\mathbf{E}\,j:: Y.j)$$

$= \qquad \{\text{range of } i \text{ nonempty}\}$

$$(\mathbf{A}\,i:: f.(X.i) \wedge f.(\mathbf{E}\,j:: Y.j))$$

$= \qquad \{\text{monotonicity of } f \text{ and } (9)\}$

$$(\mathbf{A}\,i::\,f.(X.i))$$

with, as our third and last constraint on Y,

$$(\mathbf{A}\,i::\,[X.i \;\Rightarrow\; (\mathbf{E}\,j::\,Y.j)])\,. \tag{9}$$

But for the demonstration of the existence of Y, we have completed the proof in seven steps (six of which are equivalences). Now for the existence of a Y satisfying (5), (7), and (9).

In order to ease satisfaction of (9), we define Y as the weakest solution of (5); i.e., we define $Y.j$ for any j by

$$[Y.j \;\equiv\; (\mathbf{A}\,i::\,X.i) \;\vee\; \neg X.j]\,. \tag{10}$$

In order to verify that this Y indeed satisfies (5), we observe for any j

$\qquad X.j \wedge Y.j$

$=\qquad \{(10)\}$

$\qquad X.j \wedge ((\mathbf{A}\,i::\,X.i) \vee \neg X.j)$

$=\qquad \{\wedge$ distributes over $\vee\,\}$

$\qquad (X.j \wedge (\mathbf{A}\,i::\,X.i)) \vee (X.j \wedge \neg X.j)$

$=\qquad \{j$ in i's range; predicate calculus$\}$

$\qquad (\mathbf{A}\,i::\,X.i)\,.$

In order to verify that condition (7) is met, i.e., that $Y.j$ $(0 \le j)$ is indeed weakening, we observe for any j and k

$\qquad [Y.j \;\Rightarrow\; Y.k]$

$=\qquad \{(10)\}$

$\qquad [(\mathbf{A}\,i::\,X.i) \vee \neg X.j \;\Rightarrow\; (\mathbf{A}\,i::\,X.i) \vee \neg X.k]$

$\Leftarrow\qquad \{$monotonicity of $\vee\,\}$

$\qquad [\neg X.j \;\Rightarrow\; \neg X.k]$

$=\qquad \{$contrapositive$\}$

$\qquad [X.j \;\Leftarrow\; X.k]$

$\Leftarrow\qquad \{X.i\;(0 \le i)$ is strengthening$\}$

$\qquad [j < k]\,.$

Finally, in order to verify that Y satisfies (9), we observe

$\qquad (\mathbf{E}\,j::\,Y.j)$

$=\qquad \{(10)\}$

$\qquad (\mathbf{E}\,j::\,(\mathbf{A}\,i::\,X.i) \vee \neg X.j)$

$=$ {*j*'s range is not empty}

   $(\mathbf{A}\,i::X.i)\ \vee\ (\mathbf{E}\,j::\neg X.j)$

$=$ {de Morgan}

   $(\mathbf{A}\,i::X.i)\ \vee\ \neg(\mathbf{A}\,j::X.j)$

$=$ {Excluded Middle}

   true .

And this concludes the exciting part of the proof.   ☐

Van der Woude's proof is very beautiful, and I think it worthwhile to ponder over the question why this is so. It is beautiful in the way in which the proof has been divided into two parts, with Y and its three properties forming the interface between them. It is a meaningful division in the sense that our dealing with f is entirely confined to the first part. Also, the interface between the two parts is the right one, void of any overspecification: It only mentions the existence of a Y with the properties relevant for the first part. Finally, the second part, which no longer deals with f but is concerned with the existence of a Y, is pleasingly constructive. It is really a beautifully structured argument.

I think also our derivation of the proof very beautiful. The development of the first part, which deals with f, is fully driven by the need to exploit that f is given to be finitely conjunctive and *or*-continuous, and the interface was constructed as we went along. Furthermore, the second part, which constructs a Y meeting the three requirements, does so in the most straightforward manner without pulling a single rabbit out of a hat; finally it contains three mutually independent verifications that the Y constructed meets the three requirements indeed. A very nice disentanglement!

Remark   I would like to draw attention to the second step of the final calculation, which establishes [$(\mathbf{E}\,j::Y.j)\ \equiv\ $ true] . Because this cannot be established if the range for j is empty —existential quantification over an empty range yields false— the calculation has to exploit that j's range is not empty. The knowledge that disjunction distributes over existential quantification only in the case of a nonempty range —and this belongs to the general knowledge the predicate calculator should have at his disposal— all but dictates that second step.

Finally, I would like to point out that, though carried out in great detail, the whole formal proof consists of fewer than twenty steps: The whole calculation is really quite short. I beg the reader to remember this whenever he is faced with a defense of informality on the supposed grounds that formal proofs are too lengthy and too tedious to be of any practical value. This supposition is wrong.

Fillers at the YoP Institute

17

Edsger W. Dijkstra
The University of Texas at Austin

0 Why Numbering Should Start at Zero

When we have to characterize a set of adjacent natural numbers, say {2, 3, 4, 5, 6, 7, 8, 9, 10}, we have four options, depending on whether the bounds are included or not:

$$1 < x < 11,\qquad\qquad\text{(a)}$$

$$1 < x \le 10,\qquad\qquad\text{(b)}$$

$$2 \le x < 11,\qquad\qquad\text{(c)}$$

$$2 \le x \le 10.\qquad\qquad\text{(d)}$$

Natural numbers have the property that there is a smallest natural number. Different civilizations have made different choices for that minimum value; for the classical Greeks, for instance, it was 2, because, for them, 1 was not a number. (Consequently, Euclid had to introduce a case analysis in the justification of his algorithm for the greatest common divisor of two numbers, viz., the case that the two numbers had a common divisor versus the case that they had not, i.e., that they were relatively prime.)

This observation makes the convention of excluding the lower bound, as illustrated in (a) and (b), unattractive: If the range includes the smallest natural number —as the example would for the Greeks— the convention of excluding the lower bound requires the introduction of an unnatural lower bound —as the examples (a) and (b) would do for the Greeks. This is certainly inelegant and hence we adopt the principle of *inclusion of the lower bound*.

So we are left with the choice between (c) and (d). If we include the upper bound and consider the generalization $2 \leq x \leq n$, we see that for $n = 2$ the range still contains the value 2. If we wish to represent the empty range by shrinking n still further, it would require $n = 1$, which would be very unnatural for the Greeks. In general, the convention of including the upper bound requires the introduction of an unnatural upper bound; since this is certainly inelegant, we adopt the principle of *exclusion of the upper bound*.

In short, (c) is the winner: Ranges of natural numbers will be indicated by

$m \leq x < n$

with natural bounds m and n, with $m \leq n$. Further advantages are

the number of values in the range equals the difference of the bounds, and

if the upper bound of one range equals the lower bound of another range, the ranges are contiguous.

After these preliminary investigations we ask ourselves how we characterize the first n natural numbers. For the classical Greeks this would be

$2 \leq x < n+2$;

were we to adopt the convention that the natural numbers start at 1, we would get the equally ugly

$1 \leq x < n+1$.

Obviously,

$0 \leq x < n$

is the most elegant formula; it corresponds to accepting zero as the smallest natural number. (This choice has further advantages.)

And this is why my manuscripts start with page 0. It is really quite easy. When writing a manuscript, I have the completed pages behind me, spread out on the floor. The number on each new page equals the number of completed pages on the floor.

1 *Fermat and Wilson*

From graph theory, we use

0. a finite, directed graph in which each node has both in-degree and out-degree equal to 1 consists of cycles;

1. consider along a cycle a path of p edges: If the path ends at the node at which it starts, the length of the cycle —i.e., the number of nodes on it— is a divisor of p; in particular, if p is prime, the cycle is of length p or is of length 1 (i.e., is a "self-loop").

We can use this to prove for natural n and prime p

$$(n^p - n) \bmod p = 0 \qquad\qquad \text{(Fermat)}$$

$$((p - 1)! - (p - 1)) \bmod p = 0 . \qquad\qquad \text{(Wilson)}$$

For the proof of the theorem of Fermat we take as nodes the n^p strings of p characters from an alphabet of size n, and introduce a directed edge from Rr to rR for any character r and string R (of length $p - 1$). According to **0** and **1**, the graph consists of cycles of length p and of self-loops. Because the self-loops correspond to the strings in which all characters are the same, and because the size of the alphabet is n, the number of nodes occurring in self-loops equals n. The remaining $n^p - n$ nodes are therefore partitioned into cycles of length p, which proves Fermat's theorem.

For the proof of the theorem of Wilson we take as nodes the $(p - 1)!$ cyclic arrangements of the numbers from 0 through $p-1$; for each directed edge we obtain (the cyclic arrangement corresponding to) the target node by increasing each number in (the cyclic arrangement corresponding to) the source node by 1 modulo p. According to **0** and **1**, the graph consists of cycles of length p and of self-loops. Because the self-loops correspond to the cyclic arrangements with constant difference (modulo p) between adjacent numbers, and because 1 through $p-1$ are the possible values of that difference, the number of nodes occurring in self-loops equals $p - 1$. The remaining $(p - 1)! - (p - 1)$ nodes are therefore partitioned into cycles of length p, which proves Wilson's theorem.

2 *Maximizing the Product for Given Sum*

Question

How do we construct a bag of positive integers with given sum so that their product is as large as possible?

Answer

Because with sum ≤ 1 the bag is unique, we analyze only the cases with sum ≥ 2 .

   Because $1 \cdot x < 1 + X$, and (because of sum ≥ 2) our target bag differs from $\{1\}$, our target bag contains no 1.

   Because $2 \cdot (x-2) \geq x \equiv x \geq 4$, our target bag need not contain integers ≥ 4.

   Because $2 + 2 + 2 = 3 + 3$ and $2 \cdot 2 \cdot 2 < 3 \cdot 3$, our target bag contains at most two 2's.

The above constraints are met by a bag of $(2 \cdot \text{sum}) \bmod 3$ 2's and for the rest 3's.

Remark   The predominance of 3's in the target bag reflects that 3 is the closest integer approximation of *e* —the base of the natural logarithm— which is the solution of the corresponding continuous problem. For the same reason it is theoretically preferable to implement Heapsort with a ternary tree instead of a binary one.

3 *On "Poor Man's Induction"*

   We consider n points along the circumference of a circular cake and cuts along all the chords between them, the points being chosen in such a way that all internal intersection points of pairs of chords are distinct.
   With f the number of pieces, Fig. 1 suggests $f = 2^{n-1}$. The reader may verify that $n = 5$ indeed yields $f = 16$. However, $n = 6$ yields $f = 31$! How does f depend on n?
   This problem is most easily solved in two steps: The first step expresses f in terms of

$$c \quad = \quad \text{the number of chords}$$
and
$$p \quad = \quad \text{the number of internal intersection points,}$$

and the second step expresses c and p in terms of n.

0. For the increase Δf of f caused by a new chord we observe

$$\Delta f$$

$= \quad$ {the new chord cuts pieces into two}

   the number of pieces cut by the new chord

$= \quad$ {a piece is cut by a segment of a new chord}

   the number of segments on the new chord

$=$ {segments are separated by intersection points}

1+the number of intersection points on the new chord

$=$ {internal intersection points of pairs of chords are distinct}

$\Delta c + \Delta p$.

From this and $c = 0 \Rightarrow p = 0 \wedge f = 1$ we derive by mathematical induction

$$f = 1 + c + p .$$

1. From the one-to-one correspondence between chords and pairs of points on the circumference we derive

$$c = \binom{n}{2} \; ;$$

from the one-to-one correspondence between internal intersection points and quadruples of points on the circumference we derive

$$p = \binom{n}{4} .$$

Combining the results from **0** and **1** we establish

$$f = 1 + \binom{n}{2} + \binom{n}{4}$$

or —by properties of binomial coefficients— equivalently

Figure 1. Cakes

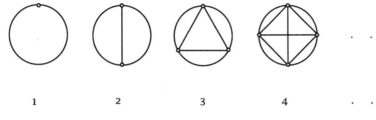

$n =$	1	2	3	4	. . .
$f =$	1	2	4	8	. . .

$$f = \binom{n-1}{0} + \binom{n-1}{1} + \binom{n-1}{2} + \binom{n-1}{3} + \binom{n-1}{4} \; ;$$

i.e., f equals the sum of the first five values on a line of the Pascal triangle, lines which each add up to a power of 2.

The above argument owes its extreme elegance to its high degree of disentanglement: **0** is not concerned with n and **1** not with f, while their combination is no more than two substitutions. Note that this partitioning into two mutually independent arguments was possible only thanks to the introduction of c and p, which carry the interface.

Acknowledgment

We owe the above beautiful solution to A. Blokhuis.

4 *The Binary Search*

Let A be a nonempty ascending integer sequence of length N; more precisely, let

$N > 0$ and $(\mathbf{A}\, i,j:\ 0 \le i < j < N: A.i \le A.j)$;

let X be an integer. We are requested to design a program solving the equation

$present: (present \equiv (\mathbf{E}\, i:\ 0 \le i < N: A.i = X))$.

We distinguish between two cases, $A.0 > X$ and $A.0 \le X$; the latter case being the harder one, we deal with that one first.

It is hard to visualize an algorithm correctly establishing *present*, i.e., determining that the value X indeed occurs in the sequence, without determining at the same time where X occurs, i.e., without establishing for some integer, i say,

$A.i = X \wedge 0 \le i < N$.

As intermediate result, this is too strong to aim for: if $\neg present$ is to be established, no such value for i exists. The best we can do in that case is to let i determine the pair of adjacent values in the sequence "between which X is missing", i.e., to establish

$A.i < X < A.(i+1) \ \wedge \ 0 \le i < N$,

for which purpose we define $A.N$ so that

$X < A.N$.

Combining the two intermediate results we construct the more realistic target of establishing

$$R: \quad A.i \leq X < A.(i+1) \;\wedge\; 0 \leq i < N .$$

Our program can then have the form

$|[$ **var** $i :$ **int**

$;$ establish R

$; present := (A.i = X)$

$]|$.

For "establish R", the precondition $A.0 \leq X < A.N$ suggests a repetition whose invariant P is obtained from R by replacing $(i+1)$ by a fresh variable, j say. That is, with

$$P: \quad A.i \leq X < A.j \;\wedge\; 0 \leq i < j \leq N ,$$

we suggest for "establish R"

$|[$ **var** $j :$ **int**

$; i,j := 0, N \,\{P\}$

$;$ **do** $j \neq i + 1 \rightarrow shrink\,(j-i) \,\{P\}$ **od** $\{R\}$

$]| \;\{R\}$.

Let us now investigate for "$shrink\,(j-i)$" to what extent a change of i will do the job. To this end we derive the weakest precondition such that $i := h$ decreases $(j-i)$ under invariance of P:

$$j - h < j - i \;\wedge\; A.h \leq X < A.j \;\wedge\; 0 \leq h < j \leq N ,$$

which follows from

$$P \;\wedge\; i < h < j \;\wedge\; A.h \leq X .$$

For $j := h$ we derive in the same manner

$$P \;\wedge\; i < h < j \;\wedge\; X < A.h .$$

These two preconditions lead for "$shrink\,(j-i)$" to

$|[$ **var** $h :$ **int**

$;$ solve $h : (i < h < j)$

$;$ **if** $A.h \leq X \rightarrow i := h$

$[\!]\;\; X < A.h \rightarrow j := h$

fi

$]|$.

We observe first that, its guards being each other's complement, the alternative construct does not abort, and second that the precondition of *shrink(j–i)* —in particular: $i < j \land j \neq i + 1$, or, equivalently, $i + 1 \leq j - 1$— implies that equation $h : (i < h < j)$ has at least one solution. For reasons of efficiency we implement "solve $h : (i < h < j)$" neither by $h := i + 1$ nor by $h := j - 1$ but rather by

   $h := \text{avg}.i.j$.

The nice thing about the above demonstration is that it makes it so clear that the termination of the repetition and the establishment of *R* are totally independent of the sequence *A* being ascending. Even if the algorithm establishes *present* we need not know that *A* is ascending; only the outcome ¬*present* requires for its trustworthiness that *A* is indeed ascending.

In the case $A.0 > X, A.0 > X \land 0 \leq i < N$ is an invariant and the above program establishes ¬*present* , as it should.

5 *The Theorem of Pompeiu*

Theorem
Consider an equilateral triangle and an arbitrary point in the plane of the triangle. Then the three distances from the vertices of the triangle to the fourth point satisfy the triangle inequalities.

Proof   The proof is by constructing a figure that contains a triangle with the three distances as its edge lengths. To this end we consider two instances of the triangle/point configuration, rotated over 60° around one of the vertices of the triangle.

Because the triangle is equilateral, one instance of one of the other two vertices coincides with the other instance of the third vertex. The triangle formed by this point of coincidence and the two instances of the fourth point has the desired edge lengths, as we see as follows.

Because the rotation is over 60°, the distance between the two instances of the fourth point equals their distance from the center of rotation, which is one of the vertices. Because in the point of coincidence, different instances of the two remaining instances coincide, its distances from the two instances of the fourth point are the distances from the fourth point to the two other vertices of the equilateral triangle.   □

Acknowledgment

The above construction is due to G. R. Veldkamp.

Remark

In my filler at the YoP Institute I used a picture, which was annoyingly over-specific: For instance, one cannot avoid choosing the fourth point inside or outside the triangle. Later in the institute, Jan L. A. van de Snepscheut showed how he could describe a class of mutual-exclusion algorithms with his hands in his pockets. The above presentation of Veldkamp's proof of the Theorem of Pompeiu has been inspired by that performance; it is a striking example of avoiding avoidable case analyses.

6 *The Monotonicity of Extreme Solutions*

In the following, capital letters P, Q, X, Y, Z denote predicates on some space. Universal quantification over that space is denoted by surrounding the universally quantified predicate by a pair of square brackets, known as "the *everywhere* operator". Lower-case letters f, g denote predicate transformers, i.e., functions from predicates (or predicate pairs) to predicates; functional application is denoted by an infix period.

Let f be monotonic in both its arguments, i.e.,

$$[P \Rightarrow Q] \Rightarrow [f.P.Y \Rightarrow f.Q.Y] \land [f.X.P \Rightarrow f.X.Q]$$

for all P, Q, X, Y.

Let $g.X$ be the strongest solution, for all X, of the equation

$$Y : [f.X.Y \Rightarrow Y] ,$$

i.e.,

$$[Z \Rightarrow f.X.(g.X)] \quad \Rightarrow \quad [Z \Rightarrow g.X] \quad \text{for all } X, Z \tag{0}$$

$$[f.X.Y \Rightarrow Y] \quad \Rightarrow \quad [g.X \Rightarrow Y] \quad \text{for all } X, Y . \tag{1}$$

Remark   Monotonicity of f in its second argument implies the existence of that strongest solution; (0) is equivalent to $[f.X.(g.X) \Rightarrow g.X]$; i.e., it states that $g.X$ is a solution; (1) states that $g.X$ implies each solution.

Then

Theorem

g is monotonic; i.e., for all P, Q

$$[P \Rightarrow Q] \Rightarrow [g.P \Rightarrow g.Q] .$$

Proof   We observe for any P, Q

$$[g.P \Rightarrow g.Q]$$

$\Leftarrow \qquad \{(1) \text{ with } X, Y := P, g.Q\}$

$[f.P.(g.Q) \ \Rightarrow\ g.Q]$

$\Leftarrow \qquad \{(0) \text{ with } X, Z := Q, f.P.(g.Q)\}$

$[f.P.(g.Q) \ \Rightarrow\ f.Q.(g.Q)]$

$\Leftarrow \qquad \{f \text{ is monotonic in its first argument}\}$

$[P \ \Rightarrow\ Q]. \quad \square$

The above three-step proof is in a sense the shortest one possible: The first step takes into account that the function applied to P is g, the second step takes into account that the function applied to Q is g, and the third step uses that f is monotonic in its first argument —and all three facts are indispensable.

It has been included for more than its brevity alone, however; it has been included because it is the simplest example of the standard derivation of proofs of theorems involving extreme solutions.

The shape of the consequent $[g.P \ \Rightarrow\ g.Q]$ immediately tells us that for the application of g to P, (0) is irrelevant and (1) is therefore essential, and, conversely, that for the application of g to Q, (1) is irrelevant and (0) therefore essential. The above heuristics all but dictate the design of such proofs. (We point out that these heuristics would hardly have been available, had the strongest solution been defined by "it is a solution and implies all other solutions" instead of by "it is a solution and implies all solutions".) Finally we would like to point out that the use of the follows-from symbol $\Leftarrow$ has enabled us to present the calculation without pulling a single rabbit out of a hat.

7 An Algebraic Approach to the Predicate Calculus [0]

As in the previous filler, capital letters can be viewed as standing for predicates on some space, universal quantification over which is then denoted by a pair of square brackets. Because we wish to replace what is usually called "reasoning" whenever profitable by calculation, we here present the logical operators, stressing their algebraic properties.

Postulate

Equality between predicates X and Y is expressed by "everywhere equivalent":

$[X \equiv Y].$

---

0. Adapted, with permission, from Edsger W. Dijkstra and Carel S. Scholten, *Predicate Calculus and Program Semantics*, Springer-Verlag, Berlin, 1989.

Postulate

Function application is characterized by the Rule of Leibniz, i.e., by being equality-preserving:

$$[X \equiv Y] \Rightarrow [f.X \equiv f.Y] \, ;$$

expressions are postulated to be functions of their subexpressions.

Postulate

Equivalence is postulated to be associative, i.e.,

$$[((X \equiv Y) \equiv Z) \equiv (X \equiv (Y \equiv Z))] \, ,$$

so that, from here on, parentheses in continued equivalences will be omitted, and to be symmetric, i.e.,

$$[X \equiv Y \equiv Y \equiv X] \, .$$

Parsing the last formula as

$$[X \equiv (Y \equiv Y \equiv X)]$$

and as

$$[(X \equiv Y \equiv Y) \equiv X] \, ,$$

we see that $\equiv$ has a left- and a right-identity element —viz., $Y \equiv Y$; therefore $\equiv$ has a unique identity element, which we denote by true:

$$[X \equiv \text{true} \equiv X] \, .$$

Postulate

Disjunction is postulated to be associative, i.e.,

$$[(X \vee Y) \vee Z \equiv X \vee (Y \vee Z)] \, ,$$

so that in continued disjunctions parentheses can be omitted; to be symmetric, i.e.,

$$[X \vee Y \equiv Y \vee X] \, ;$$

to be idempotent, i.e.,

$$[X \vee X \equiv X] \, ;$$

and to distribute over equivalence, i.e.;

$$[X \vee (Y \equiv Z) \equiv X \vee Y \equiv X \vee Z] \, .$$

Theorem

$[X \vee \text{true} \equiv \text{true}]$.

Proof   We observe for any X, Y

$\quad X \vee \text{true}$
$= \quad \{\text{def. of true}\}$
$\quad X \vee (Y \equiv Y)$
$= \quad \{\vee \text{ distributes over } \equiv\}$
$\quad X \vee Y \equiv X \vee Y$
$= \quad \{\text{def. of true}\}$
$\quad \text{true}. \quad \square$

Postulate

Conjunction is defined in terms of equivalence and disjunction by

$[X \wedge Y \equiv X \equiv Y \equiv X \vee Y]$,

a formula known as the Golden Rule.

Theorem

Conjunction is associative, symmetric, and idempotent.

Proof   This is left to the reader. $\square$

Theorem

$[X \wedge (Y \equiv Z) \equiv X \wedge Y \equiv X \wedge Z \equiv X]$.

Proof   We observe for any X, Y, Z

$\quad X \wedge Y \equiv X \wedge Z$
$= \quad \{\text{Golden Rule, twice}\}$
$\quad X \equiv Y \equiv X \vee Y \equiv X \equiv Z \equiv X \vee Z$
$= \quad \{\text{rearranging terms of continued equivalence}\}$
$\quad X \equiv Y \equiv Z \equiv X \vee Y \equiv X \vee Z \equiv X$
$= \quad \{\vee \text{ distributes over } \equiv\}$

$$X \equiv (Y \equiv Z) \equiv X \lor (Y \equiv Z) \equiv X$$
$$= \quad \{\text{Golden Rule}\}$$
$$X \land (Y \equiv Z) \equiv X. \quad \square$$

Theorem

$$[X \land (U \equiv Y \equiv Z) \equiv X \land U \equiv X \land Y \equiv X \land Z],$$

i.e., "$\land$ distributes over $\equiv \equiv$".

Proof   This is left to the reader. $\square$

Theorem

$$[X \lor (Y \land Z) \equiv (X \lor Y) \land (X \lor Z)]$$

and

$$[X \land (Y \lor Z) \equiv (X \land Y) \lor (X \land Z)],$$

i.e., disjunction and conjunction distribute over each other.

Proof   To prove the last one we observe for any X, Y, Z

$$(X \land Y) \lor (X \land Z)$$
$$= \quad \{\text{Golden Rule}\}$$
$$(X \land Y) \land (X \land Z) \equiv X \land Y \equiv X \land Z$$
$$= \quad \{\land \text{ is associative, symmetric, and idempotent}\}$$
$$X \land (Y \land Z) \equiv X \land Y \equiv X \land Z$$
$$= \quad \{\land \text{ distributes over } \equiv \equiv\}$$
$$X \land (Y \land Z \equiv Y \equiv Z)$$
$$= \quad \{\text{Golden Rule}\}$$
$$X \land (Y \lor Z). \quad \square$$

The preceding one can be proved similarly.

Theorem

$$[X \land (X \lor Y) \equiv X]$$

and

$[X \lor (X \land Y) \equiv X]$,

known as the Laws of Absorption.

Proof   To prove the first one —the second one can be proved similarly—
we observe for any X, Y

$\qquad X \land (X \lor Y)$

$=\qquad$ {Golden Rule}

$\qquad X \equiv X \lor Y \equiv X \lor (X \lor Y)$

$=\qquad$ {associativity and idempotence of $\lor$}

$\qquad X \equiv X \lor Y \equiv X \lor Y$

$=\qquad$ {identity element of $\equiv$}

$\qquad X. \ \square$

Finally we derive for the conjunction

Theorem

$\qquad [X \land \text{true} \equiv X]$.

Proof   We observe for any X

$\qquad X \land \text{true}$

$=\qquad$ {Golden Rule}

$\qquad X \equiv \text{true} \equiv X \lor \text{true}$

$=\qquad$ {true is zero-element of $\lor$}

$\qquad X \equiv \text{true} \equiv \text{true}$

$=\qquad$ {identity element of $\equiv$}

$\qquad X. \ \square$

Postulate

Implication is defined in terms of equivalence and disjunction by

$\qquad [X \Rightarrow Y \equiv X \lor Y \equiv Y]$.

Using the Golden Rule the reader may derive

Theorem

$$[X \Rightarrow Y \equiv X \wedge Y \equiv X],$$

and using the Laws of Absorption

Theorem

$$[X \Rightarrow X \vee Y]$$

and

$$[X \wedge Y \Rightarrow X].$$

We shall prove

Theorem

$$[X \Rightarrow (Y \Rightarrow Z) \equiv X \wedge Y \Rightarrow Z].$$

Proof   We observe for any X, Y, Z

$$X \Rightarrow (Y \Rightarrow Z)$$

$= \quad$ {relation between $\Rightarrow$ and $\wedge$}

$$X \wedge (Y \wedge Z \equiv Y) \equiv X$$

$= \quad$ {relation between $\wedge$ and $\equiv$}

$$X \wedge Y \wedge Z \equiv X \wedge Y$$

$= \quad$ {relation between $\Rightarrow$ and $\wedge$}

$$X \wedge Y \Rightarrow Z. \quad \square$$

Theorem

$$[X \wedge (X \Rightarrow Y) \equiv X \wedge Y].$$

Proof   We observe for any X, Y

$$X \wedge (X \Rightarrow Y)$$

$= \quad$ {relation between $\Rightarrow$ and $\wedge$}

$$X \wedge (X \wedge Y \equiv X)$$

$= \quad$ {relation between $\wedge$ and $\equiv$}

$$X \wedge X \wedge Y \equiv X \wedge X \equiv X$$

=   {idempotence of ∧}

$X \wedge Y \equiv X \equiv X$

=   {identity element of ≡}

$X \wedge Y$. □

Implication is transitive, i.e.,

Theorem

$[(X \Rightarrow Y) \wedge (Y \Rightarrow Z) \Rightarrow (X \Rightarrow Z)]$.

Proof   We observe for any X, Y, Z

$[(X \Rightarrow Y) \wedge (Y \Rightarrow Z) \Rightarrow (X \Rightarrow Z)]$

=   {pre-previous theorem}

$[X \wedge (X \Rightarrow Y) \wedge (Y \Rightarrow Z) \Rightarrow Z]$

=   {previous theorem}

$[X \wedge Y \wedge (Y \Rightarrow Z) \Rightarrow Z]$

=   {previous theorem}

$[X \wedge Y \wedge Z \Rightarrow Z]$

=   {Law of Absorption in implicative version}

true . □

Theorem

$[(X \Rightarrow Y) \vee (Y \Rightarrow Z)]$.

Proof   We observe for any X, Y, Z

$[(X \Rightarrow Y) \vee (Y \Rightarrow Z)]$

=   {relation between ⇒ and ∨}

$[(X \vee Y \equiv Y) \vee (Y \vee Z \equiv Z)]$

=   {∨ distributes over ≡}

$[X \vee Y \vee Y \vee Z \equiv X \vee Y \vee Z \equiv Y \vee Y \vee Z \equiv Y \vee Z]$

=   {idempotence of ∨ ; identity element of ≡}

true . □

Theorem

$$[(X \Rightarrow Y) \wedge (Y \Rightarrow X) \equiv X \equiv Y].$$

Proof   We observe for any X, Y,

$$(X \Rightarrow Y) \wedge (Y \Rightarrow X)$$

$=$ {Golden Rule; previous theorem}

$$X \Rightarrow Y \equiv Y \Rightarrow X$$

$=$ {definition of $\Rightarrow$}

$$X \vee Y \equiv Y \equiv X \vee Y \equiv X$$

$=$ {identity element of $\equiv$}

$$X \equiv Y. \quad \square$$

So much for the implication. Note that conjunction and implication have been defined in terms of equivalence and disjunction. In order to introduce the negation we therefore postulate its properties with respect to the latter two connectives only; its properties with respect to conjunction and implication can then be derived.

Postulate

Negation and equivalence are postulated to be connected by

$$[\neg(X \equiv Y) \equiv \neg X \equiv Y].$$

Theorem

$$[\neg X \equiv Y \equiv X \equiv \neg Y].$$

Proof   We observe for any X, Y

$$\neg X \equiv Y$$

$=$ {connection between $\neg$ and $\equiv$}

$$\neg(X \equiv Y)$$

$=$ {connection between $\neg$ and $\equiv$; symmetry of $\equiv$}

$$X \equiv \neg Y. \quad \square$$

Substituting $Y := \neg X$ in the above yields

Theorem

$$[X \equiv \neg\neg X].$$

Postulate

Negation and disjunction are postulated to be connected by the Law of the Excluded Middle, i.e.,

$[X \lor \neg X]$.

Exploring what we can derive from the above two postulates for the negation, we observe for any X, Y

$\qquad$ true
$=\qquad$ {Excluded Middle, $X := X \equiv Y$}
$\qquad [(X \equiv Y) \lor \neg(X \equiv Y)]$
$=\qquad$ {relation between $\neg$ and $\equiv$}
$\qquad [(X \equiv Y) \lor (\neg X \equiv Y)]$
$=\qquad$ {$\lor$ distributes over $\equiv$}
$\qquad [X \lor \neg X \equiv X \lor Y \equiv Y \lor \neg X \equiv Y \lor Y]$
$=\qquad$ {Excluded Middle; idempotence of $\lor$}

Theorem

$\qquad [\neg X \lor Y \equiv X \lor Y \equiv Y]$.

Confronting the above theorem with the definition of the implication, we get

Theorem

$\qquad [X \Rightarrow Y \equiv \neg X \lor Y]$.

We can furthermore use it to derive the Laws of de Morgan:

Theorem

$\qquad [\neg X \lor \neg Y \equiv \neg(X \land Y)]$
$\qquad [\neg X \land \neg Y \equiv \neg(X \lor Y)]$.

Proof   We shall prove the first one. To this end we observe for any X, Y

$\qquad \neg X \lor \neg Y$
$=\qquad$ {recent theorem with $Y := \neg Y$}
$\qquad X \lor \neg Y \equiv \neg Y$

$\quad=\quad$ {same theorem with $X, Y := Y, X$}

$\quad\quad X \vee Y \equiv X \equiv \neg Y$

$\quad=\quad$ {relation between $\neg$ and $\equiv$}

$\quad\quad \neg(X \vee Y \equiv X \equiv Y)$

$\quad=\quad$ {Golden Rule}

$\quad\quad \neg(X \wedge Y). \quad \square$

We leave to the reader the derivation of the analogous

Theorem

$\quad [\neg X \wedge Y \equiv X \wedge Y \equiv \neg Y],$

and so on.

The above text is somewhat more elaborate than what I showed as filler at the YoP Institute; also here the manipulation of formulae with explicit quantification has been omitted. The material has been included because it deserves to be better known than it is. We regret that classical logic has not yet become a daily calculational tool of the working mathematician, for we find it indispensable.

The reason logic is so little used is probably that it has been presented in the wrong way, viz., as formalization of how mathematicians "think" instead of a calculus in its own right. As the reader will have noticed, we have allowed the equivalence to play a very central role. For a calculational approach, this is essential: The notion of function application is defined by the fact that it is equality-preserving. And it is precisely the equivalence that is the logical connective that is the hardest to render in natural language; we have the "if and only if", but its deficiencies are clearly displayed in the following sentence: "John sees with both eyes if and only if John sees with one eye if and only if John is blind". By all linguistic standards, this sentence is total gibberish.

The purpose of logic is not to mimic verbal reasoning but to provide a calculational alternative.

Influences (or Lack Thereof) of Formalism in Teaching Programming and Software Engineering

18

David Gries
Cornell University

1 Introduction

This YoP Institute has been devoted to the judicious use of formalism in the conscious pursuit of elegance in our everyday activities in mathematics and programming. We say "judicious" because not everything is formalized; the game is to formalize only as much as necessary —no more and no less— to make an argument as clear, simple, and elegant as possible. It is a game of economy of thought, concept, and pen. It is a game in which the syntactic proof, consisting of a sequence of syntactic transformations according to given rules, plays a large part. You have seen the game played on sequential programs, concurrent programs, distributed programs, VLSI design, and mathematics itself. Not everyone has used the same theories, but with each speaker the common game of judicious use of formalism has been evident. And we believe that the programmer and software engineer would benefit by playing this game.

Now, in spite of Edsger's claims that the nine speakers of this Institute consist of four Americans, one Scot, one Irish, only one Dutchman (who isn't even a man), and what have you, I am sure you have noticed the dearth of American speakers. The other speakers can split up the single Dutchman whichever way they want, but I alone am the four Americans, and the only reason they let me in was because my degree was earned in Munich, Germany. Not even a Ph.D., but Dr. Rerum Natura, or Dr. Rare Nut as it is often abbreviated in my absence.

Where are all the Americans in programming and software engineering who play the same game? Of course, all profess the need for simplicity and elegance, but there are few who play our game with the intensity seen here, who concentrate so on method, who strive so *hard* for mathematical simplicity and elegance.

What one does see in Americans —and I am one— is a more hurried emphasis on facts and mechanical tools. We are so busy doing the next thing that we don't have time to reflect on the last thing. We see this in the vitae of many researchers who write only conference papers. They don't take the time to rewrite, to polish, to submit to a refereed journal where they will be subject to the often-painful anonymous referee report, which can help them grow and mature so much. We see this in the almost universal feeling that program documentation is a pain.

We see the hurriedness in our handwriting. Your typical American has not been taught to and won't take the time to learn to write clearly. The mindset of America vis-a-vis handwriting is best exemplified by the pad of paper placed for your use on the desks in the lecture hall. It is titled "scribbletex"! The last syllable, "tex", I am told, was chosen for a reason. The company wants to computerize their product, joining T$_E$X and L^{A}T$_E$X, so that Americans can produce their own scribbled handwriting on screens and laser printers, thus making the computer more end-user-friendly!

Contrast your own handwriting with the remarkably clear foils produced by the speakers this week. Look at their handwritten letters and papers —one has even published his handwritten PhD thesis, as Lecture Notes in Computer Science 200. Realizing that absolute clarity and unambiguity are necessary if formal manipulations are to be performed, and realizing that computers are not yet helpful in this regard, the speakers have consciously worked to improve their writing. And it shows. Moreover, they all carry fountain pens and, to the astonishment of their colleagues, like to talk about them.

I have used a bit of hyperbole in talking about Americans —including myself— to make a point, and it shouldn't be taken too literally. And yet, there is a germ of truth in my comments, and some pondering on them might be worthwhile.

2 *Educating the Programmer*

One of the large and difficult tasks we have —abroad as well as here— is that of educating future computing scientists, computing engineers, programmers, and other scientists, and we should think about the effect the kind of material presented at this YoP Institute could have on programming education. For the speakers at this Institute, the notion of program proof is so ingrained that they can't think otherwise. This does not mean that every line of a program is proved formally, of course, but the ideas have been so assimilated that they have become a habit, like reading or brushing teeth. And it shows: There has been evidence enough in this Institute that this habit can simplify the development and presentation of programs and mathematics.

And yet, our general programming texts and texts in data structures make little use of formalism and program proof. They are ten to fifteen years behind the times, and some are so old-fashioned that it is almost a crime to force the students to read them. I am afraid that too many people with half a mind to write an introductory programming textbook do so.

More and more texts for introductory and second-semester programming courses do introduce the term "loop invariant", but these texts often have a negative impact on the students' view of formalism and proof. Although a chapter might be devoted to the loop invariant, the author hasn't assimilated its use himself, and the technique either is not used in the text or is used incorrectly. Consequently, the student receives the impression that the loop invariant is a theoretical idea only, to be forgotten as soon as possible. And this impression is often backed up by the instructor.

A few months ago, I saw a new programming text by a respected computer scientist. They[1] received the Ph.D. some twelve years ago, and they do research in algorithms and complexity. I immediately turned to the presentation of binary search, which often reveals a writer's habits. The presentation began with an invariant, but, halfway through, the question of termination of a loop arose, and immediately a variable *found* was introduced, was set to true when the desired value was detected in the array, and was introduced into the loop condition. But the loop invariant was not changed to reflect the addition of the new variable, so the proof of correctness in terms of the invariant was completely wrong —the proof had nothing to do with the program! In consequence, the author was forced to conclude the presentation with a discussion about "the subtleness" of the algorithm —by which they meant that the job had been botched completely.

This computer scientist, working in algorithms and complexity, had not had enough practice with the formal proof of programs to realize that their proof was completely and obviously full of holes! It was not a subtle mistake,

---

1. The words "they", "them", and "their" are used (instead of "he", "him", and "his") with singular antecedents to denote someone of either sex. This practice has been in use, according to the Oxford English Dictionary, since the eighteenth century.

a minor mishap of the kind that happens to all of us, but a reflection of the fact that an 18-year-old tool of utmost importance had not been assimilated. Why? Probably because they had not the time: Like the rest of us, they had no time to pause, to reflect, to learn; they were too busy finding the next fact, dealing with students, and performing administration. Like all of us, they were overwhelmed with the rush of things.

But that is not the end of the story. This person exhibited a further characteristic that is all too prevalent in our educational system in computing. Upon being confronted with a far more effective algorithm for binary search, they replied that they knew that version, but had presented a different one because it relied more heavily on the students' intuition —you know, the old search-in-the-telephone-book metaphor.

I believe it is fundamentally wrong to teach a science like programming by reinforcing the students' intuition when that intuition is inadequate and misguided. On the contrary, our task is to demonstrate that a first intuition is often wrong and to teach the principles, tools, and techniques that will help overcome and change that intuition! Reinforcing inadequate intuitions just compounds the problem.

Naturalness in most endeavors must be learned. For example, consider the new golfer. The swing feels just right, and yet the ball doesn't go where it should. However, after many lessons from a professional, and much practice, the strange movements forced on the golfer by the pro begin to feel "natural", and the golfer finds that the acquired swing is the *only* way to swing; it is impossible to return to the old way.

The same goes for programming: Good habits, based on a serious study of the task, have to be taught —and then consciously practiced.

My friend also claimed that, although the presentation of binary search could have been better, the algorithm was correct. But correctness is not the only issue in our field; we must get *everything* right, including the arguments that compel belief in correctness, and there are right ways and righter ways to present such arguments. As we have seen this week, our arguments, our program documentation, can indeed be a joy to present and listen to, to write and read, and the simpler and more elegant the arguments, the more fun it is.

Not everyone in our field thinks this way about documentation. Let me read to you a paragraph from a paper presented at a conference on software engineering by a computer scientist who works in software engineering and cognitive science. This paper was presented at a Conference on Software Engineering Education, and the proceedings with the same title was edited by N. E. Gibbs and R. E. Fairley.[2]

Documentation (unlike good literature) is boring to write and read because we

2. Springer-Verlag, 1987; reprinted with permission.

have so little insight on how people construct facts to understand technical material. We should devise more "intuitive" notations for documentation. By intuitive I mean the nonverbal and partially verbal knowledge about how the software really works. This knowledge can then be used by the reader to construct or reconstruct an understanding of the software. With high resolution dynamic displays we have a new medium in which to rethink our approach to documentation. Together with a more sophisticated view of human memory processes, we may be able to make some significant progress on documentation.

Now, if our teachers all believe that writing is boring, that the object of teaching is to reinforce the students' intuition, that technical problems are to be solved by more intuitive notions of nonverbal and partially verbal knowledge displayed on high resolution dynamic displays, then, I say, we are in trouble!

3 *On Software-Engineering Education*

Let me say a bit more about software-engineering education. First, I do agree that knowledge of and experience with psychology, management, personal communication, and the like are important. But I believe they are secondary, and that the technical problems are of primary importance. Thus, I believe the current emphases within software engineering circles are missing the mark.

The Conference on Software Engineering Education mentioned above contained a description of a curriculum under development for a Masters of Engineering program being developed by the Software Engineering Institute (SEI) in Pittsburgh.[3] The curriculum contained some 35 modules, each of which was to be roughly equivalent to one or two semester hours in an academic semester or one work week in industry.

The core of the program, which every student was to take, consisted of ten technical modules and three management modules. Exactly *one* of these core modules mentioned program verification; it included a "survey of approaches for reasoning about and certifying software correctness, including testing, program verification, walkthroughs/inspections, and simulation". I estimate that at most five hours would be devoted to issues of program verification within the core of the SEI curriculum!

The core did not mention the predicate calculus, manipulating logical formulae, or developing program and proof hand in hand. After attending this Institute, does that make any sense to you?

One might argue that this material should be taken by every computer science undergraduate, that it is prerequisite material. I agree wholeheartedly,

---

3. A copy of this speech was given to Norman Gibbs of the SEI after the fact, and he responded. The SEI's proposed curriculum on software engineering has changed markedly since the Conference took place —they have distanced themselves quite far from the curriculum presented at the Conference. In fact, their new proposal contains at least one course on formal methods in software engineering. This should be taken into account when reading this speech.

but generally this material is *not* being taught to undergraduates —if it were, the sales of my text *The Science of Programming* would be better. Further, this argument was not made by the authors of the SEI curriculum, and the presentation conveys the impression that this is not their view.

The authors of the SEI curriculum simply didn't realize that a careful, *in-depth* study of predicate calculus and formal derivation of algorithms, with proof and program being developed hand in hand, can have a marked influence on more than half of the core modules they want to teach —communication techniques, software engineering, software interface engineering, software requirements engineering, software generation, tool building, engineering software evolution, and software quality factors. But such an in-depth study requires *at least* a full-semester course, and not only five hours. And this in-depth study should be reinforced by using the techniques and concepts in every other module.

I have made my views known to the SEI many times and have been prepared to cooperate with them on revising the curriculum. As it stands, in my opinion this SEI curriculum has the wrong emphasis. And I am not alone in disagreeing with software engineering curricula. Fred Brooks, who gave the keynote speech at the conference, said that he was "in fundamental disagreement with a good deal of what [was] proposed, described, and practiced" in software engineering, as given by the predistributed position papers for the conference. He also said,

> If you do not know what to teach in a SE curriculum and, if in putting one together, you find a lot of modules that are short on principles —where one can teach only tools or methodologies or today's practices— instead of most of those modules teach nothing at all. Instead, encourage the students to spend those hours learning something such as physics, mathematics, accounting, where they *do* know what to teach.

4 *Teaching Rigor in Proofs and Programs*

What should we be teaching to programmers and software engineers? We certainly don't have all the answers. But this Institute should leave you with the impression that our technical problems need technical solutions, that these technical solutions will rest on sound mathematical foundations, and that mastery of the predicate calculus lies at the core of our solutions. Hence, we should be teaching mastery of the predicate calculus *before* programming; the rules of formal manipulation should be taught and practiced until they have been assimilated. And then we should teach programming in terms of developing program and proof hand in hand.

Now, some people question the use of the syntactic proof, which involves pure manipulation of symbols according to given laws. They see it as too cumbersome, complex, and difficult exactly in programming, where there are so many details. They feel such symbol manipulation is best left to the computer. And indeed, students have trouble with formula manipulation. Once they have made a textual substitution, say, they no longer "understand what the formula means" and are hesitant to make further manipulations for fear of making mistakes. Because of this, they equate rigor with rigor mortis, with a stiffening of their abilities.

I have given courses in which I had actually to guide a student's hand as the first textual substitution was made in connection with the assignment-statement axiom. This was depressing, for symbol manipulation is what programming is all about! Such courses, expected to be on the development of programs, had to spend far too much time on the predicate calculus and symbol manipulation. And these were not dumb or inexperienced students; they simply hadn't received a proper education.

We are not alone in our emphasis on formal methods and syntactic proofs. Let me quote the famous mathematician David Hilbert, who first proposed the use of formal proofs, from his lecture at the Second International Congress of Mathematicians in Paris in 1900, in which he outlined his famous ten problems:

> It remains to discuss briefly what general requirements may be justly laid down for a solution of a mathematical problem. I should say first of all, this: that it be possible to establish the correctness of the solution by means of a finite number of steps based upon a finite number of hypotheses that are implied in the statement of the problem and that must be exactly formulated. This requirement of logical deduction by means of a finite number of processes is simply the requirement of rigor in reasoning. Indeed, the requirement of rigor, which has become a byword in mathematics, corresponds to a universal philosophical necessity of our understanding ... only by satisfying this requirement do the thought content and the suggestiveness of the problem attain their full value....
>
> It is an error to believe that rigor in the proof is the enemy of simplicity. On the contrary, we find it confirmed in numerous examples that the rigorous method is at the same time the simpler and the more easily comprehended. The very effort for rigor forces us to discover simpler methods of proof. It also frequently leads the way to methods which are more capable of development than the old methods of less rigor. [Quoted from *Hilbert*, by Constance Reid, Springer-Verlag, New York, 1983; reprinted by permission.]

Thus, it is not just a bunch of computer scientists that are stressing formal methods. The concept was developed some 90 years ago by one of the greatest mathematicians, and it has been pursued from time to time by many, albeit not at the same level of intensity as you have seen this week.

During his time, Hilbert's program for formalizing mathematics received its share of criticism, with some mathematicians objecting to his "reducing the science to a meaningless game played with meaningless marks on paper".

However, Hilbert claimed that it was precisely the shuffling of meaningless symbols according to given rules that provided confidence and understanding. We feel the same way about our proofs of programs (and their development). By relying more on the formula manipulation to do the work, we find proofs and programs being much shorter and simpler than they used to be. And we hope that the practical evidence provided by this week's speakers will convince you too.

5 *Conclusion*

This is the last of several YoP —Year of Programming, Year of Proof, Year of Predicate Calculus, Year of Parties— Institutes. All have eschewed non-technical issues of programming and software engineering and instead have concentrated on technical issues, usually dealing with correctness concerns. Tony Hoare's YoP Institute on concurrency, my YoP Institute on encapsulation, Huet's YoP Institute on logical foundations of functional programming, Gordon and Hunt's YoP Institute on formal specification and verification of hardware, Turner's YoP Institute on declarative programming, and this, Dijkstra's YoP Institute on formal development, all have stressed the formal, theoretical aspects. One can ask whether this mYoPic view of programming can indeed be beneficial, or whether it is only a form of nearsightedness that fails to understand the significance of broader issues. That answer to this question I leave to you, the audience, the audiences of this and the other YoP Institutes. I for one come away with gratitude to the sponsors and organizers of the YoP for giving us this opportunity and with renewed enthusiasm for the use of formal techniques in programming, and I will work even harder to extend my own use of formalism and to inculcate my students with the same view.

The Authors

ROLAND C. BACKHOUSE is professor of computing science at the Rijksuniversiteit Groningen in the Netherlands. He has written two books, both of which are in the Prentice Hall International Series in Computer Science edited by C. A. R. Hoare: *Syntax of Programming Languages* (1979) and *Program Construction and Verification* (1986). He is a member of the editorial board of the journal *Formal Aspects of Computing* and his interests are in the area of formal methods for the calculation of computer programs. Address: Subfaculteit Wiskunde en Informatica, Rijksuniversiteit Groningen, Postbus 800, 9700 AV GRONINGEN, The Netherlands.

Edsger W. Dijkstra
(1930) has worked in theoretical physics,
algorithm design, compiler construction,
process synchronization, operating
system design, programming language
semantics, programming methodology,
and mathematical methodology
in general, such as the design of adequate
notations and the exploitation of proof
theory to guide the design of streamlined
formal arguments. Currently he occupies the
Schlumberger Centennial Chair in Computer
Science and is Professor of Mathematics,
both at The University of Texas at Austin.
Address: Department of Computer Sciences,
Taylor Hall 2.124, The University of
Texas at Austin, Austin, Texas 78712-1188.

Wim H. J. Feijen received
a Bachelor's Degree in Mechanical
Engineering and a Master's
in Applied Mathematics, both at
Eindhoven University. From 1970
until 1984 he was an assistant of
Professor Dijkstra's —in Eindhoven
also— helping to develop
the mathematics of program
construction. During recent
years he has become more and
more interested in smoothening
mathematical reasoning, for the
benefit of the design of programs
and proofs. Address: Department
of Mathematics and Computing
Science, Eindhoven University of
Technology, Postbox 513, 5600 MB Eindhoven, The Netherlands.

A. J. M. VAN
GASTEREN, born in 1952, is
living and working in the Netherlands.
In 1978 she received a master's degree
in mathematics, having specialized
in computing science under
the supervision of Edsger W. Dijkstra.
In 1979 and 1980 she took part
in an automation project. From 1981
to 1987 she was a BP Venture Research
Fellow at the University of Technology
in Eindhoven, investigating the design
and presentation of programs and
mathematical proofs in collaboration
with Prof. Dijkstra and W. H. J. Feijen.
In 1988 she received her Ph.D. from

the aforementioned university with a dissertation entitled "On the shape of
mathematical arguments." Currently she works at the universities of Groningen
and Utrecht, doing research in programming methodology. Address:
Rijksuniversiteit te Utrecht, Vakgroep Informatica, Postbus 80.089,
3508 TB Utrecht, The Netherlands.

DAVID GRIES, a native of
New York, received his doctorate from
the Munich Institute of Technology
in 1966. He was an assistant professor
at Stanford from 1966 to 1969 and
has been at Cornell since then, serving
as department chairman in 1982–87. He
is known for his research in compiling
and in programming methodology
and for his texts *Compiler Construction
for Digital Computers* (1971),
*An Introduction to Programming,
a Structured Approach* (1973, with Dick
Conway), *Programming Methodology*
(1978, editor), and *The Science
of Programming* (1981). He was a
Guggenheim Fellow in 1984–85, received the 1985 AFIPS Education Award,
received the 1986 Clark Award for excellence in undergraduate teaching in the
Cornell College of Arts & Sciences, and was a co-recipient of the 1976 ACM
Programming Languages and Systems Best Paper award. He is currently Chairman
of the Computing Research Board and is on the editorial boards of several journals
and book series. Address: Cornell University, Department of Computer Science,
Ithaca, New York 14853-7501.

ALAIN J. MARTIN graduated from the Institut National Polytechnique de Grenoble in 1969. He is currently a professor of computer science at the California Institute of Technology. His research interests include concurrent and distributed programming and its application to the design of VLSI circuits. Address: California Institute of Technology, Computer Science Department, Pasadena, CA 91125.

JOSEPH M. MORRIS holds a Ph. D. from Trinity College, Dublin, having done part of his graduate study at the Technische Universiteit, Eindhoven. He has since worked in industry and education in Europe and the United States, and currently lectures in computing science at the University of Glasgow. His research interests include formal specifications, programming calculi, and curricula for computing science. Address: Computing Science Department, University of Glasgow, Glasgow G12 8QQ, U.K.

MARTIN REM studied
mathematics at the University of Amsterdam
and holds a Ph.D. in computing science
from Eindhoven University of Technology.
He is currently professor of mathematics
and computing science at Eindhoven,
part-time visiting professor at California
Institute of Technology, and consultant
for Philips Research. He is editor of the
journals *Integration* and *Science of Computer
Programming*. For the latter journal
he writes a column 'Small Programming
Exercises'. His research interests are
parallel programs and VLSI design. Address:
Technological University Eindhoven,
Department of Mathematics and Informatics,
Postbox 513, 5600 MB Eindhoven, The Netherlands.

JAN L. A. VAN DE SNEPSCHEUT
is professor of Computing
Science at Groningen University.
He received a PhD from
Eindhoven University. In 1983/84
he was a visiting assistant
professor at the California
Institute of Technology.
Address: Rijksuniversiteit
Groningen, Van Deyssellaan 90,
9721 WX Groningen,
The Netherlands.

*A*ll six of the Programming Institutes were recorded on videotape, and edited versions of these tapes have been prepared by MPA Productions, Inc., under the auspices of the Computer Sciences Department of The University of Texas at Austin. They are available for purchase in various combinations ranging in size from individual lectures to the complete set. Tapes can be provided in all formats and standards; for most sessions, photocopies of the speakers' overhead-projector transparencies are also available.

For a complete listing of the available tapes, including prices, please write to

Year of Programming (Tapes)
3103 Bee Caves Road, Suite 235
Austin, TX 78746
U.S.A

or call (512) 328-9800.